PAH Publishing
Classic Muscle Car
Illustrated Restoration Guide Series

TRANS AM AND FORMULA
Restoration Guide
1970-1981

Joe Moore

First Published in 2004 by PAH Publishing
International
711 Hillcrest, Monett, Missouri 65708 USA

The information in this book is true and
complete to the best of our knowledge. All
recommendations are made without any
guarantee on part of the author or Publisher,
who also disclaim any liability incurred in
connection with the use of this data or
specific details. Always use jack stands and
exercise caution when working on your
automobile.

Trans Am And Firebird Formula
Restoration Guide 1970-1981
ISBN:0974773026

Cover Photo: 1973 Formula with a 455-ci
S.D. one of 43 built. Owned by Don Bennett
of Vienna, MO

Printed and bound in the United States of
America

Contents

Acknowledgments

This book would have not been possible without the assistance of the following people. David Osborne of Jim Osborne Reproductions who, generously supplied the decals that were used in this guide. They offer a great selection of quality decals for your Firebird. Benny Henderson, a good friend that allowed us to go take photos of the salvaged Firebirds in his yard. Another good friend Ed Witte of CST Auto Salvage, the guys at Texas Trans Ams whom we met at the POCI Nationals in Joplin MO, and answered some questions about wheels And a special thank you to Paul and Kelly Carmi; Greg Richey; Terry and Shelly Nicoll, Bruce Smith (who has a fine example of an untouched 1970 Trans Am); Steve Porter; David and Katharnia Perryman ,Ron and Cyndi Douglas, Wayne Anderson, Doug Kamphus, Robert Chumley, and Joe Geiger all of whom attended the POCI Nationals, where we got the opportunity to enjoy viewing and photographing their cars for use in this guide. Also thanks to the Pontiac Oakland club who hosted the event. A special thanks to Don Bennett who owns the car on the cover of this book, a 1973 Formula with a Super Duty 455 it was one of 43 built. Probably less than five survive today. This book is dedicated to to my wife Karla, without her help, this book would have never seen the light of day. She is my everything.

Preface

There was no other car like the Pontiac Firebird. Born as a sibling of the GM family it was over shadowed by its cousin, the Chevrolet Camaro. It packed the punch of the GTO, but Camaro always seemed to get the nod with both the customers and the critics. However, a total restyle in 1970 brought new life to the Firebird, especially a model name that had seen the light of day the year before. Trans Am was no longer overshadowed by its Chevrolet cousin. Its road racing looks demanded and got attention. The shaker hood scoop that bolted up through the hood gave evidence that something sinister was hiding under the hood; front and rear spoilers along with wheel flares just completed the race car image. Even though the critic's choice was the Trans Am, sales were not that strong, but they weren't that strong for its cousin the Z-28 either. It seemed that the Trans Am and its sister 'hot rod' Formula with its fiberglass hood with twin scooped hood had missed the mark, and could be facing the chopping block. The Z-28 would disappear for the 1975 model year, and it seemed that the Trans Am was headed that way.

It was the creative golden touch of Jim Wangers that save the Trans Am, and in fact put it on the road to stardom. It seems that a director in Hollywood had this idea about a car chase movie. He wanted to use a foreign car as the star, but Wangers saw a different way. American muscle. A black Trans Am. And when the movie debuted it wasn't Burt Reynolds, Sally Fields or Jackie Gleason that viewers rememberedfrom *"Smokie and The Bandit"*, it was that black and gold Trans Am. Suddenly sales of Trans Ams rocketed, it became hard to find a black Trans Am, as local dealers quickly tied the Special Edition (which had nothing to do with the movie) into the movie, calling it a *Bandit Special.* Suddenly the Trans Am was the star of the show, as the number one Firebird being sold. It was ironic that the soaring sales of the Trans Am would bring the dismissed Z-28 back, but I the Chevy would never catch up with the Trans Am. Firebird would continue as would the Trans Am only to fade from view at the turn of the new century. The times changed, names changed. But I wouldn't count the bird out just yet. It's legendary name means "bird from the ashes" Firebird will rise again.

Information for this guide was drawn from Pontiac factory material inclined parts catalog and service bulletins. Part numbers listed may not match the ones on your car, as part numbers differed for the various vendors that made the part, also when parts ran out other parts were substituted.

Every effort was made to ensure that information used in this guide is correct. Therefore, no responsibility can be taken on the action of the authors or the publisher if any inaccuracies occur.

Documentation and Decoding

Vehicle Identification Number

Luckily for all "bird lovers" and Fire Chicken Wranglers everywhere you can quickly spot a true Trans Am or Formula by decoding the VIN, which is not difficult at all once you know how. Location for the VIN plate was the same from 1970-1981, riveted to the driver's side instrument panel. However three different formats were used. This information is limited by the 1970-1971, you can quickly determined a fake Trans Am with this format. With the 1972-1980 format you can determine model and original engine size, which can be a great bonus when selecting a true 400-ci equipped car in the later years. Both the model and engine size is also covered by the 1981 format, but it also adds the country of origin and type of seat belts. We will cover each format separately.

1970-1971 MODELS

All VIN plates in this group will begin with the division code which is the number "2" standing for Pontiac. This is followed by a two-digit code for the model series. Unlike the previous generation the 2nd generation Firebirds came in any body style you like as long as it was a sleek back coupe, so all Firebirds will have the body code 87 third and fourth digits of the VIN, even those models that were specially made into convertibles, this was an after market production and no special code was given to these models. It was this four digit code of the VIN that make up the model number, and it is this number that can determine the car's originality. Refer to chart number 1 for the 1970-1971 model numbers. Sixth digit is the last year of the model year 0-1970 1-1971.

Seventh digit is a letter code that represents the assembly plant. All 1970-1971 Firebirds were built at the Norwood, OH assembly plant and will be coded with the letter "N" in the VIN plate. The last six digits of the VIN were the serial number most V-8 models began at 100001. There is some misinformation about the serial number and they way they apply to production. VIN numbers were not given at assembly plant but given out as the car was sold, not produced. This is why the VIN and the Fisher Body Tag numbers (discuss later on) do not agree. The VIN was given to the car when it was ordered. The Fisher Body number was given at the plant and is a sequential production. Thus the VIN 226870L10014 does not mean that it was the 14th car built at the Van Nuys assembly plant it means that it was the 14th car ordered or sold that was to be produced by that plant.

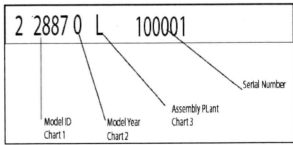

Typical 1970-197 VIN breakdown

Chart 1
1970-1971 Model Numbers

Code	Model	Year Used
2387	Basic Firebird	1970-1971
2487	Esprit	1970-1971
2687	Formula 400	1970-1971
2887	Trans Am	1970-1971

Chart 2
1970-1981 Model Year

Code	Model Year
0	1970
1	1971
2	1972
3	1973
4	1974
5	1975
6	1976
7	1977
8	1978
9	1979
A	1980
B	1981

Chart 3
1970-1981 Assembly Plant Codes

Code	Assembly Plant	Year Used
L	Van Nuys, Ca	1973-1981
N	Norwood, OH	1970-1981

1972- 1980 MODELS

The biggest change in the format was the addition of the original engine size. Since no more characters were added and the format stayed as is; the 13-digit placement code, formats had to be altered to make room for the engine code. This way the model code was reduced to a single letter instead of a pair of numbers as the years before. Regardless of the changes, the VIN still starts with the number 2 for the Pontiac division. This is followed by the model code and the body style code, all Firebirds used the code "87" as it did before, this three digit code, which will begin with a letter is considered the model number and should be consulted when determining the models true identity. Please refer to chart number 4 for the codes. The fifth digit code represented the original engine check chart number 5 for details. The sixth digit was the last number of the model year. However the 1980 model year is the exception and the letter "A" was used instead of a number to represent the model year.

The seventh digit was the assembly plant code and the last six digits were the serial number, again most begin at the number 100001. The exceptions are the 1972 model year, which began at 500001.

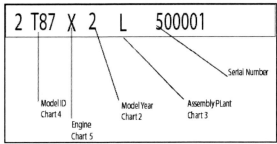

Typical 1972-1981 VIN format

Chart 4
1971-1981 Model Numbers

Code	Model	Year Used
S87	Basic Firebird	1972-1981
T87	Esprit	1972-1981
U87	Formula	1972-1979
V87	Trans Am	1972-1974
	Formula	1980-1981
W87	Trans Am	1975-1981
X87	10th Anniversary T/A	1979
X87	Turbo Pace Car	1980
X87	Trans Am Special Edition	1981
Y87	NACAR Pace Car	1981

1981 MODELS

With ever increasing government regulations on the cars safety a new VIN format was needed in 1981. It will begin with the code country of origin, which will be the number "1" for USA. This is followed by the letter "G" for General Motors and the number "2" for Pontiac This is followed by the letter "A" indicating manual seat belts. Fifth through seventh characters in the VIN represents the model, which can be found in chart number 4. The eight-digit is the original engine size which can be found in chart number 5 ; the ninth is a check digit; the tenth digit is the letter "B"indicating the 1981 model year, and the last digits are the serial number, which will begin with the number 100001.

Chart 5
1972-1981 V-8 Engine VIN Codes

Code	Engine	Year Used
M	350-ci 2-bbl S.E.	1972-1976
N	350-ci 2-bbl D.E.	1972-1975
R	400-ci 2-bbl S.E.	1972-1975
T	400-ci 4-bbl D.E.	1972-1975
X*	455-ci 4-bbl D.E.	1972-1975
S	400-ci 4-bbl S.E.	1972-1975
Y	455-ci 4-bbl D.E.	1973-1975
P	400-ci 2-bbl D.E.	1973-1975
J	350-ci 4-bbl	1976
H	350-ci 2-bbl	1976
W	455-ci 4-bbl	1975-1976
H	350-ci 2-bbl	1976
P	350-ci 2-4-bbl	1976
N	400-ci 2-bbl	1976
Z	400-ci 4-bbl	1976
Y	301-ci 2-bbl	1977
L	350-ci 4-bbl	1977-1979
R	350-ci 4-bbl	1977-1979
X	350-ci 4-bbl	1977-1979
Z	400-ci 4-bbl	1977-1979
K	403-ci 4-bbl	1977-1978
U	305-ci 2-bbl	1978
W	301-ci 2-bbl V-8	1979-1981
Y	301-ci 2-bbl V-8	1979-1980
G	305-ci 2-bbl V-8	1979-1981
H	305-ci 4-bbl V-8	1979-1981
K	403-ci 4-bbl V-8	1979
T	301-ci Turbo	1980-1981
S	265-ci 2-bbl V-8	1980-1981

S.E.- Single Exhaust D.E. Dual Exhaust * Super Duty
also used this code

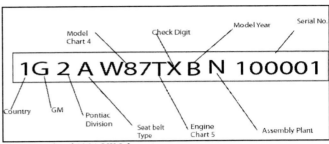

An example of 1981 VIN format

*Not all Body tags follow the rules. We found this
example on a 1975 model.*

Body Number Plate

Except for the build sheet no other item can provide as much information about your firebird as the Body number plate. Also know as a data plate or trim plate it was installed by the Fisher Body group before the final assembly of your car.

Basic information on the tags were the same at all assembly plants and contain the basic information of model, assembly plant code, unit number, trim seat, seat style and exterior color. However other information is coded into this plate and it each plant is different, as are group of model years.

1970-1972 NORWOOD

Top line of information starts with the letters "ST" this is followed by the last two digits of the model year "70"-1970 "71" 1971 "2"- 1972 following this is the model number:

1970-1972 Firebird Model Numbers

Code	Model
22387	Base Firebird
22487	Esprit
22687	Formula
22887	Trans Am

In the middle of the first line of information is the assembly plant code . Both "N" and "BN" have been seen on tags, both codes stand for Norwood Ohio assembly plant   At the end of this line is the Fisher sequence number, which the actual number of the car built that year; this code will not usually match the last six digits of the VIN.

Second line of information begins with the letters "TR" which stands for trim. This is followed by a three-digit code for the interior trim; this is sometime followed by an additional code representing seat or headrest type.

1970 Interior Trim Color

Code		Color
Vinyl	Knitted Vinyl	
201	211	Blue
N/A	213	Dark Saddle
N/A	214	Red
205	215	Saddle
206	216	Green
207	217	Sandalwood
	227*	*-Cloth and Vinyl
208	218	Black
	228*	*-Cloth and Vinyl
209	219	Black

At the end of the second line are the letters PNT that stands for paint. Preceding these letters is the exterior paint code. Except those models with a vinyl roof it will have the same paint code in both places for example the code 10-10 would mean that the bottom and top portions of the car were paint white. Those with a vinyl roof or special two-tone paint (a rare item on Firebirds) would have a different code in the second place indicating that a different color was used on the roof. (See charts for decoding these numbers.)

The third line of information begins with the beginning build date. This is listed as the month January 01- 12 December and is followed by a letter code that represents the number of week in the month, A-first week to E-fifth week. At the end of this line are groups of numbers the meanings of these numbers is unclear and may have no significant use except to factory workers.

1970 Exterior Color Codes

Code	Color Name
10	Polar White
14	Palladium Silver
19	Starlight Black
25	Bermuda Blue
26	Lucerne Blue
28	Atoll Blue
34	Mint Turquoise
43	Keylime Green
45	Palisade Green
47	Verdoro Green
48	Pepper Green
50	Sierra Yellow
51	Goldenrod Yellow
53	Coronado Gold
55	Baja Gold
58	Granada Gold
60	Orbit Orange
63	Palomino Copper
65	Carousel Red
67	Castilian Bronze
75	Cardinal Red
78	Burgundy
Spec.	Special Color

1971 Interior Trim Color

Code		Color
Vinyl	Knitted Vinyl	
201	211	Blue
N/A	212	Ivory
203	213	Saddle
N/A	214	Sienna
206	216	Jade
207	217	Sandalwood
	227*	*-Cloth and Vinyl
208	218	Black
	228*	*-Cloth and Vinyl
209	219	Black

1971 Exterior Color Codes

Code	Color Name
11	Cameo White
13	Nordic Silver
16	Bluestone Gray
19	Starlight Black
24	Adriatic Blue
26	Lucerne Blue
29	Regency Blue
39	Aquarius Green
42	Limkist Green
43	Tropical Lime
49	Laurentian Green
53	Quezal Gold
55	Baja Gold
59	Aztec Gold
61	Sandalwood
62	Canyon Copper
66	Bronzini Gold
67	Castilian Bronze
75	Cardinal Red
78	Rosewood
Spec.	Special Color

An example of Van Nuys Body Number Tag. It is belived that the first two digits of the last group of numbers on the last line is the production date. The production date here would be February 12, 1970

1972 NORWOOD

All lines of the Norwood tag decode the same as the previous year, including sales codes appearing on the bottom lines. Also the code A51 for bucket seats may follow the date code.

1972 Interior Trim Color

Code		Color
Standard	Custom	
121	221	Ivory
131	231	Dark Saddle
141	241	Green
161	261	Black
	361*	Cloth and Vinyl
N/A	251	Dark Blue
	351*	Cloth and Vinyl
207	217	White
	227*	
208	218	Black
	228*	*-Cloth and Vinyl
209	219	Black

1972 Exterior Color Codes

Code	Color Name
11	Cameo White
14	Revere Silver
18	Antique Pewter
19	Starlight Black
24	Adriatic Blue
26	Lucerne Blue
28	Cumberland Blue
36	Julep Green
48	Wilderness Green
50	Brittany Beige
53	Quezal Gold
54	Arizona Gold
55	Shadow Gold
56	Monarch Yellow
57	Brasilia Gold
62	Spice Beige
63	Anaconda Gold
65	Sundance Orange
69	Cinnamon Bronze
75	Cardinal Red
SPEC.	Special order paint
SHOW	Show- used on show cars
Cust.	Custom
PRIME	Primer only

1973 NORWOOD

The Norwood body number tag has a slightly different appearance due to new models numbers. The basic layout is the same as in previous years, however the bucket seat option code now follows the interior trim code, instead of the date code. Codes following the date code are sales code for the Trans Am package (WS4) or the Formula ram Air hood (WU3) were some times used. Again, just because your car does not have the codes on the tag, dose not mean your car was equipped without these options or is a phony, some cars were coded other were not. Stripe color will sometimes follow these codes, if the car is so equipped with stripes.

1973-1974 Firebird Model Numbers

Code	Model
2FS87	Base Firebird
2FT87	Esprit
2FU87	Formula
2FV87	Trans Am

1970-1972 Vinyl Top Colors Codes

Code	Color Name
1	White
2	Black
5	Sandalwood
7	Dark Gold
9	Dark Green

1973 Interior Trim Color

Code		Color
Standard	Custom	
232	242	White
233	243	Saddle
236	246	Black
N/A	247	Oxblood
N/A	255	Beige

1973 Exterior Color Codes

Code	Color Name
11	Cameo White
19	Starlight Black
24	Adriatic Blue
26	Lucerne Blue
29	Admiralty Blue
42	Verdant Green
44	Slate Green
46	Golden Olive
48	Brewster Green
51	Sunlight Yellow
56	Desert Sand
60	Valencia Gold
64	Ascot Silver
66	Burnished Umber
68	Burma Brown
74	Florentine Red
74*	Honduras Maroon
75	Buccaneer Red
81	Mesa Tan
97	Navajo Orange
SPEC.	Special order paint
SHOW	Show- used on show cars
Cust.	Custom
PRIME	Primer only

*-Used after build date 07B (2nd week in July 1973)

1974-1978 NORWOOD

Not much changed in the way the tag decodes. The biggest change was the addition of a color code for the steering column that ends the build date line. The numbers below this are not known at this time. Be aware that there is a change in model numbers in 1975.

1975-1978 Firebird Model Numbers

Code	Model
2FS87	Base Firebird
2FT87	Esprit
2FU87	Formula
2FW87	Trans Am

1974-1978 Steering Column Color Codes

Code	Model
BLK	Black
SAD	Saddle
GRN	Green
RED	Red
BLU	Blue
OXB	Oxblood
BUK	Buckskin
	Firethorn
TAN	Tan
CAR	Carmine
LTB	Light Blue

Be aware also that there was a mistamping of the body plates on cars built at the Norwood assembly plant in 1975 From the start of production to February 28, 1975 up to VIN 2N87S51V532929 those models with a vinyl top were not so code. The code for the vinyl roof was not listed it was stamped with a _ or left blank. Cars without a vinyl roof were not affected and have the paint code stamped. After this VIN and date the vinyl code was stamped onto the body plate.

1976-1978 LOS ANGELES

This tag used the same model numbers, trim code, and exterior codes that were used on the Norwood tags. They decoded in much the same way. However there are slight differences. You may notice the letter "W" preceding the paint code this is for water based painted, the code "L" means that a lacquer-based paint was used. Don't confuse this with the letter "L" following the code; this indicates the lower portion of the car, as the letter "U" indicates the upper part. See 1979-1980 LOS ANGELES for more information about decoding the trim codes.

The last line is also unique to Van Nuys cars. It will begin with the build date, which is the month and a letter indicating the number week in the month, A-1st, B-2nd, C- 3rd and so on. The letter code that follows this code is the steering wheel and instrument panel color. Following this is a dash on most cars and the number "3" if power windows were ordered. Base Firebirds will have another dash following this code.

Steering Column Color Code Van Nuys

Code	Model
B	Black
U	Blue
T	Tan
C	Red
G	Green

1978 Body tag for Los Angeles assembly plant, note that his car was painted with a water-based paint which indicated by the letter W" proceeding the paint code.

1979-1980 ANGELES

Revamp in the way the tag is laid out. The top line begins with the last two digits of the model year "79"-1979, "80"-1980; this is followed by the built date. Although the build date location changed it decodes the same as in previous years. Following this is the model code, assembly plant code and the unit number. Although they sometimes ran tighter and look like a VIN , they are the same as the last six digits of this number is for the Fisher Body assembly plant and is the sequential number built at that plant. Do not worry if this number does not match that on the VIN, this is common.

Second line begins with the trim code, which is now a two-digit and letter code, no TR letter appear on this line as in years past. This code breaks down further as follows. First two digits are the base interior trim colors, the code after this is the type of material.

The trim code is followed by the lower and upper body color marked with the letters "L" and "U" (sometimes T) respectively. And the end of this line is the code for the type of paint used. The following codes were used: "W" water based; "L" lacquer based and "S" special paint.

The third line of information is now the seat type code. All Firebirds were given the code A51 for bucket seats. If the car is ordered with T-Tops then the code "CC1" will appear next, if not, then three dashes will appear here. Next to this is the single letter code for the steering column color. The number "3' will appear next if power windows were ordered, if standard windows were then a dash was used. The last of the numbers on this line are not known.

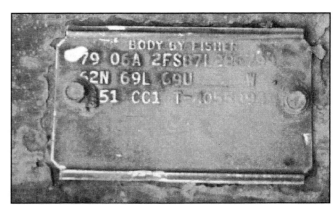

1979 Trans Am built at the Los Angeles assembly plant. Note the CC1 code indicating t-top roof panels.

1979 Trans Am built at the Norwood, Ohio assembly pant Note the option code of A31 and WS4 that are stamped on the tag.

1979-1980 NORWOOD

The Ohio based assembly plant also got a new tag. It's appearance and the way it decodes look pretty much like the Van Nuys (Los Angeles) tag. The difference is in the last line. The line still began with the seat code for bucket seat (A51) and if T-tops were ordered then the code CC1 would follow; after this other option codes like WS4 for Trans Am A31 Power windows and other sales codes may follow. The color of the steering column will appear at the end of this line or just below it in an abbreviated form.

1981 LOS ANGELES

 This tag looked much like the 1979-80 format, except that the seat type code A51 was on a line by itself, if T-tops were ordered then the code CC1 will also appear here. The steering column code and option codes were dropped down to a separate line.

1981 NORWOOD

 There very little change in the way this tag looked also. The A51 seat type code and if so equipped CC1 T-top codes were on a line by themselves. The sales code list was dropped down on a line by itself, but the steering column color also appeared on this line.

1973 Vinyl Top Colors Codes

Code	Color Name
A	White
B	Black
F	Chamois
G	Green
H	Maroon
T	Neutral

1974 Exterior Color Codes

Code	Color Name
11	Cameo White
19	Starlight Black
24	Adriatic Blue
26	Lucerne Blue
29	Admiralty Blue
36	Gulfmist Aqua
40	Fernmist Green
44	Lakemist Green
46	Limefire Green
49	Pinemist Green
50	Carmel
51	Sunstrom Yellow
55	Denver Gold
59	Crestwood Brown
64	Ascot Silver
66	Fire Coal Bronze
69	Shadowmist Brown
74	Honduras Maroon
75	Buccaneer Red
97	Navajo Orange
SPEC.	Special order paint
SHOW	Show- used on show cars
Cust.	Custom
PRIME	Primer only

1974 Interior Trim Color

Code		Color
Standard	Custom	
573	593	Saddle
	583*	*-Cloth and Vinyl
576	596	Black
	586*	*Cloth and Vinyl
572	592	White
N/A	594	Green
N/A	590	Red

1974 Vinyl Top Colors Codes

Code	Color Name
A	White
B	Black
D	Blue
E	Beige
F	Brown
G	Green
H	Maroon
L	Russet
R	Saddle
W	Taupe

1975 Exterior Color Codes

Code	Color Name
11	Cameo White
13	Sterling Silver
15	Graystone
19	Starlight Black
24	Arctic Blue
26	Bimini Blue
29	Stellar Blue
31	Gray
39	Burgundy
44	Lakemist Green
45	Augusta Green
49	Alpine Green
50	Carmel
51	Sunstrom Yellow
55	Sandstone
58	Ginger Brown
59	Oxford Brown
63	Copper Mist
64	Persimmon
66	Fire Coal Bronze
72	Roman Red
74	Honduras Maroon
75	Buccaneer Red
80	Tampico Orange
SPEC.	Special order paint
SHOW	Show- used on show cars
Cust.	Custom
PRIME	Primer only

1975 Interior Trim Color

Code		Color
Standard	Custom	
11V	11W	White
19V	19W	Black
N/A	26W	Blue
63V	63W	Saddle
N/A	73W	Oxblood

1975 Vinyl Top Colors Codes

Code	Color Name
11T	White
13T	Silver
19T	Black
28T	Dark Blue
44T	Med. Green
55T	Sandstone
68T	Cordovan
74T	Maroon
75T	Red

1976 Exterior Color Codes

Code	Color Name
11	Cameo White
13	Sterling Silver
16	Med. Gray
19	Starlight Black
28	Athena Blue
35	Polaris Blue
36	Firethorn Red
37	Cordovan Maroon
40	Metallime Green
49	Alpine Green
50	Bavarian Cream
51	Goldenrod Yellow
55	Anniversary Gold
57	Cream Gold
65	Bucksin Tan
67	Durango Bronze
72	Roman Red
74	Honduras Maroon
75	Buccaneer Red
78	Carousel Red
SPEC.	Special order paint
SHOW	Show- used on show cars
Cust.	Custom
PRIME	Primer only

1976 Interior Trim Color

Code		Color
Standard	Custom	
11N	11M	White
19N	19M	Black
91N	91M	
26N	N/A	Blue
92N		
64N	64M	Buckskin
71N	N/A	Firethorn
97N		

1976 Vinyl Top Colors Codes

Code	Color Name
11T	White
13T	Silver
19T	Black
35T	Dark Blue
36T	Firethorn
37T	Mahogany
65T	Buckskin

1977 Exterior Color Codes

Code	Color Name
11	Cameo White
13	Sterling Silver
15	Gray
19	Starlight Black
21	Lombard Blue
22	Glacier Blue
29	Nautilus Blue
32	Royal Lime
36	Firethorn Red
37	Cordovan Maroon
38	Aquamarine
44	Bahia Green
48	Berkshire Green
50	Cream Gold
51	Goldenrod Yellow
61	Mojave Tan
63	Buckskin
64	Feist Orange
69	Brentwood Brown
72	Roman Red
75	Buccaneer Red
78	Mandarin Orange
SPEC.	Special order paint
SHOW	Show- used on show cars
Cust.	Custom
PRIME	Primer only

1977 Interior Trim Color

Code		Color
Standard	Custom	
11R	11N	White
19R	19N	Black
	19B*	Cloth and Vinyl
N/A	24N	Blue
	92N	
64R	64N	Buckskin
71R	71N	Firethorn
97R	97N	*-Cloth and Vinyl
	71B*	

1977 Vinyl Top Colors Codes

Code	Color Name
11T	White
13T	Sliver
19T	Black
22T	Light Blue
44T	Med. Green
61T	Light Buckskin

1978 Exterior Color Codes

Code	Color Name
11	Cameo White
15	Platinum
16	Gray
19	Starlight Black
21	Dresden Blue
22	Glacier Blue
24	Martinique Blue
29	Nautilus Blue
30	Lombard Blue
44	Seafoam Green
45	Mayfair Green
48	Berkshire Green
50	Gold (1)
51	Sundance Yellow
55	Gold (2)
56	Burnished Gold
58	Blue (2)
61	Desert Sand
67	Ember Mist
69	Chesterfield Brown
75	Mayan Red
77	Carmine Red
79	Claret
85	Med. Blue Irid
SPEC.	Special order paint
SHOW	Show- used on show cars
Cust.	Custom
PRIME	Primer only
(1)	S/E Firebird
(2)	Accent color

1978 Interior Trim Color

Code		Color
Standard	Custom	
11R	11N	White
19R	19N	Black
	19B*	Cloth and Vinyl
N/A	24N	Blue
	92N	
62R	62N	Dark Camel
	62B*	*Cloth and Vinyl
74R	71N	Dark Carmine
	97N	*-Cloth and Vinyl
	71B*	

1978 Vinyl Top Colors Codes

Code	Color Name
11T	White
15T	Silver
19T	Black
22T	Light Blue
44T	Med. Green
61T	Light Buckskin
79T	Dark Carmine

1979 Exterior Color Codes

Code	Color Name
11	Cameo White
15	Silver
16#	Gray
19	Black
21	Pastel Blue
22	Light Blue
24	Bright Blue
29	Dark Blue
40	Pastel Green
44	Medium Green
50**	Gold
51	Bright Yellow
54	Lt. Yellow
61	Med. Beige
63	Camel
69	Dk. Brown
75	Red
77	Carmine
79	DK. Carmine
80**	Red
85#	Med. Blue
56	Gold (2)
SPEC.	Special order paint
SHOW	Show- used on show cars
Cust.	Custom
PRIME	Primer only
**- Special Order Colors only	
#-Two Tone only	
(2) Accent color only	

1979 Interior Trim Color

Code		Color
Standard	Custom	
12R	12N	Oyster
19R	19N	Black
	19B*	*-Cloth and Vinyl
	24N	Lt. Blue
	24B*	*-Cloth and Vinyl
62R	62N	Dk. Camel
	62B*	*-Cloth and Vinyl
74R	74N	Dk. Carmine
	74B*	*-Cloth and Vinyl
N/A	152	Silver

1979 Vinyl Top Colors Codes

Code	Color Name
11T	White
15T	Silver
19T	Black
22T	Light Blue
40T	Pastel Green
61T	Med. Beige
79T	Dark Carmine

1980 Exterior Color Codes

Code	Color Name
11	White
15	Platinum
16#	Gray
19	Black
21	Lt. Blue
22#	Med. Blue
24	Bright Blue
29	Dark Blue
37	Accent Yellow
40	Lime Green
44	Dk. Green
50	Yellow
51	Bright Yellow
56	Yellow;
57	Gold
59	Beige
63	Lt. Camel
67	Dk. Brown
72	Red
75	Claret
76	Dk. Claret
77	Cinnabar
79	Red Orange
80	Rust
84	Charcoal
85	Vapor Gray
PRIME	Primer only
#-Two Tone only	

1980 Interior Trim Color

Code		Color
Standard	Custom	
12R	12N	Oyster
	12C*	*Cloth and Vinyl
19R	19N	Black
	19B*	*Cloth and Vinyl
26D	26N	Dark Blue
26R	26B*	*Cloth and Vinyl
62D	62N	Dark Camel
62R	62B	*Cloth and Vinyl
74R	74N	Dark Carmine
	74B*	*-Cloth and Vinyl

1980 Vinyl Top Colors Codes

Code	Color Name
11T	White
19T	Black
12T	Light Blue
44T	Dark Green
63T	Camel
76T	Dark Claret
85T	Gray

1981 Exterior Color Codes

Code	Color Name
11	White
16	Stardust Silver
19	Black
20	Vibrant Blue
22	Kingston Blue
29	Nightwatch Blue
35	Pastel Waxberry
36	Shadow Gold
37	Burnished Umber
40	Yellow Bird Yellow
41	Yellow Accent
45	Lt. Jadestone Met.
47	Dk. Jadestone Met.
48	Pinehurst Green
51	Tahitian Yellow
54	Baniff Blue
56	Yellow
57	Navajo Orange
58	Burnt Orange
63	Pastel Sandstone
67	Barclay Brown
68	Med. Sandstone
72	Lt. Maple Met.
75	Spectra Red
77	Autumn Gold
84	Ontario Gray

1981 Interior Trim Color

Code		Color
Standard	Custom	
15V	15W	Silver
19N	N/A	Black
		*Cloth and Vinyl
26R	26D	Dark Blue
	26N	*Cloth and Vinyl
	26B	
63B	N/A	Lt. Sandstone
64D	64N	Buckskin
64R	64B	
75R	75N	Med. Red
	75B	

1981 Vinyl Top Colors Codes

Code	Color Name
11T	White
19T	Black
29T	Dark Blue
36T	Waxberry
45T	Jadestone
63T	Pastel Sandstone
64T	Doeskin
77T	Dark Maple
85T	Med. Slate

Frames

All second generation Firebirds are built on GM's F-body format, which it shares with its GM cousin the Chevrolet Camaro. This platform consists of unitized construction. A sub frame supported the front-end sheet metal, front suspension, engine and in some cases the transmission. Because of this design it is essential that the sub-frame be properly aligned, to ensured correct suspension location. If you are buying or restoring a Firebird you believed has been in a collision it is a must that you check the alignment, and if needed have it realigned. This is a repair that is best left to professionals, as the over all strength of the frame is essential to the way the car will handle and body panels will align. If the frame is beyond repair then it is best to replace the whole unit. Be aware that many different frames were used and have little interchange due to the way sheet metal and other components attach to it.

Front Sub-Frames Part Numbers

1970	3989418
1971-1973	3964800
1974	462835
1975	462835
1976-1979	14000882
1980-1981	14013090

The transmission assembly was supported at the rear of the sub frame by a cross-member. The part number for this part is dependent on the transmission type. Both the frame assembly and the transmission cross-member should be painted first with a good quality primer. Then both assemblies should be painted with semi-gloss black (Chassis Black) for detail.

Transmission Cross-Member Part Numbers

3-speed	3964816	1970-1975	
Manual	344677-	1976-79	
4-speed	3964816	1970-1975	
Manual	344677-	1976-79	
3-speed	3964819*	1970-75	All
Automatic	344677**	1976-81	
3-speed	3964816#	1970-75	All
Automatic	344677#	1976-81	

*- M35 **M38 # M40

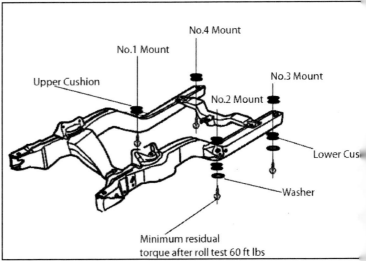

Four rubber cushion body mounts were used.

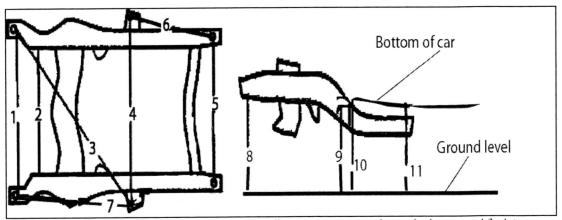

1970-1972 Front sub frame alignment measurements. All measurements are taken to dead center and flush to adjacent surface.

Fig Ref.	Dimension	Fig Ref.	Dimension
Horizontal Dimensions		**Vertical Dimensions**	
Front Sub Frame			
1	37-11/16	8	9-11/16
2	28-13/16	9	9-1/16
3	57-1/4	10	9-15/16
4	45-1/4	11	3-9/16
5	33-7/16		
6	32-7/8		
7	39-5/8		
Rear Frame Rails			
A	37-1/16	F	3-5/16
B	60-13/16	G	17-1/16
C	43-11/16	H	13-1/4
D	45-3/8		
E	45-7/16		

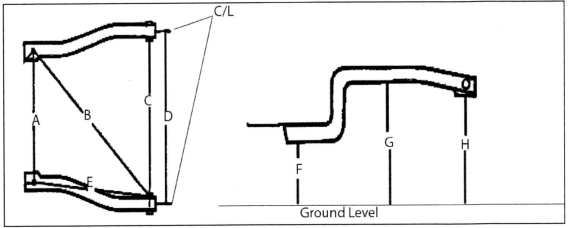

1970-1972 Rear frame rail dimensions

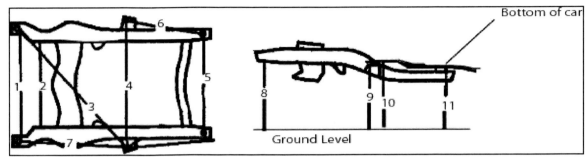

1974 Front sub frame alignment measurements. All measurements are taken to dead center and flush to adjacent surface, 1975 similar

Fig Ref.	Dimension	Fig Ref.	Dimension
Horizontal Dimensions		**Vertical Dimensions**	
Front Sub Frame			
1	37-11/16	8	9-11/16
2	28-13/16	9	9-1/16
3	57-1/4	10	9-15/16
4	45-1/4	11	3-9/16
5	33-7/16		
6	32-7/8		
7	39-5/8		
Rear Frame Rails			
A	37-1/16	F	3/4
B	60-3/4	G	13-3/4
C	43-9/16	H	10-1/4
D	38.00		
E	45-7/16		

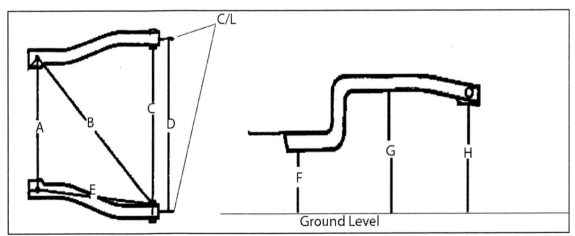

1974 Rear frame rail dimensions, 1975 is similar.

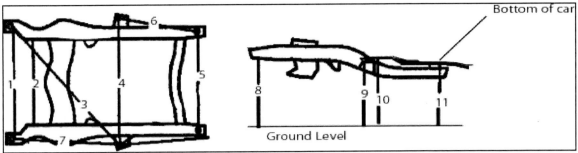

1978 Frame dimensions 1976, 1977 and 1979 are similar

Fig Ref.	Dimension	Fig Ref.	Dimension
Horizontal Dimensions		**Vertical Dimensions**	
Front Sub Frame			
1	37-11/16	8	9-11/16
2	28-13/16	9	9-1/16
3	57-1/4	10	9-15/16
4	45-1/4	11	3-9/16
5	33-7/16		
6	32-7/8		
7	39-5/8		
Rear Frame Rails			
A	37-1/16	F	7/8
B	60-7/16	G	13-3/4
C	43-9/16	H	10-1/4
D	38.00		
E	45-1/4		

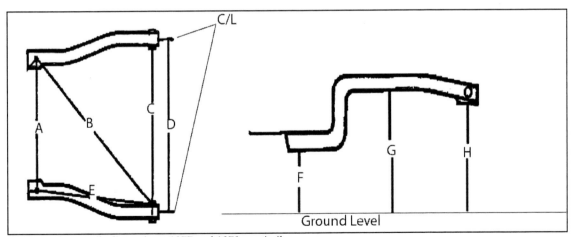

1978 rear frame rails dimensions, 1977 and 1979 are similar.

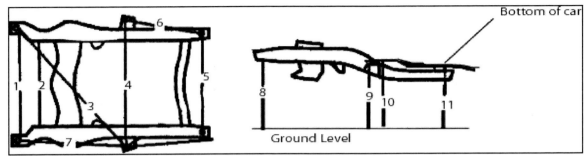

1981 front frame dimensions 1980 is similar.

Fig Ref.	Dimension	Fig Ref.	Dimension
Horizontal Dimensions		**Vertical Dimensions**	
Front Sub Frame			
1	37-11/16	8	9-11/16
2	28-13/16	9	9-1/16
3	57-1/4	10	9-15/16
4	45-1/4	11	3-9/16
5	33-7/16		
6	32-7/8		
7	39-5/8		
Rear Frame Rails			
A	37-1/16	F	7/8
B	60-7/16	G	13-3/4
C	43-9/16	H	10-1/4
D	38.00		
E	45-1/4		

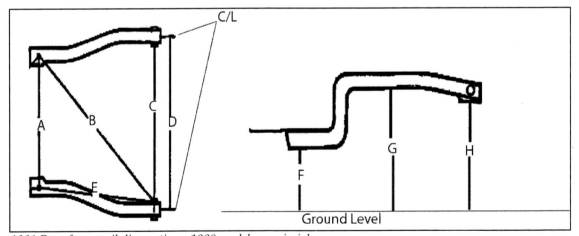

1981 Rear frame rail diamentions, 1980 models are simialr

Suspension and Steering Systems

Front Suspension

All second generation Firebirds had the same type of front suspension system. That consisted of wishbone type upper and lower control arms with a coil spring wedge in between. Based on proven designs like countless other GM models, this design is highly stable and except under great stress provided a good handling ride. Different rates of springs were used according to the suspension option and power plant that was ordered. For example springs were higher rated in a car with a 455 ci V-8 than those with a 350-ci V-8.

The upper and lower control arms originally were dipped, at the part manufacturing plant, in a semi-gloss black paint to keep the parts from rusting on the shelves. Dipping these parts in paint should not be an option to the restorer, as the results will be less than expected. To duplicate the like new appearance, spray the arms with chassis black. For the upper arm the entire assembly should be painted black. The lower control all of the arms except approximately 2-inches at the ball joint end should be painted chassis black. Originally this end was the end that was held when the part was dipped and was left natural and unpainted, painting that end detail gray can duplicate this look. For other details use a small brush and dab silver model paint on the heads of the rivets that hold the ball joint. The mounting bolts had a flat black finish. However, in some later built models parts were never painted. You have a choice here; you can either paint the parts gloss black for detail, or paint them to duplicate the look of unpainted metal.

Upper And Lower Control Arms

Part Number		Position
Left	Right	
1970-1972		
3964833	3964834	Lower
3964827	3964828	Upper
1973		
3964833	3964834	Lower
3312877	3312878	Upper
1974-1979		
6260591	65260592	Lower
335893	335893	Upper
1980-1981		
14039015	14039016	Lower
14039013	14039014	Upper

SPRINGS

Several different rates of springs were used according to the options that were installed on the car. Springs should have a natural appearance, which can be duplicated by painting them detail gray. Up to 1973 models the spring usage was determined by model, engine size and transmission type. Beginning in 1973 the front coil springs were computer selected, according to certain options and their weight on the front wheels. According to technical bulletin Number 73-T-29 a scraping noise could occur on the Left-hand coil spring on spring codes AV or AW; to fix this the springs were replaced with codes AU and CR, respectively. AU springs were implemented into production beginning at VIN 3N122540 and beginning with VIN 3N122529 the CR spring was implanted into production. Thus either an AV or AU or AW or CR code would be correct for an early built Firebird, but only the AU or CR codes are correct for later built Firebirds. However, the AV and AW codes were deleted, so only the AU or CR codes should be used.

1970 Firebird Front Coil Spring Usage Chart										
Manual and Two-Speed Automatic Transmissions										
Model	6-cyld.	350-ci	Trans Am or with 400-ci*	Formula 400		350-ci with a/c	Trans Am With a/c Or with 400-ci*	Formula 400 with a/c		
				Ex. Ram Air IV	Ram Air IV			Ex. Ram Air IV	Ram Air IV	
	3996362	3996365	344537	344537	344537	344537	3988100	3968104	3988100	
With M38 Automatic Transmission										
	3996362	344537				344537				
With M-40 Automatic Transmission										
			344537	3988100	3988104		3988104	3988100	3988104	
*- Except with Ram Air IV Check Formula 400 with Ram Air IV for Trans Am with Ram Air IV										

1970 Front Coil Springs part numbers

1971-1972 Firebird Front Coil Spring Usage Chart									
Manual and Two-Speed Automatic Transmissions									
Model	6-cyld.	350-ci	Trans Am or with 455-ci	Formula 400/455		350-ci with a/c	Trans Am With a/c Or with 455-ci*	Formula 400/455 with a/c	
				400-ci	455-ci			400-ci	455-ci
	3996362	3996365	344537	344537	344537	344537	3988100	3968104	3988100
With M38 Automatic Transmission									
	3996362	344537				344537			
With M-40 Automatic Transmission									
			344537	3988100	3988104		3988104	3988100	3988104

1971-1972 Front coil spring part numbers

1973 RPO Selection Chart For Firebird Springs			
		Spring Option Weights	
Code	**Option**	**Front**	**Rear**
CF7	Sun Roof	2.5	3.0
C60	Air Conditioning	54.0	2.0
D55	Console	3.5	2.5
JL2	Power Disc Brakes	4.5	1.0
L30	350-ci 2-bbl	99.0	11.5
L65	400-ci 2-bbl	101.0	11.8
L78	400-ci 4-bbl	1060	13.0
L75	455-ci 4-bbl	112.5	13.0
M38	Automatic	8.0	3.5
M40	Automatic	14.0	6.0
N41	Power Steering	14.5	0
V01	H.D Radiator	7.5	0
WS4	Trans Am Package	4.0	38.5
W66	Formula Package	2.0	11.0
Y89	Handling Package	4.0	3.5
Front Coil Spring Sprung Weight Chart			
Model	**Sprung Weight**	**Codes**	**Code Part Numbers**
V-8	0-940	AR, AU	AU- 396365
	941-100	AV, AW	AW-344537
	1001- Over	CR, CS	CR-3998629

1973 Firebird front coil springs. Add up listed option weights add to base weight of 795. Check weight total in chart check service code. Cross-reference service code and find part number

RPO OPTION WEIGHTS- 1974 Firebird

Option	Front	Rear
C60 Air Conditioning	54.0	2.0
D55 Front Console	3.5	2.5
JL2 Power Disc Brakes	4.5	1.0
LS2 455 4-bbl Super Duty Engine	112.5	13.5
L30 350-ci 2-bbl Engine	99.0	11.5
L65 400-ci 2-bbl Engine	101.0	11.5
L75 455-ci 4-bbl Engine	110.0	13.0
L78 400-ci 4-bbl Engine	111.0	13.0
M38 T.H. 350 Lt. Duty Transmission	8.0	3.5
M40 T.H. 400	14.0	6.0
U57 Stereo Tape Player	4.0	1.5
U63 Radio	3.0	1.0
V01 Heavy-Duty Cooling	6.5	0.0
WX3 Shaker Hood	4.0	0.0

1974 Firebird Front coil spring part numbers add up total option weights to base weight of 812.Look in chart below for part number

Sprung Weight and Part Numbers 1974 Firebird

Model	Spring weight Total	Spring Part Number
Six Cylinder	All	3996362
V-8 with F78x14 or GR70x15 Tires	0-937	3996365
	938-999	344537
	1000-Over	3998629
V-8 with E78x14 or FR78x14 Tires	0-906	3996365
	907-969	344537
	970-Over	3998629

RPO OPTION WEIGHTS- 1975 Firebird

Option		Front	Rear
A31 Power Windows		2.4	2.6
C60 Air Conditioning	Six-Cylinder	42.5	5.0
	V-8	50.0	2.0
D55 Front Console		3.6	2.5
JL2 Power Disc Brakes		5.0	1.0
K19 A.I.R. Emissions	Six Cylinder	6.0	0.0
	V-8	7.0	0.0
L30 350-ci 2-bbl Engine		99.0	12.7
L76 350-ci 4-bbl Engine		91.5	13.0
L78 400-ci 4-bbl Engine		106.8	13.7
M38 T.H. 350 Lt. Duty Transmission		7.0	3.0
N10 Dual Exhaust		4.0	6.4
TP1 Maintenance Free Battery	Six Cylinder	5.6	0.0
	V-8	5.7	0.0
U57 Stereo Tape Player		4.0	2.0
U63 Radio		3.0	1.0
V01 Heavy-Duty Cooling		7.5	0.0

1975 Front coil springs add total option weights to base total of 854 to get spring weight totals.

Sprung Weight and Part Numbers 1975 Firebird

Model	Spring weight Total	Spring Part Number
With FR78x15 or F78x14 Tires	0-969	3988104
	970- Over	3988106
With GR70x15 Tires	0-981	3988104
	982-1040	3988106
	1041-Over	3988108

1976 Firebird Base Weight For Spring Selection

Model	Base Spring Weight	
	Front	Rear
Firebird Coupe Six Cylinder	857	585
Esprit Coupe	865	599
Formula Coupe	952	607
Trans Am Coupe	952	602

RPO OPTION WEIGHTS- 1976 Firebird

Option	Front	Rear
A31 Power Windows	2.4	2.6
C60 Air Conditioning Six-Cylinder	37.5	4.0
V-8	56.0	4.5
D55 Front Console	3.6	2.5
JL2 Power Disc Brakes	4.5	1.0
K19 A.I.R. Emissions Six Cylinder	6.5	0.0
V-8	7.0	0.0
L30 350-ci 2-bbl Engine	77.5	13.0
L76 350-ci 4-bbl Engine	79.5	13.0
L78 400-ci 4-bbl Engine	83.5	13.7
M38 T.H. 350 Lt. Duty Transmission	7.0	3.0
U57 Stereo Tape Player	4.0	2.0
U58 AM/FM Stereo	3.4	3.4
U63 AM Radio	2.5	1.0
U69 Am/Fm Radio	3.9	1.0
V02 Super Cooling Radiator	7.5	0.0
W66 Formula Option Group	1.0	3.0

Add base weight for spring selection according to model, than add total option weights to obtain spring section

Sprung Weight and Part Numbers 1976 Firebird

Model	Spring weight Total	Spring Part Number
With FR78x15 or F78x14 Tires	0-920	3988113
	921-957	462508
	958-Over	462509
With GR70x15 Tires	0-981	3988104
	982-1040	3988106
	1041-Over	3988108

1977 Firebird Base Weight For Spring Selection

Model	Base Spring Weight	
	Front	Rear
Firebird Coupe	812	575
Esprit Coupe	819	588
Formula Coupe	872	587
Trans Am Coupe	910	590

RPO OPTION WEIGHTS- 1977 Firebird

Option	Front	Rear
A31 Power Windows	2.4	2.6
C-60 Air Conditioning	56.0	4.5
D55 Front Console	3.6	2.5
JL2 Power Disc Brakes	7.0	2.0
A.I.R Emissions	8.0	0.0
L27 301-ci 2-bbl Engine	43.0	5.0
L34 350-ci (R)	59.0	7.0
L76 350-ci 4-bbl Engine	82.0	12.0
L78 400-ci 4-bbl Engine	89.0	9.5
L80 403-ci 4-bbl Engine	68.0	7.0
M38 T.H. 350	7.0	3.0
U57 Stereo Tape Player	4.0	2.0
U58 AM/FM Stereo	4.4	3.9
U63 AM Radio	2.5	1.0
U69 Am/Fm Radio	3.0	1.0
V02 Super Cooling Radiator	7.5	0.0

Add total option weight to base spring weight according to model to obtain total sprung weight

Sprung Weight and Part Numbers 1977 Firebird

Model	Spring weight Total	Spring Part Number
With six-cylinder or 301-ci V-8 (except Firm Ride or Trailer tow)	0-886	354161
	887-919	3982354
	920-Over	3988104
With 350-ci, 400-ci or 403-ci (except Firm Ride or Trailer Tow)	0-950	3988113
	950-Over	462509
With Firm Ride Or Trailer Tow	0-975	6262428
	976-Over	6262430

1978 Firebird Base Weight For Spring Selection

Model	Base Spring Weight	
	Front	Rear
Firebird Coupe 231-ci	810	587
Esprit Coupe	808	584
Formula Coupe	878	593
Trans Am Coupe	905	592

RPO OPTION WEIGHTS- 1978 Firebird

Option	Front	Rear
A31 Power Windows	1.8	2.0
BS1 Acoustical Body	1.6	9.6
B37 Floor Mats Front And Rear	2.3	2.5
CC1 Hatch Roof	6.4	10.3
C-60 Air Conditioning	46.9	2.8
D55 Front Console	3.6	2.5
D80 Rear Spoiler	0.0	5.1
JL2 Power Disc Brakes	4.5	.5
A.I.R Emissions	7.5	0.0
LG3 305-ci 2-bbl Chevy Engine	60.0	7.0
LM1 350-ci 4-bbl Chevy Engine	70.0	8.0
L78 400-ci 4-bbl Engine	93.3	10.0
L80 403-ci 4-bbl Engine	68.0	7.0
M33 Transmission	7.0	3.0
UA1 Heavy Duty Battery	6.0	0.0
U58 AM/FM Stereo	4.4	3.9
WS4 Trans Am Option	2.0	3.9

Sprung Weight and Part Numbers 1978 Firebird

Model	Spring weight Total	Spring Part Number
With 231 or 305 or #50-ci Chevy eninge)	0-854	354161
	855-919	3982354
	920- over	3988104
With 400 or 403-ci	0-950	3988113
	951- Over	462503

Although still selected by weight of the vehicle in 1979, charts were not used to select the spring. Instead you either select it from the original production code that was taped to the spring or locate the "GAWRF" weight on the sticker that is located on the driver's door. Note this weight was in kilograms (kg). Weight was spelled according to model and engine size. This method of selecting springs was used from 1979-1981.

1979 Firebird Front Spring GAWRF Range

Except 400/403 or Special Performance	Part Number
0-926	354161
927-986	3982354
987-Over	3988104
400/403 or Special Perforamnce	
0-953	3988113
954-Over	462509

1979 Firebird Front Spring Code

Production Code	Part Number
EV, HI,ATK	354161
ATM,ATX	3982354
HL,ATY	3988104
KU,KV	3988113
KW,KX, AUM	462509

1980 Firebird Front Spring GAWRF Range

With Standard Suspension	Part Number
0-892	462503
893-954	354161
955-1013	3982354
1014-Over	3988104
Formula/Trans AM with Standard Suspension	
0-892	462503
93-954	354161
955-1013	3982354
1014-Over	3988104
Special Performance Suspension (WS6)	
0-1002	3988111
1003-1041	3988113
1042-1144	432509
1145-Over	462511

1980-81 Firebird Front Spring GAWRF Range

Production Code	Part Number
Standard Suspension	
AUB, AUC	462503
	354161
ATM,ATX	3982354
ATY	3988104
Formula/Trans AM with Standard Suspension	
AUB, AUIC	462503
EV, ATK	354161
ATM,ATX	3982354
ATY	3988104
Special Performance Suspension (WS6)	
KJ, KT	3988111
KU,KV	3988113
KW, KX	432509
AUN,AUR	462511

1980-81 Firebird Front Spring GAWRF Range

Production Code	Part Number
Standard Suspension	
AUB, AUC	462503
	354161
ATM,ATX	3982354
ATY	3988104
Formula/Trans AM with Standard Suspension	
AUB, AUIC	462503
EV, ATK	354161
ATM,ATX	3982354
ATY	3988104
Special Performance Suspension (WS6)	
KJ, KT	3988111
KU,KV	3988113
KW, KX	432509
AUN,AUR	462511

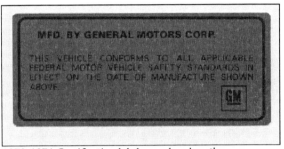

1970-1974 Certification label was placed on the driver's door Decal Courtesy of Jim Osborne Reproductions

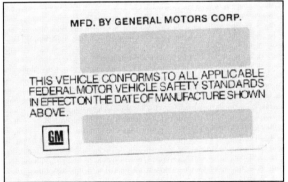

1975 Certification label was also used on the driver's door. Upper the manufacture date below is the VIN Decal Courtesy of Jim Osborne Reproductions

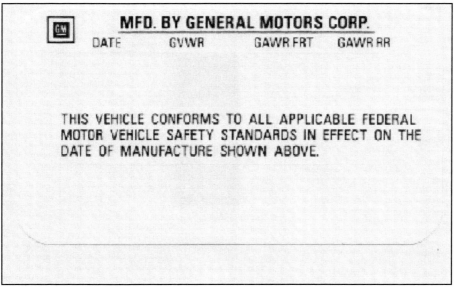

1976-1981 Certification label, springs were regulated by the GAWR ratings. Decal Courtesy of Jim Osborne Reproductions

SHOCK ABSORBERS, FRONT

There were several different manufacturers of shock absorbers Most of them were made by the Delco-Ramey and the body of the shock assembly should have a semi-gloss dove gray appearance. However, others were painted semi-gloss black. Shocks were sent directly from the manufactures to a dealer that was replacing the part, they were not considered a standard GM part. Part number 5535623 (1154078 merchandise number) was used on all 1970-1977 Firebirds; in 1978 the part number was changed to 4993544 and continued into 1979 model year. For 1980 two different shocks were used standard was part number 5535623 while Trans Am, Formula or those with special performance suspension (WS6 or WS7) used part number 4993544, these same shocks with the same restrictions were used again in 1981 models.

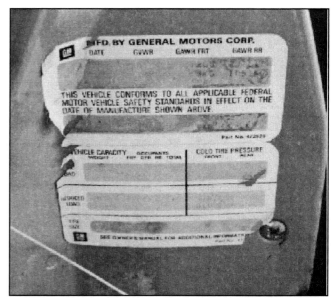

1978 certification label shown in place on the driver's door.

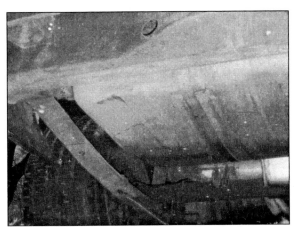

All second-generation Firebirds used multiple leaf rear springs.

SWAY BAR, FRONT

Various sizes were used according to suspension package and/or model. The bar should have a semi-gloss black appearance; duplicate this by painting it chassis black. However, some bars were left natural, this can be duplicated by painting it detail gray.

Trans Am models used the largest diameter bar, which was also optional on Formula 400 and 455 models. The Formula bar was used on base and Esprit models with firm ride package.

Front Sway Bar Part Numbers

Model Year	Diameter	Part Number	Notes:
1970-74	15/16	3965651	(1)
1970-74	1-1/8	3975523	(2)
1970-74	1-1/4	3986480	(3), (4)
1975-1981	1.00	356530	(1)
1975-1981	1-1/4	356534	(2) (3), (4)

(1) Except Formula Trans Am or with Firm Ride
(2) Formula
(3) Trans Am
(4) Firm Ride

Rear Suspension

The F-body (what Pontiac calls the Firebird line) rear suspension consists of multi-leaf rear spring design. The springs are rubber mounted at the underbody side rail attachment points. This design insured uniform spring loading while minimizing the transmission of road noise to the passenger compartment. The springs are positioned to the axle by a locating bolt placed close to the center of the spring.

Several different springs were used. Usage depends on model; Formula and Trans Am models utilized heavier-duty springs than say an Esprit model, engine size also dramatically affected the rear spring usage. However, more individual leaves does not necessarily means that the springs are higher rated. In fact the heavy-duty units used on Trans Ams had five individual springs on each side while the six-cylinder had six individual springs, yet the Trans Am springs are heavier-duty and provide better handling characteristics.

The springs should have a natural appearance this can be duplicated by painting them detail gray, which gives the illusion of unpainted steel. The spring shackles and brackets were painted semi-gloss black (chassis black) the U-bolt that holds the springs together should have a natural appearance.

Just as with the front coil springs beginning in 1973 the rear springs were no longer regulated by the model but were selected by computer based on total sprung weight, at the factory. But weight did not affect the rear springs as much as front coil units, and basically the main factor affecting rear springs was again model and engine size. Later on tire size would be more a factor. To select by weight use the RPO Option chart located in the "Front springs' Section of this chapter. Listed below is the rear Base Sprung weight of each model year.

Total Rear Sprung Weight

1973	542
1974	596
1975	590
1976	585-6-cyld
	599-Esprit
	607-Formula
	602-Trans Am
1977	575-Base
	588 Esprit
	587-Formula
	590-Trans Am
1978	587-Base
	584 Esprit
	593-Formula
	592-Trans Am

Although still selected by weight of the vehicle in 1979, charts were not used to select the spring. Instead, you either select it from the original production code that was taped to the spring or locate the "GAWRR" weight on the sticker that is located on the driver's door. Note this weight was in kilograms (kg). Weight was spelled according to model and engine size. This method of selecting springs was used from 1979-1981.

1970-1971 REAR SPRING PART NUMBERS

Side	6-Cyl.		350-ci		400-ci		Formula 400 Ex F60x15 Tires		Trans Am And Formula 400 F60x15 Tires	
Left	482545	5	482545	5	482546	6	482546	6	481132	5
Right	480878	6	480878	6	482548	6	482548	6	481132	5
Number following part number is total; spring count										

1972 REAR SPRING PART NUMBERS

Side	6-Cyl.		350-ci Exc. Sport Option		350- ci Sport Option Exc. Hand. Pkg. And 400-ci		350- 400-ci Sport Option Exc. Hand. Pkg.		455-ci	
Left	480878	6	480878	6	482528	6	481132	5	481132	5
Right	480878	6	480878	6	482528	6	481132	5	481132	5
Number following part number is total; spring count										

Spring ID Codes

Part Number	Code	Part Number	Code	Part Number	Code
480878	PA	482528	PR	481132	PL

1973-1974 REAR SPRING PART NUMBERS

Side	6-Cyl.		350-ci Except Formula		Formula 350 400-ci 2-bbl		Trans Am or Formula except 350	
Left	480878	6	480878	6	482528	6	481132	5
Right	480878	6	480878	6	482528	6	481132	5
Number following part number is total; spring count								

Spring ID Codes

Part Number	Code	Part Number	Code	Part Number	Code
480878	PA, PB	482528	PR, PF	481132	PJ

1975 REAR SPRING PART NUMBERS

Side	6-Cyl. Or 350-ci exc. Formula 350		Formula 350*		Firebird 400-ci with Gr70x15 Tires and automatic transmission		Formula 350** or Firebird w/ 400-ci V-8 With FR78x15 Tires or 4-speed	
Left	480878	6	480878	6	482528	6	481132	5
Right	480878	6	480878	6	482528	6	481132	5
Number following part number is total; spring count * with GR70x15 Tires **with FR78x15 Tires								

1976 REAR SPRING PART NUMBERS				
Side	6-Cyl. Or 350-ci exc. Formula 350	Formula 350	Firebird 400-ci with Automatic transmission	Firebird 400-ci Manual transmission or 455-ci V-8
Left	494776	480884	480884	481132
Right	494776	480884	480884	481132

1977 REAR SPRING PART NUMBERS				
Side	6-Cyl. , 350-ci* 400-ci#* or 403#*	Formula exc. 400-ci 4-speed	Trans Am*#	Trans Am (4-speed) Formula 400 (4-speed) Firm Ride pkg.
Left	494776	480884	480884	481132
Right	494776	480884	480884	481132
*- Except Firm Ride or trailer tow pkg. #- Automatic transmission only.				

1978 REAR SPRING PART NUMBERS				
Side	231-ci, 305-ci, 350-ci except 4-speed	350-ci 4-speed Formula 305 400-ci * 403-ci*	Trans Am*	Trans Am (4-speed) Formula 400 (4-speed) Firm Ride pkg.
Left	494776	480884	480884	481132
Right	494776	480884	480884	481132
*- Automatic transmission only.				

1980-1981 Rear Spring GAWRR Range					
Standard F-body		Formula/Trans Am Standard Ride		RPO WS6 Special Performance Package	
Range	Part Number	Range	Part Number	Range	Part Number
0-1016	480878	0-1042*	482548	0-1083	481132
1017-1062	494776	1043-Over	480884	1084-Over	480885
1063-1107	480880	*- Except with P205/75R tires all weight used part number 480884			
1108-Over	480881				

Spring ID Codes					
Part Number	Code	Part Number	Code	Part Number	Code
480878	PA	482528	PR	481132	PL
480880	PB,PC	480881	UC,PE	482548	PR
494776	UA	480884	PF, PG	480885	YP

Typical rear suspension.

SHOCK ABSORBERS, REAR

All 1970-1975 Firebirds used part number 3188143; it was changed to part number 4993545 in 1976 and remained till the end of the 1981 model year. The shock assembly was either painted dove gray or black in a semi-gloss finish.

Build date is stamped on the cover. Cover was aluminum. The mounting bolts should have a natural appearance. Painting them with silver model car paint can duplicate this.

REAR SWAY BAR

A rear mounted sway bar greatly helped in the handling aspect of the second generation Firebird, it was this bar that would allow it to out do the Z-28 and come in only second to the Corvette as the best handling American built model at that time.

Several different bars and diameters were used, which depended on the model and the model year. The bar was part of the firm ride which was standard on the Formula and Trans Am models. The Formula 350/305/301 models used a 19/32-in diameter bar, while the 400-ci used a 5/8-in diameter bar, except those with the firm ride package, which used a 13/16-in. diameter bar. This set up was used up 1978, when a slightly slimmer ¾-in bar replaced the 13/16-in. bar. The 13/16 and the 19/32-in bars were never released, as a replacement the 5/8 bar part number 3983084 was the only one released and it replaced the other two bars. The ¾-in diameter bar was listed as part number 10000606. The rear bar was left either natural or was painted semi-gloss black, up to the early 1975 models, after that all bars were left unpainted to save cost in assembly.

Steering Systems

Power steering was a popular option in the 1960's and 1970's, so much in fact that Pontiac upped the scale and made it standard for all Firebird models. This is not to say that all Firebird steering gearboxes were the same, some Trans Am and Formula models required special steering gearboxes that provide better handling properties due to quicker ratios. The steering gear box assembly should have a natural unpainted steel finish, which can be duplicated by painting it detail gray, except the cover, which should have a dull aluminum finish. The built date code appears on the cover The cover holding bolts should have a natural unpainted finish, which can be duplicated by painting them detail gray. The end plug should also have a dull silver appearance. The end plug retainer ring should have a natural finished steel appearance.

Several different steering columns were used according to the type of transmission and steering that was ordered in the car. From 1970-1972 was an odd ball of sorts and that is a Firebird with a column mounted shift lever. It was available in two forms: the three-speed manual which is a rare sight and those with automatic, which again is rare but more plentiful than the standard three on a tree type. In 1973 all Firebirds came with a floor shift.

Steering Gear Boxes

Part #	Usage	Model Years
7807742	2-bbl V-8	1970
7807741	4-bbl V-8	1970
7810872	2-bbl V-8	1971
7811210	400-ci V-8	1971
7826332	Except Formula or Trans Am	1972-1976
7818141	Formula or Trans Am	1972-1975
7826636	Formula or Trans Am	1976
7826636	Except Formula or Trans Am or Special Perf. Pkg.	1977-1978
7833311	Formula or Trans Am.	1977-1978
7829773	Special Performance pkg.	1978
7833311	Except Formula or Trans Am or Special Perf. Pkg.	1979
7833310	Formula or Trans Am	1979
7833312	Special Performance pkg.	1979
7833145	Except Formula or Trans Am or Special Perf. Pkg.	1980-1981
7848140	Special handling or Perf. Pkg.	1980-1981

The columns have a unique pattern of finish. The area under the hood, and visible is usually painted semi-flat black. The pitman arms idler arms, intermediate rods and inner and outer tie-rod ends were left natural from the factory; painting them cast iron gray can duplicate this. When painting tie rods be careful not to get paint on the rubber seals, as paint can deteriorate them, use masking tape to seal this area off when painting. The tie rod clamps should have a natural or flat black finish; both styles were used. Tie rod nuts should be painted with silver model paint to emulate the fresh factory appearance. The holding carter pins should have a dull silver appearance.

Steering Column Part Numbers

Model Year	Part Number	Transmission Type	Shifter Location	Notes
1970	7807885	3-speed Manual	Column	
1970	7807884	Automatic	Column	
1970	7807882	All	Floor	Without Tilt
1970	7808583	All	Floor	With Tilt
1971-1972	7812228	3-speed Manual	Column	
1971-1972	7812225	Automatic	Column	
1971-1975	7812229	All	Floor	Without Tilt
1971-1976	7812204	All	Floor	With Tilt First Design
1976-1977	7826997	All	Floor	2-nd Design with tilt
1978	7828751	All	Floor	1-st design Clamp type spline tooth shaft
1978	7829523	All	Floor	2-nd design thru bolt rectangular shaped shaft Without Tilt
1978	7828813	All	Floor	1-st design Clamp type spline tooth shaft with tilt
1978	7829593	All	Floor	2-nd design thru bolt rectangular shaped shaft With Tilt
1979-81	7832656	Automatic	Floor	Without tilt
1979-81	7832305	Manual	Floor	Without Tilt
1979-81	7832661	Automatic	Floor	With Tilt
1979-81	7832304	Mnaual	Floor	With Tilt

Identification number at bottom of steering gear may not always match the part number.

Typical power steering pump, shown is from a 1978 Trans Am with 400-ci V-8

Power Steering Pumps

All 1970 V-8 Firebirds used one single power steering pump listed as part number 7808536. This was changed to part number 7811290 in 1971 and was used on all V-8 Firebirds till 1976. In 1974 part number 7811290 continued to be used but only on true Pontiac built powerplants, this discounted the 305-ci Chevy, 350-ci (R – code) and the 403-ci Oldsmobile powerplants. Part number 7826701 was used on the Oldsmobile built powerplants. The only engine to used part number 7811290 in 1978 was the 400-ci V-8, the 305-ci and the 350-ci were built by Chevrolet and used part number 7832189, while the 403-ci Oldsmobile V-8 used the same part number it used the year before. The 301-ci and the 400-ci were true Pontiac powerplants and again used part number 7811290; all other powerplants used the same part numbers as the previous year. The 265-ci and 305-ci Chevrolet built V-8s used part number 7839788 in 1980 and 1981. The pump assembly was painted 60-degree gloss black. The mounting brackets that supported the pumps should also be painted 30-degree gloss black

Power Steering Pump Pulleys

One single pulley part number 480513 was used on 1970 V-8 Firebirds. For 1971 the part number was changed to 481042, which was used on all 1971 Pontiac models with a V-8 and power steering. In 1972 this was changed to part number 493243 and was used on all 1972-1974 Pontiac V-8's with power steering, except 1972-73 Ventura II with 307-ci V-8. This part became the replacement part for 1971 models.

For 1975 part number 496411 was used again it was used on all Pontiac models with a V-8 and power steering, except the Ventura II models. From 1976 on the pulley was not sold as a separate part but was part of the pump assembly, this was done to avoid the possibility of installing a Pontiac pulley on a Chevrolet or Oldsmobile built power steering pump. By keeping the pump and pulley and combined parts this would not happen.

Power Steering Pump
Belt Part Numbers

Part Number	Usage	Notes
480537	1970 w/o a/c	1/2x49-3/4
480538	1970-71 with a/c	1/2x48.00
480537	1971 400-ci w/o a/c	1/2x49-3/4
9433755	1972-74*	7/16x51-1/2
539130	1972-**	7/16x48
9433754	1973-74 with a/c	7/16x51
9433754	1975 w/o a/c	7/16x51
9433753	1975 with a/c	7/16x51-1/2
GL-9433754	1976 V-8 w/o a/c	
Gk-9433753	1976 V-8 with a/c	
Gk-9433753	1977 301-ci V-8 w/o a/c	
GH-9433753	1977 301-ci V- 8with a/c	
FT-9433725	1977 305-ci w/o a/c	
FT-9433737	1977 305-ci with a/c	
GL-9433754	1977 350-ci or 400-c V-8 w/o a/c	
Gk-9433753	1977 350-ci or 400-c V-8 with a/c	
GC-9433746	1977 403-ci V-8 with ot w/o a/c	
GF-9433749	1978 400-ci V-8	
FZ-9433743	1978 403-ci	
FZ-9433742	1978 403-ci with a/c	
FZ-9433743	1978 305-ci or 350-ci w/o A.I.R. emissions	
GF-9433749	1978 305-ci or 350-ci w/o A.I.R. emissions and a/c	
GF-9433747	1978 305-ci or 350-ci w/o A.I.R. emissions w/o a/c	
GE-9433748	1979 301-ci	
GE-9433749	1979 400-ci, 1979 305-ci or 350-ci with a/c	
GD-9433747	1979 305-ci or 350-ci w/o a/c	
10009102	1979 403-ci V-8	
10014015	1980 -814.9 liter	
FV-9433739	1980-81 305-ci V-8	
GK-9433753	1980 -814.3 liter, or 301-ci V-8 w/o a/c	
GJ-9433752	1980-81 4.3 Liter or 301-ci V-8 with a/c	

Wheels and Wheel Covers

Wheels

Several different styles of wheels were used on the 1970-1981 Firebirds. The most common is standard stamped steel wheel. A 14x6 inch wheel was standard on the base Firebird and the Esprit models, till 1976. From 1977-1981 all Firebirds including the base and Esprit models came standard with 15-inch wheels. Although there was still one 14-inch wheel, a 14x5-in unit used with the Space Saver Spare option but this was available only on 1977 models. From 1978 on only a 15 in wheel was used. A stamped steel wheel 15-inch was also available from 1971-1976 if the handling package, or from 1975 to 1976 when radial tires were ordered on the base or Esprit models.

Styled wheels were available all 12 years. The first styled wheel was a carry over design from the first generation. The Rally II wheel featured a five spoke design that resemble the classic Magnum 500 and Carger SS which were so popular in the early 1970's. These wheels were a standard affair on Trans Ams in a 15-in. variety, except a few specialty models. This wheel was also available as a 14-inch diameter wheel up to 1976. Beginning in 1977 this wheel was standard on all Formula models in a 15x7 in formats, these wheels were no longer available on the Trans Am models The 14-inch Rally II wheel was optional on all Firebirds, except the Trans Am or those with the handling package, which upgraded to 15-inch wheels.

One of the most desired wheels was the very popular "honeycomb wheels'. Designed by Bob Porter these wheels featured the look of a bee-hive that was cross-sectioned, thus the name. Introduced in 1971 as a late fall option, they were available in 14x7 and available on all models except the Trans Am. The Trans Am was optional, not standard, with the 15x7 in. versions of this wheel. Most of the wheels made were of the 15x7 in, which was optional, on the 1971-1972 Formula 400 models and Trans Ams. The honeycomb wheels continued until the end of the 1976 model year.

Beginning in 1977 the most popular of the custom wheels appeared. The Snowflake wheel so called because it looked like a snowflake was made from cast aluminum, Pontiac as an aluminum wheel commonly refers it to. It required a special warning sticker in the trunk. These wheels came in a natural silver shade or a variety of colors that corresponded with the exterior color of the car. They were available on all Firebirds as optional equipment in a 15x7 inch size. but were standard on the Trans Am models with the special performance or handling packages from 1977-1978 in a 15x8 in format; however, they were limited to either Gold or Gray. The 15x8 wheels were not available from the factory on other Firebird models.

In 1979 another styled wheel option appeared. The Appliance Wheel Company made the Turbo alloy wheels. Available only as a 15x8 in. wheel, these wheels featured a multiple slotted design around the outer edge. They were available from 1979-1981. They were available on the

Trans Am or Formula models with the performance package only, till 1981 when late in the year a 15x7-1/2 in. wheel became available and was optional on all Firebird models with the handling package, except Trans Am or Formulas with the WS6 package All wheels can be identified by their design, size and a code that is usually stamped near the valve stem opening, or on the back of the wheel.

1970 Trans Ams used this Rally II wheel. Note the large inner face of the rim.

1971 Trans Ams used this wheel note the smaller inner face. This wheel is incorrect for a 1970 model.

Later Rally II wheels, like this 1976 version came with trim rings.

Snowflake wheel, shown is the 15x7 series.

Homey comb wheels were a popular option on 1971-1976 models.

1979 Turbo cast wheels.

Body colored Rally II wheels were also optional.

Some wheels like this snowflake wheel are coded on the back of the wheel

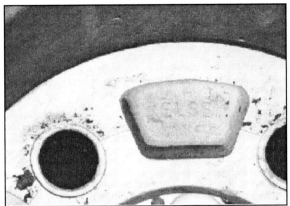

Kelsey Hayes was one manufacturer of snowflake wheels. The company name will appear on the back of the wheel.

Other wheels like the stamped steel and this rally II wheel the Id code can be found near the valve steam.

Western Wheel Company also supplied Snowflake wheels to Pontiac.

Conventional spare, was the standard set up.

Space Saver Spare Tire was popular option, shown is the 1972 version.

41

1970-1981 Wheel Part Number And Codes-Stamped Steel Type

RPO	Wheel Name	Size	Part Number	Code	Mode Years	Notes
Standard*	Stamped Steel	14x6	326857	XD	1973	*_Base and Esprit
Standrd*	Stamped Steel	14x6	326857	EL	1974	*_Base and Esprit
Standard *	Stamped Steel	14x6	397635	AM	1970-1972	*_Base and Esprit
Standard*	Stamped Steel	14x6	397635	UA	1975-1976	Without Radials only
Standard*	Stamped Steel	14x7	334397	KG	1973	*-Formula
Standard*	Stamped Steel	14x7	334397	EM	1974	*Formula
Standard*	Stamped Steel	14x7	3975667	CL	1970-1972	*-Formula
Standard	Stamped Steel	15x6	9590205	RF	1978-1981	Base and Esprit
Standard*	Stamped Steel	15x6	9590597	FL,RF	1975-1976	Std. With Radials
Standard*	Stamped Steel	15x6	9590597	RF,TF, FL	1977	Standard wheel
	Compact Spare	16x4	9590927	TV,JJ	1981	All
N65	Space Saver Spare	14x6	9793592	KC	1970-1972	
Standard	Stamped Steel	15x6	9590205	RF	1978-1981	Base and Esprit
	Stamped Steel	15x7	326875	AE	1971-1974	With Handling package only. Or 1974 Formula with Radials

1970-1981 Wheel Part Number And Codes-Styled						
RPO	Wheel Name	Size	Part Number	Code	Mode Years	Notes
PO5	Honeycomb	14x7	483084	JX	1971- 1973	N/A T/A or with handling package
PO5	Honeycomb	14x7		KS	1974	N/A T/A or with handling package
PM7	Honeycomb	15x7	484452	KP	1971- 1974	
	Honeycomb	15x7	326875	AE	1975- 1977	With rings
	Honeycomb	15x7	497154	HP	1975 -1976	Without rings
N98	Rally II	14x7	485455	JS	1970- 1972	N/A on T/A
	Rally II	14x7	525709	HN	1975- 1976	Without Radials only
N98	Rally II	14x7	485455	KS	1973- 1974	N/A on T/A
	Rally II	15x6	526566	KG	1977- 1981	Base and Esprit
PM7	Rally II	15x7	525710	HM, HF, HW	1973- 1976	Std. On Trans Am
Standard	Rally II	15x7	525710	HW	1978- 1981	Formula
Standard	Rally II	15x7	525710	HW	1978- 1981	Formula
PM7	Rally II	15x7	485454	JW	1970- 1972	Std. On T/A
PM7	Rally II	15x7	489252	HM	1973- 1975	Std. On T/A
N90	Snowflake	15x7	10010053	JA	1979-1981	Red
N90	Snowflake	15x7	10010054	KH	1979- 1981	Gold
YJ8	Snowflake	15x7	10000213	JB	1977- 1979	Blue
	Snowflake	15x7	527040	KJ,JR	1977- 1978	Gray
N90	Snowflake	15x7	10013030	KH	1980- 1981	Gold
N90	Snowflake	15x7	10013033	PD	1980- 1981	Natural
N90	Snowflake	15x8	10013035	JT	1980- 1981	Trans Am
N90, Y82	Snowflake	15x7	547928	KH	1977- 1978	Gold
Standard	Snowflake	15x8	10003208	JF	1977- 1978	Gold
YJ8	Snowflake	15x7	10010053	JA	1977	Red
Standard	Snowflake	15x8	10002467	JJ	1978	Gray Trans Am IV only
Standard	Snowflake	15x8	10002467	JJ	1978	Gray Trans Am IV only
Standard	Snowflake	15x8	10003208	JF	1978	Gold
YJ8	Snowflake	15x7	10006758		1978	Red
Standard	Snowflake	15x8	10002467	JJ	1978	Gray Trans Am IV only
Standard	Snowflake	15x8	10003208	JF	1978	Gold
N90	Snowflake	15x8	10005786		1979	Silver Ex. WS6 or WS7
N90, WS6	Snowflake	15x8	10005783	JT	1979	Gray Trans Am with WS6
N90, WS6 or WS7	Snowflake	15x8	10007513	JZ	1979	Ex. Y89
N89	Turbo	15x7-1/2	10019435	PY	1981	Gold
N89	Turbo	15x7-1/2	10019434	PX	1981	Natural
N89	Turbo	15x7-1/2	10020798	PZ	1981	White
N89	Turbo	15x8	10007389	HA	1980- 1981	Trans Am
N89	Turbo	15x8	10012285		1980- 1981	White Trans Am only
N89	Turbo	15x8	10013036	PL	1980- 1981	Trans Am Only
N89, Y89	Turbo	15x8	10007389	HA	1979	Trans Am with Y89
N89	Turbo	15x7	10013029		1980	Yellow Ex. Trans Am.

REFINISHING WHEELS
The standard stamped steel wheel, which was used with a full-wheel cover should be thoroughly cleaned and free of rust, then lightly sand the surface with 400-grit sandpaper. Then apply two thin coats of a durable enamel semi-gloss black paint. Do not use acrylic lacquer, as the surface will have to be buffed out, buffing out a wheel is hard to do with all the nooks and crannies that a wheel contains. Enamel provides a hard surface that wears well, plus does not require buffing to shine.

The standard 7/16-20 thread hex-head lug nuts part number 358501 should have a natural finish

The Rally II wheels can be repainted this way (this information was taken from a 1975 dealer Installed Technical bulletin # 75-T-14 dated 10/27/75).

1. Clean the wheel thoroughly to remove all grease and dirt.
2. Thoroughly scuff sand total area to be refinished with # 400 grit sandpaper. If spokes do not need refinishing they can be masked at this time. If rust is present, sand rusted area to bare metal and clean the exposed metal with Prep-Sol or equivalent.
3. If paint is sanded through to bare metal spray area to be color coated with high quality dark gray surface-primer such as Ditzler DZL32 or equivalent. When dry, thoroughly sand the surface primer with 400 grit sandpaper to insure proper adhesion of color coat.

4. If bright argent spokes need to be repainted, spray with Ditzler DQ-8568. Allow to dry completely (author note: allow 12-24 hours).
5. Mask spokes as required. Scuff sand remainder of wheel to insure proper adhesion.
6. Spray charcoal gray areas (author note use Ditzler DDL32947)
7. Allow to dry (author note at least overnight) or bake at 180-degrees for 30-minutes.

The above does not apply to those ordered under option RPO N67 which feature inserts that were body colored and available from 1976- 1981. They were painted in the same fashion as described above but instead of the charcoal gray, body color was applied here instead. DO NOT USE THE SAME PAINT THAT YOU USED ON THE EXTERIOR OF THE CAR, the proper finish here is acrylic enamel not acrylic lacquer. Note, before applying paint color you may have to first remove the old paint with a chemical stripper. The Rally II wheel used special 7/16-20 thread hex-head lug nuts part number 9789086 for 1970 and changed to part number 414188 in 1971 and remained till 1981. These later units were used on the Honeycomb and Snowflake wheels also.

Snowflake and Honeycomb
If you are looking for 100 percent like original appearance it is best to have a specialty shop remachine the wheel and then repaint it. However, this procedure can be expensive, and may not be available in all areas. The second choice is to do it yourself.

Clean the wheel thoroughly to remove all grease and dirt. You may have to use wax and grease remover also to remove as much of the deposits of the road, and it may take more than one application. Note: some cleaners can harm the surface of the wheel so try a hidden spot first. One of the best ways to remove dirt and grime is with a sandblaster, but DO NOT use sand, instead use glass beads. Sand is too harsh for aluminum and can damage it.

Small nicks and imperfections can be removed using a small die grinder that can be found in hobby shops with a brass or copper bristle wheel, do not use the steel carbon wheel it is too coarse and will cause greater damage to the wheel. Work carefully and slowly using only the edges of the brush and do not apply too much pressure. Be very careful when working around the lug nut mounting holes, this is where the greatest number of nicks is likely to occur, but do not enlarge the bolt hole diameter, or the wheel may not fit properly.

Spots and stains (for example from previously used stick on balancing weights) can be removed by wet sanding with 400 to 600-grit wet or dry sandpaper. Use a backing sponge and be sure to follow the contour of the wheel, and keep the sand paper as clean as possible.

Next, if the wheel is one of painted options then use a good quality paint stripper. Some extra-heavy duty strength strippers will attack aluminum, so read on the container to be sure it is safe for aluminum surfaces. Follow the directions on the stripper and be prepared to apply at least three coats. Wash the wheel thoroughly again to remove any chemical residue that is left from the stripper.

Wet sand the wheel again, being sure to follow the contour of the wheel, with an extra fine grit (like 1500) wet and dry sand paper. Than repeat using a super fine grit (like 2000) wet or dry sandpaper, and sand wet. Be sure to use a backing sponge both times. With Snowflake wheels that were left natural or gray than you do not have to paint the wheels. Those that were colored will have to be repainted.

The paint area of Snowflake wheels depends on the wheel size. Those wheels that were 15x8-in. should be painted gold including the ribbed edges, those that were 15x7 should have polished edges instead of being painted. This is accomplished by either masking the wheel off, or carefully wiping the paint off the edges with a rag dipped in paint thinner, before the paint sets. If you choose to do this wipe the paint off immediately after spraying one single wheel, than move on to the next wheel. Do not get the rag too soaked to avoid the reducer dripping and spoiling your new paint job. As with other wheels it is best to use acrylic enamel paint for wheels. Some restorers apply clear coat to their wheels over the color coat, hoping to give the wheels a longer life. It doesn't work that well and will give the wheels an incorrect gloss and they will look too shiny.

Buffing the wheel is the last step. Polishing compounds can remove the tiny scratches that were left in the restoration process, and can remove unwanted paint on the rim. It is best that the wheel be mounted to something sturdy. One of the best ways is to have a make up of a mounting frame that is made of steel and lug bolts and that can be mounted securely to a workbench, then bolt the wheel in place using lug nuts. Polish the rim, working around the contour of the rim, till you get the desired shine.

45

When painting honeycomb wheels remember that the outer finish is polyurethane. Painting procedures for this type of paint are the same with any other kind of paint except remember that this paint has a short pot life, of only 2-3 hours, so mix up only what you need at a time. Spray at 35-lbs of pressure at the gun and give the wheel 2 or 3 coats allowing 2-3 minutes flash time between each coat. Allow the wheel to dry at least 2-4 hours before touching it. Do not compound wheel, this will reduce the gloss. It is VITAL that you wear a quality type painters mask when spraying this type of paint. Because of the isocyanates contained in this paint, a disposable type mask, or a cheap painters mask is not recommended, even if you shot the wheels outside you should still wear a good quality painter's mask. And note that some people may have an allergic reaction to the isocyanates. Read the label of the additives, if you are known to have an allergy to any of these chemicals then do not spray the paint yourself, or be exposed to the vapors or mist. This flexible finish paint was also used on the bumpers of certain models.

Ditzler
Paint Color Part Numbers

Color	Ditzler Paint Number
Silver*	DQE-8906
Charcoal Gray (1)	DQE-32947
Bright Argent (1)	DQE-8568
Blue	2815
Gray	2954
Gold	82352

All other colors are the same as the exterior color.
*- Honeycomb Wheels Only
(1) Rally II Wheels only except body colored.
Reproduction companies like OEM Paints have the correct gold finish.

Hub Caps And Wheel Covers

A dog dish style hubcap part number 9774609 was standard on all 1970 Firebirds except the Trans Am. A trim was included with the Esprits. For 1971-1972 the standard hubcap was listed as part number 5738083; this 10-1/2 in diameter cap had the word Pontiac imprinted into it, it was standard on all but the Trans Am. A custom wheel cover part number 483426 was optional for all models except the Trans Am or with the handling package, for both 1971 and 1972. This design featured a center hub with multiple spokes protruding from it to the edge of the cover. The Deluxe cover was the same unit used on the Tempest line and was listed as part 486553, it featured a design with raised center dome with the Pontiac crest in the center with multiple blades, this same cover was used again in 1972 and 1973 as a dealer installed option. The deluxe cover in 1972 was listed as part number 9890699 which featured the Firebird crest; it was also available as the deluxe cover for 1973.

Standard hubcap for 1973 was part number 485200, which featured the Pontiac crest with an indentation in the center\, this was the standard hub cap up to 1975 for all models except Trans Am. Available for all except the Trans Am was the Deluxe wheel cover part number 488595, which featured the Pontiac crest and was surrounded by three rings. The custom cover was listed as part number 497542, and was available for cars with 14-in wheels only. If 15-in wheels were ordered along with the custom wheel cover, then part number 486554 was used. Both covers had the same design as part number 486553 in 1972. All these covers were used again in 1974, except the Deluxe cover which was now listed as part number 496031. This cover featured multiple legs along the outer edge with a large center dome.

In 1975 the Deluxe cover was listed as part number 496031, and the custom cover was part number 486554, and was available only with 15-in wheels.

The standard hubcap was listed as part number 498800 from 1976-1981, and was used on the Base Firebird and the Esprit only. The Deluxe cover for 1976 was listed as part number 496972 with 15-in wheels and part number 496931 with 14-in wheels. No custom cover was available.

The Deluxe cover remained available for 1977 but was restyled. Listed as part number 527060, this cover filled with round holes was available only with 15-in wheels and continued over into the 1978 model year. For 1979 the deluxe cover was listed as part number 10005598 which held a Pontiac medallion part number 527062 in the center; this cover remained optional on the Firebird and Esprit models till 1981. A second additional cover part number 549372, which simulated wire wheels was also available. The wire wheel cover continued into the first part of 1981, where part number 10013584 took its place. The first type had large glue-in type center medallion while the later style had a smaller snap-in type. It is incorrect for a 1980 Firebird to have the snap in type wheel cover. Part number 549372 was also available on 1977-1979 Firebirds.

Drivetrain

Transmission, Three-Speed Manual

1970-1971

The Saginaw built 3-speed manual transmission was the standard unit on models with the 350-ci 2-bbl V-8. Part number 3974485 was used both years. It had the following gear ratios.

1st	2.54
2nd	1.50
3rd	1.00
Rev.	2.63

This unit will have the code letters "RA" painted in yellow on the right-hand side of the case. The letters should be 2.00 in. height.

The heavy-duty three-speed was built by the Muncie plant. This transmission was standard on cars with a 400-ci or 455-ci, except the 1970 Trans Am. Two units were used; part number 477781 was used in 1970 and part number 3952657 was used in 1971. These transmissions were coded two ways. The source code is stamped on the flat surface of the case just below the rear lower corner of the side of the case. This code will begin with the Letter code "H" indicating the heavy-duty Muncie three speed. This is followed by the date of manufacture, which consist of the last digit of the year (9-1969, 0-1970 and 1-1971) a letter code for the

month of manufacture and the day of the month (01-31). Remember this: this is the manufacture date so the year and model year may not always agree. The code H9T17 would be December 17, 1969 and would be for a 1970 model. Any number following this code is the individual serial number of the unit. Note: the date on the transmission must be BEFORE the assembly date on your Firebird to be considered correct. The letter A or B will follow, this represents the first gear ratio. A- 3.03 and B-2.42. Another ID code was painted on the front upper side of the right-hand side of the transmission case. The letters "DG" for 1970 and "RM" for 1971 were painted here in 1.00 in. high yellow letters.

Muncie Transmission Date Codes					
Month	Code	Month	Code	Month	Code
Jan.	A	May	E	Sep.	P
Feb.	B	June	H	Oct.	R
March	C	July	K	Nov.	S
April	D	Aug.	M	Dec.	T

A floor mount lever shifted all heavy-duty three-speed transmissions. The Hurst built shift assembly was listed as part number 405765 both years and the shift lever was listed as part number 479048 and knobs were the same units that were used on the Saginaw three-speed floor shifted models.

1972-1979

The Saginaw built 3-speed manual transmission was still the standard unit on models with the 350-ci 2-bbl V-8. Part number 332556 was used for all 1972 and early 1973 models, these models must not use a later style unit, which was listed as part number 346313, which was also used in 1974 models. Ratios were the same as they were in 1971.

Painted ID codes were in the same location as in previous years, except different codes were used. The 1972-early 1973 model used "TA" while the later built 1973 models and 1974 models used the code "TN".

The floor mounted shift lever was the same unit and used the same part number as in previous years; the shift knob was listed as part number 482346. The Muncie transmission was still used in A-bodies in 1972; it was not used in the Firebird line. Instead an automatic transmission became standard on the 400 and 455-ci models, with the 4-speed as an option. Big changes hit the 1975 models the only powerplant that could be had with a three-speed manual transmission were the six-cylinders. This continued through till the end of 1981.

A black colored *knob was also available for 1972-1973 models.*

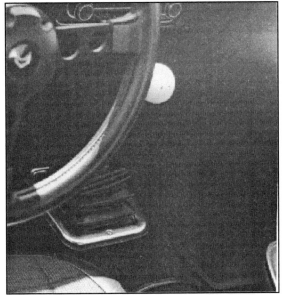

Trans Am and Formulas used a white colored shift knob for 1970-1973, with a four-speed transmission

According to service bulletin number 73-T-25 dated 3/23/73, a common problem with the three-speed manual transmission was that it would lock up in gear (usually 2nd gear) and could not be shifted. This was due to the fact that the detent cam (interlock) spring in the transmission case, was too weak. The solution was to replace the production detent cam spring with part number 3831718 which was rated at 20-lbs instead of 10-lbs like the production unit was. At first this was believed to be only on A-body models, but was later found to be on the Firebird and the Ventura II models also. This affected 1970-1973 models where the transmission dent cam spring was changed.

REFINISHING THREE-SPEED TRANSMISSION

Saginaw and Muncie used a cast iron main case and tail shaft. The transmission was left unpainted when new, you can paint it to duplicate the fresh factory look of cast iron. After thoroughly cleaning the case and noting any paint marks (we will discuss this later on) the case assembly should be painted cast iron gray, there are many manufacturers of this type of paint just be sure to use a good quality version like the one from Eastwoods.

Code letters, given in previous text, should be added after the transmission is painted. You can find stencil lettering at an art supply or even a hardware store, the cardboard type stencils work excellently. Yellow model spray paint is a close match to the color. Location of these codes and their size varies according to manufacturer. You may also find white marks that appear to be just a swab of paint on the units. These are not a mistake; they are line shift inspection marks indicating that the proper parts were put together. You will likely find one on the main case and one on the tail shaft. All shift rods should have a natural metal appearance.

Transmission, Four-Speed Manual

1970-1971

A Muncie built four-speed transmission was standard in the 1970 Trans Am and was optional on all 1970 Firebirds with a V-8 powerplant, including the 350-ci V-8. Two different transmissions were available. The wide ratio unit part number 3952659 and the close ratio unit part number 3968011. In 1971 the part numbers were changed to 3981709 for the wide ratio and 3978766 for the close ratio, yet it was still available for all V-8 powered Firebirds.

The transmission unit will have yellow code letters painted on top of the case. The letters should be 1.00 in height. The following codes were used.

Muncie Transmission ID Codes

	1970
Wide Ratio	WB
Close Ratio	DL
	1971
Wide Ratio	WT
Close Ratio	WO

Gear shifting was done through a floor-mounted lever part number 405728 for the shifter mechanism and part number 479048 for the lever. It was topped with a white colored knob both years

Muncie 4-speed Gear Ratios

Gear	Wide Ratio	Close Ratio
1st	2.52	2.20
2nd	1.88	2.64
3rd	1.46	1.28
4th	1.00	1.00
Rev.	2.59	2.27

1972-1974

The Muncie transmission was no longer available on the models with the 350-ci 2-bbl powerplant. Instead a Saginaw built unit was used. The 1972 unit continued over into the 1973 model year, and then was replaced by part number 332558 about midway through the year. In 1974 the Saginaw 4-speed transmission was available as an option on all models with the 350-ci powerplant.

The ID code was done in yellow paint and consisted of two letters one-inch in height on the right-hand side of the transmission case. The following codes were used.

Saginaw Transmission ID Codes

1972	WC
1973	TF
1974-1975	WC

The shift lever was listed as part number 479048 all three years and was used by both the Muncie and the Saginaw units.

Muncie transmission was again available in 1972 to 1974 only with those models with a 400-ci or 455-ci V-8 powerplant. It was available as a wide ratio or a close-ratio unit for 1972 and 1973 but only as a wide ratio unit for 1974. As before codes were applied to top of the Muncie transmission case that consisted of two letters that were 1.00 in height. The following codes were used.

Muncie Transmission ID Codes

1972-1973	
Wide Ratio	UA
Close Ratio	FC
1974	
Wide Ratio	WD

1975-1981

As the performance era began fading away, rock solid transmission like the Muncie begins to be regulated to memories that belong to the used car lot. The Warner 4-speed took the Muncie place in 1975 as the heavy-duty unit used on models with the 400-ci V-8 and only in the Firebird line. The good news was that when you ordered the 4-speed you got a close ratio unit. The bad news was they were not available with the 455-ci powerplant or the 403-ci V-8 and there were some restrictions on the use of a 4-speed in California.

As performance rolled to a sudden stop in 1980 with the deletion of the mega cube powerplants, the Borg-Warner 4-speed (called a 83MM model) continued to be offered on only the 305-ci V-8. No four-speed was offered for the 1980 models, at first but one was graduated in near the end of the year for the 301-ci V-8.

Identification codes were placed on the right-hand side of the case in two-inch high yellow letters. The following codes were used.

Borg-Warner Transmission ID Codes

1975-1976	HW
1977-1978	ZT-400-ci
	ST-301-ci
1979	UF
1980-1981	DC

The shift lever was listed as part number 479048 for 1975 and used a simulated leather shift knob listed as part number 481595. In 1976 the shift lever was changed to part 405728 and used shift knob part number 481595, this same lever and knob was used up till 1979. Beginning in late 1980 part number 405728 was used for 4-speed applications. Although the lever was switched it continued to use the same shift knob as before.

Typical leather covered shift knob used on 1971-1981 4-speeds, note the proper positioning of the knob.

Top view of later style 4-speed knob notes the shift pattern. This knob became the replacement for all 1970-1981 4-speed models.

REFINISHING TRANSMISSION

The Saginaw transmission has the same finishing characteristics that were used on the three-speed manual transmission and should be followed. The Borg and Warner also had a cast iron case and should be painted like the Saginaw unit.

The Muncie unit is different though. The case of the Muncie transmission was made of aluminum, and was left unfinished from the factory. To duplicate this finish and keep the unit looking new paint it aluminum silver in a semi-flat finish, or after carefully cleaning and applying ID codes give the case a coat of clear paint. The clear can have the benefit of protecting the code marking as well as the case itself, the drawback is that clear paint may give it an incorrect gloss, but most people will not notice.

As for the code lettering it should be on top of the case, not on the sides and should be in yellow lettering in letters that are one-inch in height. The letters were stenciled on, use 1-inch high stencils that can be obtain from an office supply or a hardware store. Testor's yellow model spray paint works well for this application. You may also find white inspection marks on the main case and extension; these marks were just a swipe of paint that was applied by the line inspector. When applying these do it in one quick swipe of a small (1/4 in. wide) brush.

Clutch

A diaphragm spring-type clutch is used on all Firebirds with a manual transmission. The clutch assembly consists of a driven plate, cover–pressure plate and release mechanism. Four different clutch driven plates were used, which depended on the engine size and output.

Clutch Driven Plates

Application	Diameter	Part Number
350-ci	10.4 in	544185
400-ci	10.4 in.	9777438
455-ci	11.0	482034

The clutch cover and pressure plate of all models is the diaphragm spring type. Two types were used according to engine combinations. The flat finger diaphragm spring design was used on the 350-ci V-8s while the bent finger diaphragm spring design was used on the 400-ci and 455-ci powerplants.

Clutch release bearing usage was determined on the clutch and pressure plate design. Those with the flat finger type will use a release bearing with an overall length of 1-7/8 in. and is stamped "22" on the inner side of the bearing shoulder. That using the bent finger type uses a release bearing that is 1-1/5 in. length and is stamped "CT-24K". Do not mix the two, as problems with clutch pedal engagement will results especially as the clutch wears. The clutch pedal in 1970-1971 was listed as part number 3965693 and was used with all applications. The pedal should be painted 30-degrees gloss black The pad assembly was listed as part number 3921648 for 1970-1972, no pedal trim was standard, but was available as part of a custom trim option. The trim plate was listed as part number 3923615. Part number 332519 was used from 1973 till the end of the 1981 model year. The clutch pedal pad was also changed it was listed as part number 14009148; this is a clutch pad only on earlier models. The brake pad would also fit the clutch. From 1973-1975 the clutch pad is unique, and a brake pedal pad will NOT fit. The trim plate was also unique and was listed as part number 491627. In 1976 the clutch pedal pad used part number 14009148, which remained till the end of the 1981 model year. The custom trim cover that was used with custom pads; it was listed as part number 491627 and was used from 1976-1981.

Cover and Pressure Plate Part Numbers

Application	Color Code	Part Number
350-ci	Orange	3991496
400-ci	Yellow	481833
455-ci	White	3884598

Transmission, Automatic

1970-1971

There were three distinct types of automatic transmissions available for the 1970 and 1971 Firebird line. The general type was a two-speed unit known as option code M35, which featured a single piece aluminum case. It can be identified by its serial code, which appears on the right front side of the case, it was available only for cars with a 350-ci V-8.

M35 Automatic Transmission Codes

Application	ID Code	Part Number
1970 350-ci	EA	477621
1971 350-ci	TS	3987939

The 350-ci birds were also optional with a 3-speed automatic known as the Turbo-Hydra Matic 350 or RPO M38. This was a tougher and more reliable automatic than the M35, and gave the driver more range control. Like the M35 the M38 transmission was also a one-piece aluminum case. The identification code for the M38 transmission is located on the accumulator on the right hand side of the case. At the top of the three line code of information will be the last two digits of the manufacture(69-1969, 70-1970, 71-1971) , below this the second line will begin with the identification code. JF was used for 1970 and MA was used is in 1971. This is followed by a three digit code for the calendar date (001- Jan.1- -365 –Dec. 31). The bottom code is the shift code (D-Day N-Night). Note that the two-letter identification code was also placed on the front right-hand side of the case in the form of a stick-on decal; this decal was to be used only at the factory for quick identification and was quickly lost.

M38 Automatic Transmission Codes

Application	ID Code	Part Number
1970 350-ci	JF	6260128
1971 350-ci	MA	6260250

The 400 and 455-ci equipped cars came with a 3-speed Turbo-Hydra-Matic series 400 transmissions when an automatic transmission was ordered

The transmission is identified by a two-letter code that is stamped on a small plate that is on the right-hand side of the case just forward of the governor. The serial number will begin with the letter P, which indicates the Pontiac. This is followed by a letter code that indicates the engine family. This is followed by the model year code (70-1970, 71-1971) . The remaining numbers are the serial number of the transmission, which can be useful in determining running changes in the line.

Speaking of which: there was a change in the Sun gear and Sun gear shaft on the T.H. 400 transmission in 1971. According to Dealer Service Bulletin Number 71-I46 dated 3/4/71 new models were being built with new sun gear and the sun gear shafts. Quoting from the bulletin "the new design sun gear has a full compliment of mating splines and, for this reason the old design sun gear will NOT assemble to it. However, the new design sun gear WILL assemble to either the old or new design sun gear shaft." This being part number 8626807 took the place of 8623177 (the old sun gear) and dealer were encouraged to use up existing parts. Therefore it is unlikely you will find part number 8623177 today, but if you do remember it will not fit transmission with serial numbers later than those below.

M40 New Sun Gear Beginning Serial Numbers-1971

ID Code	Serial Number	ID Code	Serial Number
PQ	1890	PR	1344
PT	3094	PW	3429
PX	19816	PY	2182

T.H. 400 Automatic Transmission Codes

Application	ID Code	Part Number
455-ci H.O.	PQ	8626686*
		8627088**
400-c 2-bbl	PT	8627090
400-ci 4-bbl (1)	PX	8626691
455-ci (2)	PR	8627089
455-ci (3)	PW	8627091
400- 4-bbl; (4)	PY	8627093
455-ci (5)	PF	8627109

*-1970 only **-1971 Only (1)- 3.08 or 3.23 axle
(2)- 3.3 or 3.42 axle (3)- 3.07 or 3.08 axle
(4)- 3.42 or 3.55 axle (5)- 2.56 or 2.73 axle

Standard shift lever for all types of automatic transmissions was a column mounted shift lever. The 1970 part number was listed as 480677 and 482967 in 1971 and was used on all types of automatics. Column shifted Firebirds are a rare item most came with the optional console. This shift in the floor lever was listed as part number 481176 both years on the Turbo-Hydra-Matics and part number 481224 for the two-speed M35 transmission. While they used different levers they all used the same knob listed as part number 481172. Note a floor shift automatic was available only if the optional console was ordered.

Typical automatic shift lever used in second generation Firebirds. Shown is a 1979 model.

1972-1974

With the deletion of the two-speed automatic only the M38 and M40 transmissions remained. Identification code locations were in the same positions as they were in 1971. The big thing to watch for is the change over in transmissions in the 1973 model year. Due to EPA regulations there was a major change in the emission controls on March 15, 1973. All vehicles built after this date would be required to used the new emission control systems, which greatly influenced some transmissions that used different internal calibrations and a TCS switch that monitored the 2 to 3 speed switch instead of the 1-2 shift. After this date the M40 transmission will have a new three digit code, as the number "2" will be placed between the two letter of the old code. If, for example, the code PG was used it would now be coded P2G. This three-digit code will be painted on the bell housing as well as the ID plate on the case. The M38 transmission used all new codes. It is vital that the proper transmission be used. An early style transmission will not fit and operate with a later style powerplant or vice versa

1972 T.H. 400 Automatic Transmission Codes

Application	ID Code	Part Number
455-ci H.O.	PQ	8626686*
		8627088**
400-c 2-bbl	PT	8627090
400-ci 4-bbl (1)	PX	8626691
455-ci (2)	PR	8627089
455-ci (3)	PW	8627091
400- 4-bbl; (4)	PY	8627093
455-ci (5)	PF	8627109

*-1970 only **-1971 Only (1)- 3.08 or 3.23 axle
(2)- 3.3 or 3.42 axle (3)- 3.07 or 3.08 axle
(4)- 3.42 or 3.55 axle (5)- 2.56 or 2.73 axle

1973 Transmission Code Changes

Application	Old Part Number	Old Code	New Part Number	New Code
			M38 T.H. 350	
350-CI	6260399	MA	1244981	MC- with 2.93 axle
			1244982	ME- with 3.08 axle
			M40 T.H. 400	
400-CI-4-bbl	8627483	PG	8627758	P2G
455-CI H.O	8627484	PQ	8627760	P2Q
455-CI 4-bbl	8627485	PR	8627684	P2Z
400-CI 2-bbl	8627486	PT	8627762	P2T

1974 Automatic Transmission Codes

Application	ID Code	Part Number
	M38 T.H. 350	
350-ci 2-bbl with 2.73 or 2.93 axle	MA	
350-ci with 3.08 axle	ME	
	M40 T.H. 400	
400-ci 4-bbl (except California)	PG	
400-ci 2-bbl (California Only)	PL	8627793
455-ci Super Duty	PQ	
400-ci 2-bbl (Except California)	PT	
400-ci 4-bbl (California Only)	PW	8627795
455-ci 4-bbl	PZ	

1975-1977

Big news for 1975 was the removal of the M40 automatic transmission, while it was still used on the LeMans and the full-size models, only the M38 automatic transmission was used on the Firebird line, including the big cube 400-ci and 455-ci powerplants. As before, a code was used to identify the M38 transmission; it is found on the accumulator, which is located on the right-hand side of the transmission case.

Original shift knobs can be restored with a little elbow grease and time. In the before knob is scuffed and dirty.

Also the transmission ID code was stamped on the governor housing, thus if the governor was ever replaced, it required that original transmission code be stamped onto the governor cover. It would be incorrect for the transmission not to have a stamping code on the cover. Also the two-digit ID code was stamped in ink on the bell housing. You will most likely have to have a custom stamp made up for this.

A floor-mounted lever listed as part number 485926 was used all three years. This shifter was also used on the 1975-1977 Lemans and Ventura II models. The knob was listed as part number 481172.

1978-1981

The Turbo-Hydra-Matic 350 was still being used as the only automatic transmission in 1978 but was now coded as option M33. As in years past the identification code was located on the governor cover, stamped in ink on the bell housing or on the accumulator cover on the right-hand side of the transmission case. The M33 transmission would carry over into the 1979 model year.

For 1980 the transmission would again be jumbled. Those models with a Chevy built engine used the T.H. 350 transmission design for the Chevrolet motor, while the others used a unit designed for the Pontiac platform. This continued into 1981.

Shift lever was a floor-mounted unit. Those 1978 models without the performance option package used the same shifter that was used in 1977. Those with the performance option package used part number 351300; this shifter would continue to be used in the 1979-81 models with the WS6 option package. Those without the package used part number 498974.

1975-1977 M-38 Transmission Identification Codes

Application	Code
1975	
350-ci 2 or 4-bbl	MA
400-ci 4-bbl	MF or MG*
1976	
350-ci 2 or 4-bbl	MA
400-ci 4-bbl	MK or MG*
1977	
350-ci 2 or 4-bbl	MA
400-ci 4-bbl	MK or MG*
403-ci	MX

1978-1981 Automatic Transmission Identification Codes

Application	Code
1978	
T.H. 350	
301-ci	MR
305-ci	KJ or JC
350-ci	MA or MJ*
400-ci	MG, MK#, MP, MT
403-xi	MZ* or LP

*-California only #- Trans Am

1979	
T.H. 350	
301-ci	ME or MJ
305-ci	JC
350-ci	JD
403-xi	LM$_{(1)}$
	LP
	LT $_{(1)}$**

*-California only #- Trans Am (1) with 2.73 or 3.23 rear axle **-High Altitude package

1980-1981	
T.H. 350	
301-ci	MS, MT*
305-ci	JD, JK$_{(C)}$

(C)- Chevy built *- Turbo Charged

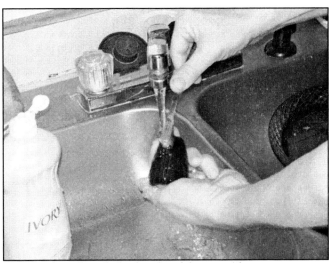

First step is to clean the knob and push button with a mild soap, an old tooth brush come in handy for getting into tight places like the crevices on the sides on the knob. Clean under running water to avoid grinding the dirt into the vinyl.

After the parts are clean, rinse and dry thoroughly. Than apply a coat of protective finish such as Amor- all All or even lemon oil based furniture spray to prevent the vinyl from drying out. Our finished project looks good as new.

Propeller Shaft

Usage was determined by model and engine type. Propeller shafts should have a natural appearance or be painted flat black; they came both ways. They should also have color code stripe on them. There was no set location for this code, most appear in the middle of the shaft or near the tail-end,

REFINISHING AUTOMATIC TRANSMISSIONS

The two-speed automatic case should have a natural look to it; painting it detail gray can duplicate this. While the Turbo-Hydra-Matic should have a brighter fresh aluminum appearance painting the case aluminum silver can do this.   White inspection marks were usually placed on the bell housing and the oil pan, these were just a dab of white paint and when reapplying do it in one quick motion. Also, you may find chalk marks on the bell housing that will be the code letters that identify the transmission, on those up to 1974. After this date the code was stamped in ink or a small decal that was placed on the bell housing.

of the shaft towards the rear axle. You may also find a dab of yellow paint on the shaft that will match up with a dab of paint on the axle pinion, this was done because the shaft is balanced and it is essential that the same location be used, if the shaft was ever removed.

Propeller Shaft Color Codes

Usage	Transmission		Color Codes
		1970-1972	
Firebird (Base)	All		1-Orange
Esprit	Automatic		1- White
			1-Black
Except Base Firebird	3-spd Man.		1-Orange
			1-Blue
			1-Purple
Except Base Firebird	3-spd Man.		1-Orange
	with 3.73 axle		1-White
			1-Brown
Firebird/Esprit 350-ci	4-speed Man		1-Orange
Formula 400/ Trans Am	4-speed Man.		1-Blue
Formula 400*/Trams Am	Automatic		1-Brown
Esprit 400-ci 2-bbl	Automatic		1-Ortange
Formula 400	Automatic		1-White
Formula 400 *	4-speed Man.		1-Yellow
Trans Am**/Formula 400**	Automatic		
Formula 400/ Trans Am	4-Speed C.R.		1-Orange
			1-Brown
			1-Yellow
		1973	
350-ci 2-bbl	All		1-Orange
			1-White
			1-Brown
400-ci /455-ci	All		1- Orange
			1-White
			1- Yellow
		1974	
350-ci 2-bbl	All		1-Orange
			1-White
			1Yellow
400-ci /455-ci	All		1- Orange
			1-White
			1- Brown
		1975-1976	
350-ci	All		2- Brown
400-ci	All		1- Yellow
			1-Yellow

Rear Axle
1970-1974

All Firebirds were equipped with a "C" type semi-floating differential rear axle, which was supported with rear leaf springs. The differential carrier is made of nodular iron. The axle tube housings are pressed into the sides to form a complete axle assembly. A removable cover is made from stamped heavy steel and is held to the axle housing with bolts. The C-type axle came in two forms the standard axle (where one wheel pulls) or Safe-T-Track where both wheels pull.

Axle ratio can be determined by a code that stamped on the right-hand axle tube adjacent to the carrier on the front of the tube. The code can be used to determine a standard axle from a Safe-T-Track axle. Axle ratios came in two flavors: standard, and performance.

The axle assembly should be painted 30-degrees gloss, the axle assembly was painted as whole and assembled, thus the cover and cover bolts should also be painted semi-gloss black. A dab of yellow paint was used on the filler, which indicated a no filled axle. These dabs of paint were used only during production, and have no other significance, but should be reapplied for detail.

1970-1971 Rear Axle Identification Codes				
Ratio	Gear Combination		Codes	
	Ring	Pinion	Standard	Safe-T-Tack
1970				
2.73	41	15	COC	COD
3.07	43	14	COS	COT
3.08	40	13	COE	COF
3.31	43	13	COU	COV
3.36	37	11		
3.55	39	11		COX
3.73	41	11		COZ
4.10	41	10		COO
1971				
2.73	41	15	CZG	CAG
3.08	40	13	CXG	GYG
3.42	41	12	CKG	GJG
3.73	41	11	N/A	GGG
4.10	41	10	N/A	GBG

1971 Rear Axle Usage Chart				
Engine	Transmission	Axle		
		Std.	Performance	Air Conditioning
350-ci 2-bbl	Manual	3.42	N/A	3.42
	Automatic	2.73		2.73
350-ci 2-bbl**	Automatic	3.08	N/A	3.08
400-ci 2-bbl	Automatic	2.73	3.08	2.73
400-ci 4-bbl	3-spd Man.	3.42	3.73#	3.42
	4-spd Man W.R.	3.42	3.73#	3.42
	4-spdMan. C .R.	3.73#	3.73#	N/A
400-ci 4-bbl **	Automatic	3.42	N/A	3.42
455-ci	Manual	3.42	3.73#	3.42
	Automatic	3.08	3.42	3.08
	Special Order		4.10	

1972 –1981 Rear Axle Identification Codes

Ratio	Ring	Pinion	Standard		Safe-T-Tack
	Gear Combination		**Codes**		
				1972	
2.73	41	15	CZG		CAG
3.08	40	13	CXG		GYG
3.42	41	12	CLG		CMG
				1973	
2.73	41	15	CZG		CAG
3.08	40	13	GXG		GYG
3.42	41	12	CLG		CMG
				1974	
2.73	41	15	CZG		CAG
3.08	40	13	GXG		GYG
3.42	41	12	CLG		CMG
				1975	
2.56	41	16	PGG		PTG
2.73	41	15	PAG		PUG
3.08	40	13	PCG		PWG
				1976	
2.41			PJG		PSG
2.73	41	15	PAG		PUG
3.08	40	13	PCG		PWG
3.23			PDG		PXG
				1977	
2.41			PJG		PSG
2.56			PHG		PTG
3.08	40	13	PCG		PWG
3.23			PDG		PXG
				1978	
2.41			PJG		PSG
2.56			PHG		PTG
3.08	40	13	PCG		PWG
3.23			PDG		PXG
			PMG		PPG
				1979	
2.41			PJG		PSG
					PVG
2.56			PHG		PTG
2.73			PAG		PUG
					PRG
3.08	40	13	PCG		PWG
					PQG
3.23			PDG		PXG
					PPG
3.42			N/A		POG

Note all code above include the "G" manufactures code

Ratio			Standard		Safe-T-Tack
				1980-1981	
2.41			PJ		PS
					PV***
2.56			PH		PT
2.73			PA		PU
3.08			PC***		PO
					PW
					PQ
3.23			PD		PX
3.42			PB		PY
			PE***		PO

***-1981 only

1975-1981

Firebird still used the Chevrolet built rear axle, which is the same exact unit that was used under the Camaro. Ratio codes were still decoded the same way as before, but more and more performance ratios simply disappeared from the option list. An important thing to remember when detailing your rear axle is to watch the build date. According to Pontiac service bulletin number 75-I-27 dated 5/20/1975, all rear axles are no longer painted, thus it is incorrect for a late built 1975 or later Firebird to have the rear axle painted gloss black. Painting the axle detail gray can duplicate the look of fresh metal; also no yellow paint dab was used on the filler plug on cars built after this date. All Firebirds were equipped with a "C" type semi-floating differential rear axle that was supported with rear leaf springs. The differential carrier is made of nodular iron. The axle tube housings are pressed into the sides to form a complete axle assembly. A removable cover is made from stamped heavy steel and is held to the axle housing with bolts. The C-type axle came in two forms the standard axle (where one wheel pulls) or Safe-T-Track where both wheels pull.

Brakes

Master Cylinder

1970-1971

Two different master cylinders were used in Firebirds. Usage depended on the brake type. All models with the standard front drum brakes used part number 5471958, while those with power assist used part number 5470664. Both master cylinders used a 1-1/4-in .The master cylinder should be have a natural unpainted appearance, which can be duplicated by painting it cast iron gray. The cover was unique to the master cylinder. Those without power assist used part number 5455517 while those with power brakes used part number 5470405. Both covers should have a cadmium gold appearance. The retainer was also unique to the cylinder and was listed as part number 5468103 without power brakes

1972-1974

Standard disc brakes again used a master cylinder with a 1-1/4-in. diameter piston. It was now listed as part number 542652, all three years. Those models with the power-assisted disc brakes used the same part number as it used in 1971. Refinishing is the same as the previous years, except more were left unpainted and have the cast iron gray appearance.

1975-1976

The master cylinder was again restyled for 1975 and two master cylinders were still used; part number 18001112 was used both years without power assist; it used a 1.00 in diameter piston bore. Part number 1800884 was used on all Firebirds with power brakes; it used a –1/4 in. piston. Refinishing is the same as previous years. The cover was listed as part number 18000779 and was used on both master cylinders. The natural bail was listed as part number 5470407 for both units.

1977-1980

The master cylinder was again restyled for 1977 those without power assisted brakes used part number 18005271 this was the standard set-up on most models till the end of the 1980 model year

Those models with power assisted brakes did not remain as constant. The 1977 models used part number 18005733, which was used on the other 1977 Pontiac models with power disc brakes. In 1978 part number 18005733 was used, it was also used on the 1978-1979 full-size and Ventura II/Phoenix lines. This unit was also used on 1979 and 1980 Firebirds unless the rear disc brake option was ordered; in this case part number 18009576 was used. As for refinishing it is the same as before. The cover used the same part number as in 1976 and was used on all cylinder assemblies; the bail also used the same part number.

1981

The master cylinder was completely restyled for 1981 model year. Now made from aluminum and plastic they look nothing like their previous counterpart, and featured a translucent nylon reservoir. It employed a "quick take-up" feature in the rear chamber that replaced excess pedal travel. Several different units were used according to model and brake options, those with rear wheel disc brakes required a special master cylinder, as did those models with a turbo charger.

1981 Master Cylinder Part Numbers

Model	W/O Rear Discs	W/ Rear Disc
Except Turbo	18013426	18008060
With Turbo	18008059	18008061

Brake identification was stamped on a tag (white arrow) that was attached to the bail. This tag was easily lost and very few survive. Code may have also been stamped on the end (black arrow) of the unit its self. Only careful cleaning will reveal the code, if it is there.

Typical master cylinder should be painted cast iron gray. The cover should have a gold cadmium appearance.

Later 1981 models used a plastic reservoir, and featured decal identification on the side as shown.

Booster Chamber
1970-1974

Delco-Moraine built power booster chamber was used with power-assisted disc brakes it was listed as part number 5470735 in 1970, and 5472354 in 1971, which continued to be used till the end of the 1974 model year. The original units came with a light gold cadmium finish; this can be duplicated with spray paint.

1975-1977

The 1975 unit was listed as part number 18000021, it will fit 1971-1974 models, but the 1971-74 unit will NOT fit the 1975 models. This unit was used again on Firebird till the end of the 1977 model year. Finishing is the same as in previous years.

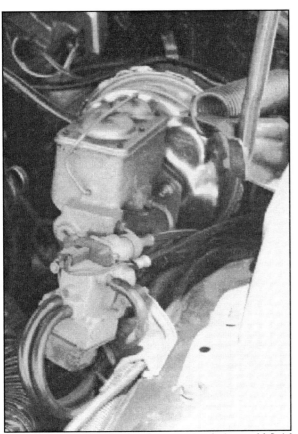

Note the booster chamber has the correct cadmium gold finish

1978-1980

A new booster chamber was used for the 1978 model year. Listed as part number 18003895, it was used only this year. Two different booster chambers were used in 1979. Those without the rear disc brakes used part number 18004083, while those with the rear disc brakes used part number 180004365. These two brake booster chambers were used again in 1980 models. Refinishing is the same as in previous years

1981

The booster chambers were again restyled and will not fit earlier models. A total of four different chambers were used. Those with rear disc brakes again required a unique assembly

1981 Booster Cylinder Part Numbers

Model	W/O Rear Discs	W/ Rear Disc
Except Turbo	18007257	18006557
With Turbo	18006322	18006557

Brake Drums, Rotors and Calipers

1970-1974

All Firebirds came standard with 9-1/2 in. diameter drum brakes at the rear wheel only. The drums were listed as part number 3841176 both years. At the front were 11-in diameter and listed as part number 3961281. Drums should be painted steel gray to duplicate the look of fresh forged steel. The disc was made of cast iron and should have a natural finish to it. Be sure to mask this area off before attempting to refinish your rotors. The lug bolts should not have a cast iron finish, nor be painted but be cleaned and given a light coating with a lubricant to prevent rusting. For detail the center of the bolt can be painted, using a small brush, with detail gray to duplicate the look of fresh steel.

The calipers were not as constant as the rotor assembly. They are unique to each side and will not swap positions

Caliper Housing and Pipe Part Numbers

Part	Right-Hand	Left-Hand
1970-1971	5472533	5472532
1972	5474056	5474055
1973-1974	2620586	2620585

The caliper should have a natural appearance, which can be duplicated by painting it detail gray; be sure to protect the inner surfaces and rubber seals of the unit when painting. The backing plate was either natural, duplicate by painting detail gray, or painted flat black, both styles were used.

1975-1981

New 9-1/2 I.D. brake drums part number 1249146 were used on the rear wheels for 1975, these cast iron units were used till the end of the 1981 models year, except with the 1979-1981 models with the rear disc brake option group.

All Firebirds models used front disc brakes. The 1975-1978 models used part number 334348 which used a cast iron 11-in. diameter finned rotor. The caliper was a sliding unit, and unlike the rotors different model years used different part numbers.

Caliper Housing and Pipe Part Numbers

Part	Right-Hand	Left-Hand
1975-1976	2620586	2620585
1977	18002421	18002420
1978	18003761	18003760
1979-1980	18005265	18005264
1981	18012309	18012308

Brake Pedals

Brake pedal differed according to what type of transmission was used. Those with manual transmission used a different part number than those with an automatic transmission; those units used with automatic transmission featured a larger step face, thus the two are not interchangeable. The 1970-1974 models used part numbers 3965697 for cars with a manual transmission and 3972201 with an automatic. The pedal pads were listed as part numbers 3921648 with manual transmission, this is the same pad that was used on the 1970-1972 clutch. Those with an automatic transmission used part number 3888682. Trim was used around the pads when the custom trim was selected. These part numbers were listed as 3923615 for manual transmission equipped cars and 3888683 with an automatic.

Beginning with the 1979 model year, rear disc brakes became optional. It was listed as option code J65 and was standard on the 10th Anniversary Trans Am models. This set up required a special rear rotor listed as part number 10005272. The rear calipers were listed as part numbers 18006748 left-hand and 18006749 right-hand. These parts were used till the end of 1981 model year.

All refinishing was the same as in previous years. The rear wheel drums should have the look of fresh cast iron, which can be duplicated by painting them cast iron gray. The rear rotors should be finished in the same manner as the front units. See the 1970-1974 section for more details.

1970-1981

The pedals were restyled for 1975 models. Those with a manual transmission used part number 347401 and those with an automatic transmission used part number 347402. The pads and the trim plates used the same part numbers as in 1974.

For 1976 the pedals were again restyled. Those with manual transmissions used part number 368063 those with an automatic transmission used part number 368064. These brake pedals were used only with the standard (non-power) disc brake set up. Those with power brakes used different pedals; they were listed as part numbers 10007527 with manual transmissions and 10005206 with automatic transmissions. Note this only applies to 1979-1981 models.

This photo shows the correct 30-degree gloss (Semi-gloss) black finish on the brake pedal. Notice how the paint doesn't cover the entire arm but stops at the top. Above this point the arm should have a natural steel finish.

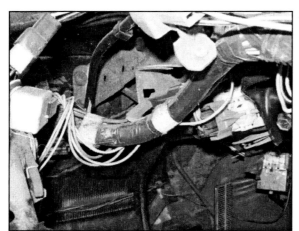

The upper brake pedal bracket was originally left unpainted and has rusted; it should have a natural appearance, and not be painted semi-gloss black.

Above is a typical parking brake cover, below is a brake pedal pad cover for a car with automatic transmission.

Engines

Short Block, V-8

1970

Standard V-8 on the base Firebird and the Esprit models, was a 350-ci 2-bbl rated at 255-hp. Next up was a 400-ci 2-bbl rated at 265 hp. Optional on the base and the Esprit and standard in the Formula 400 was the 330-hp 4-bbl version of the 400-ci. Trans Ams were standard with the 400-ci 4-bbl Ram Air III, which was rated at 335-hp. Called a 400 H.O. by Pontiac this power plant was a lot tougher than it sounds. The additional five ponies are very noticeable. The reason the Ram Air III version was listed as H.O. (High Output), was so not to confuse buyers wanting the Ram Air IV package that was simply listed as Ram Air. Rated at 345 hp, it is just as tough as the 1969 version although it had a higher horsepower rating. The 1970 version was much more livable on the street.

The casting number and date are found at the rear of the block, just behind the number eight cylinder. The date consists of a letter code that indicates the month followed by the day and the year. Remember that the year may not always agree with the model year. Code like D220 would be April 22, 1970 and would be for a 1970 model while the code J250 would be September 25, 1970and be for a 1971 model. Usually anything cast after July will be for the next year

Engine serial number and identification code will appear on the front face of the block just below the right-hand cylinder head. This two-letter code should be used for identification of the block.

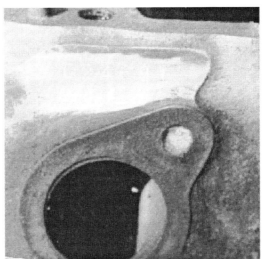

An example of an engine block identification code. The number on the top line is the engine serial number. That number may be referenced if there were a rolling change during the model year. The bottom line is the engine block identification code.

1970 V-8 Cylinder Block Casting Numbers

CID	Casting Number	Notes
350-ci	9799916	
400-ci	9799914	All except Ram IV Or Ram Air V
400-ci	9799915	Ram Air IV
400-ci	481708	Ram Air V

Ram Air V was a special order model that was used for racing only. It had to be ordered through the dealer and installed by the dealer, otherwise it would not pass government safety regulations. The horsepower rating for this powerhouse is unknown, as it was never offically released. For your Firebird to be properly equipped with this power plant, it must have been installed by the dealer and have paperwork to back up that claim.

1970 Engine Identification Codes

Horsepower	Codes	Transmission	Notes
350-ci			
255	WU	Manual	2-bbl
255	YU	Automatic	2-bbl
400-ci			
265	XX	Automatic	2-bbl Not available with man. trans.
330	WT	Manual	4-bbl
330	YS	Automatic	4-bbl
335	WS	Manual	H.O.
335	YZ	Manual	H.O.
345	WH	Manual	Ram Air
345	XN	Automatic	Ram Air

All V-8 blocks should be painted Pontiac Silver Blue 181-97219-DuPont, 13255, Ditzler, 266T21- Rinshed Mason. Oil pan 481030 was used with all V-8 powerplants, it too should be painted to match the engine block   The dip stick was listed as part number 9793342 for all models except Trans Am or those with Ram Air or air conditioning; these models used part number 9793341. The handle of the dipstick should be painted to match the cylinder block. The dipstick tube is also unique. And Trans Am models require a special upper tube due to the air cleaner design. The tube should have a natural appearance, but a little engine color over spray is acceptable as the part was in place when the engine was painted.

1970 Short Block Part Numbers

Block	Crankshaft	Rods	Pistons	Rings	Cam Shaft
350-ci					
479875	9795479	541000	478809	9794347	537441
400-ci 2-bbl					
479877	9795480	541000	478810	9794362	537441
400-ci 4-bbl					
479877	9795480	541000	478810	9794362	9779067
400-ci H.O.					
479878	9795480	541000	478810	9794362	9779068
400-ci Ram Air IV					
479879	9794054	541000	478811	9794362	9794041

1971 Engine Identification Codes

Horsepower	Codes	Transmission	Notes
350-ci			
250	WR, WN	Manual	3-spd.
250	WU YP	Manual	4-spd.
250	YU WP	Automatic	With RPOM35
250	XR YN	Automatic	With RPO M38
400-ci			
265	XX XY	Automatic	2-bbl
265	WS WX	Manual	2-bbl
300	WT	Manual	4-bbl with 3-spd
300	WK	Manual	4-bbl with 4-spd.
455-ci V-8			
325	WH	Automatic	Except H.O.
335	WL	Manual	H.O. with 3-spd.
335	WC	Manual	H.O with 4-spd.
335	YE	Automatic	H.O.

1971

Standard V-8 in the base Firebird and Esprit was again the 350-ci V-8, this is not a Chevrolet built powerplant, it is completely Pontiac. Like the year before it was available only as a 2-bbl and pushed out 250 horsepower. Next up was the 400-ci 2-bbl that produced 265-horsepower. Available as an option in all models except the Trans Am was a 4-bbl version of the 400-ci power plant that pumped out 300-horsepower. Optional in the Formula model only was the first of two 455-ci platforms, this 4-bbl unit was rated at 325-hp. The top performer was standard in the Trans AM models, which was a 455-ci 335-hp 4-bbl v-8,it was also optional on the Formula model.

The casting number and date are located at the rear of the block, just behind the number eight cylinder. The date used the same format that was before. Likewise the engine identification and production number are located in the same location as before.

Casting Date Month Codes

Code	Month	Code	Month	Code	Month
A-	January	B	February	C	March
D	April	E	May	F	June
G	July	H	August	I	September
J	October	K	October	L	December

All V-8 blocks should be painted Pontiac Silver Blue 181-97219-DuPont, 13255, Ditzler, 266T21- Rinshed Mason. Oil pan 481030 was used with all V-8 powerplants; it too should be painted to match the engine block. The dipstick was listed as part number 9793342 it was used on all V-8s without air conditioning. If air conditioning was ordered then part number 9793341 was used on all V-8s except the 455-ci H.O. It used part number 483765, which was used solely in the Firebird line. That from a GTO will NOT fit. The handle should be painted to match the cylinder block. The upper oil dipstick tube was listed as part number 480843 and was used in all models with or without air conditioning, except the 455-ci H.O., which used part number 523707. It was used in 1968-1969 Pontiacs, except those

with the Ram Air IV, set up. The tube should have a natural appearance, but a little engine color over spray as the part was placed on when the engine was painted, is acceptable.

1971 Short Block Part Numbers

Block	Crankshaft	Rods	Pistons	Rings	Cam Shaft
			350-ci		
483391	481379**	541000	478809	9794347	483555 9779066*
			400-ci 2-bbl		
483394	481380***	541000	478810	9794357	483555
			400-ci 4-bbl		
483394	481380***	541000	478810	9794362	9779067
			455-ci-4-bbl		
483394	9799103	541000	478812	478815	9779067
			455-ci 4-bbl H.O.		
483393	9799103	541000	478812	478815	9779068

*-with M38 transmission **-Stamped "79" number 1 counter weight
***- Stamped "80" number 1 counter weight

1971 Cam Shaft ID Codes

Part Number	ID Code	Part Number	ID Code
48355	W	9779066	N
9779067	P	9779068	S

1971 V-8 Cylinder Block Casting Numbers

CID	Casting Number	Notes
350-ci	481990	
400-ci	9799914	
455--ci	9799140	
455-ci	483677	H.O.

1972

The method used to list the horsepower rating changed in 1972, they were now rated with the engine under load, while the earlier rating had the engine free of accessories like alternators so that the ratings were lower than they were for 1971.

The V-8 used in the base V-8 Firebird and the Esprit models was a 350-ci rated at 160-hp with single exhaust. A 400-ci 2-bbl rated at 175-hp was optional in all but the Trans Am. A 400-ci 4-bbl rated at 250-hp was also for all except the Trans Am. The Trans Am came standard with a 455-ci H.O. rated at 300-hp; this power plant was also optional in the Formula models.

The engine block should be painted Pontiac Silver Blue which used the same part numbers as in 1971. Oil pan was listed as part number 527503 and was used on all V-8s. This pan was used on all 1972-1974 Pontiac models, except the Ventura II models. The dipstick was listed as part number 9793341 this 31-1/4 overall length rod was used on all powerplants and models. The dipstick tube was listed as the same part numbers as in 1971.

1972 Engine Identification Codes

Horsepower	Codes	Transmission	Notes
		350-ci	
160	WR	Manual	
160	YR	Automatic	
160	YU	Automatic	With NOX
		400-ci	
175	YX	Automatic	2-bbl
175	ZX	Automatic	With NOX
250	WK	Manual	
250	YS, ZS	Automatic	
		455-ci V-8	
300	WD, WM	Manual	
300	YB,YE	Automatic	

The 1970 400-ci with Ram Air

1972 Short Block Part Numbers

Block	Crankshaft	Rods	Pistons	Rings	Cam Shaft
				350-ci	
487641	481379	541000	478809	489075	483555
				400-ci 2-bbl	
487640	495201	541000	478810	489139	483555
				400-ci 4-bbl	
487640	495201	541000	478810	9794362	9779067
				455-ci-4-bbl	
487639	9799103	541000	485804	491212	9779068

1972 V-8 Cylinder Block Casting Numbers

CID	Casting Number	Notes
350-ci	481990	
400-ci	481988	
455-ci	485428	

1973

Big news for 1973 models was the introduction of the 455-ci Super Duty powerplant and a mid-year emission change that greatly affected the powerplants and their usage.

Standard V-8 in the base Firebird, Esprit and Formula was the 350-ci V-8 rated at 150 hp with single exhaust and 175 with dual exhaust. A 400-ci 2-bbl was optional on the Esprit and Formula models only, it was rated at 170-hp with single exhaust the 4-bbl version of the 400 was rated at 230-hp and came standard with dual exhaust. The 455-ci 4-bbl V-8 was standard in the Trans Am models, and optional on the Formulas. Rated at 250 hp, it should not be confused with the all-new 455-ci Super Duty. With a family history of the 421 SD the 455 SD power plant pumped out 310-ponies, which was excellent for its time, had this power house been released in 1969 its rating would have been over 400-hp. The 455 SD was special from its block to the internal goodies inside it.

It was due to government regulations from the EPA that caused a change in powerplants. Models built after March 15, 1973 will incorporate a new emission system that removed the time delay feature and the EGR solenoid. These powerplants will have special codes, and it is incorrect for a later built car to have a earlier built engine, and

in some states today actually be considered illegal, as it will not pass the emission test. While the codes were changed most of the internal parts did not, but the color that engine the was painted was changed. Early models (those up to 3/15/73) used the same color shade as in previous years. Later models (after 3/15/73) were painted with a darker shade of blue than before. This color is very hard to find. It is listed as 14817-Dupont and 14580- Ditzler. It is essential for correctness that the proper shade be used.

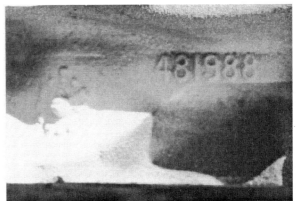

An example of a cylinder block casting number. The item at the left, is a casting clocking indicating it was cast at two- o'clock a shift indicator elsewhere will tell if it is a.m. or p.m.

By the arrow code we can determine that this was cast by the day shift meaning that the clock in the photo above was 2 p.m. It was cast at GM-4 foundry.

Some blocks like this 1973 unit have the cubic inch displacement cast into the sides of the block. But not all blocks at all foundries were marked.

1973 Engine Identification Codes

Horsepower	Codes		Transmission	Notes
	Early	Late		
		350-ci V-8		
150/175	XR	ZB	Manual	
150/175	YL	WL	Automatic	High Altitude
150/175	YR	WD, YW	Automatic	Except Calif. or High Altitude
150/175	ZR	WA	Automatic	NOX
		400-ci V-8		
170	YX	X4	Automatic	2-bbl, Except High Attitude or Calif.
170	YZ	W5	Automatic	2-bbl High Attitude
170	ZX	X3	Automatic	2-bbl, With NOX
230	WP	YG	Manual	4-spd.-EARLY
230	WK	Y6	Manual	3-spd-EARLY
230	YS	XN	Automatic	EARLY Except High Attitude or Calif.
230	YT	XK	Automatic	High Attitude
230	YY		Automatic	
230	Y3	XX	Automatic	
230	ZS		Automatic	NOX
		455-ci V-8		
250	WT	ZE	Manual	EARLY-Unit Distributor
250	WW	ZZ	Manual	EARLY Non-Unit Distributor
250	YA	XE,X7	Automatic	EARL;Y-Unit Distributor
250	YC	XL	Automatic	EARLY-Non-Unit Distributor
250	YD	XM	Automatic	High Altitude
250	YK		Automatic	NOX
250	ZA		Automatic	NOX
250	ZC		Automatic	NOX
250	ZS		Automatic	NOX
310	W8	ZJ	Manual	Super Duty
310	Y8	XD	Automatic	Super Duty

1973 Short Block Part Numbers

Block	Crankshaft	Rods	Pistons	Rings	Cam Shaft
				350-ci	
491947	481379	541000	478809	489075	483555
				400-ci 2-bbl	
487640	495201	541000	478810	489139	491255
				400-ci 4-bbl	
487640	495201	541000	478810	9794362	9779066-Autoamtic Transmission 9779068-With Manual transmissions
				455-ci-4-bbl	
487639	9799103	541000	485804	491212	9779068- Except Calif. Cars 9779066-Calif. Cars only
				455-ci Super Duty	
491948	490164	485225	493421	493421	9779068

1973 V-8 Cylinder Block Casting Numbers

CID	Casting Number	Notes
350-ci	481990* 488986**	*-Early **-Late
400-ci	9799914* 481988**	
455-ci	9799140* 485428**	
455-ci S.D.	490132	

SPECIAL INSTRUCTIONS FOR 455-ci SUPER DUTY

This power plant used forged aluminum pistons instead of cast, and special oil rings, and special heavy-duty 80 psi oil pump. The connecting rods were forged steel rather than cast and featured .437 diameter bolts instead of .375 that were used on other models. Prevailing torque nuts were used, so that you can reuse the rod nuts again if they are removed, such as during a rebuild. You also must measure the bolt stretch rather than torque the bolts down. This is done using a micrometer to measure the bolt ends. The nuts have to be in place but not tightened; measure the length of the bolt. Next tighten each nut alternately in 10-lb ft steps with a torque wrench till 60-lbs ft rating is reached. Again measure the bolts they should now be .006-to .008 in. longer than before. If the bolts did not stretch to at least .006 in. then retighten in 5-ft.lbs steps till this goal is reached. It is a must that this procedure is done, or your Super Duty may end up being worth a pile of doody.

Available only two years 1973 and 1974 very few just as the plate says very few super duties were made. This a 1973 Super Duty Formula, one of 43 built that year.

1974

Standard V-8 in the base Firebird, Esprit and Formula was the 350-ci V-8 rated at 150 hp with single exhaust and 170 with dual exhaust. A 400-ci 2-bbl was optional on the, Esprit and Formula models only; it was rated at 175 hp, and came with single exhaust. This power plant was more a highway cruiser than a performer and is more common in the Esprit than the Formula.

The first of the 4-bbl equipped platforms was the 400-ci V-8 rated at 225-hp, it came standard with dual exhaust. It was optional in the Formula model only and standard in the Tran Am models. Two 455-ci V-8s were available the standard 455-ci 4-bbl which was rated at 250-hp and the 455-ci Super Duty which was now rated at 290-hp. This drop in horsepower was due to a milder camshaft. That was required to make the Super Duty legal in acceptance of emissions. Oh, those wonderful government regulations.

1977 and later engines are painted GM blue, regardless of the manufacturer.

1974 Engine Identification Codes

Horsepower	Codes	Transmission	Notes
		350-ci	
155/170	AA	Automatic	High Altitude
155/170	WA	Manual	
155/170	YA	Automatic	
155/170	ZA	Automatic	Calf.
		400-ci	
175	AH	Automatic	2-bbl, High Altitude
175	YH	Automatic	2-bbl
175	ZJ	Automatic	2-bbl, Calif.
225	AT	Automatic	High Altitude
225	WT	Manual	
225	YT	Automatic	
225	YZ	Automatic	
225	ZT	Automatic	Calf.
		455-ci V-8	
250	AU	Automatic	High Altitude
250	YW, YY	Automatic	
250	ZU	Automatic	Calf.
250	ZW	Automatic	Calf.
290	W8	Manual	Super Duty
290	Y8	Automatic	Super Duty

1974 V-8 Cylinder Block Casting Numbers

CID	Casting Number	Notes
350-ci	488986	
400-ci	481988	
455-ci	485428	
455-ci S.D.	490132	

1972-1975 Cam Shaft ID Codes

Part Number	ID Code	Part Number	ID Code
48355	W	9779066	N
9779067	P	9779068	S
491266	Z	493323	N

1974 Short Block Part Numbers

Block	Crankshaft	Rods	Pistons	Rings	Cam Shaft
				350-ci	
491947	481379	541000	478809	489075	483555* 494957**
				400-ci 2-bbl	
487640	495201	541000	478810	489139	491255
				400-ci 4-bbl	
487640	495201	541000	478810	9794362	9779066-Autoamtic Transmission 9779067-With Manual transmissions
				455-ci-4-bbl	
487639	9799103	541000	485804	491212	493323
			455-ci Super Duty		
491948	490164	485225	493421	491212	9779068

1975

Mid way through the "me-generation" decade spiraling upward gas prices insurance agents waiting with baited breath to surprise you with the outrageous rates on a Super Duty T/A, and stronger and stronger EPA regulations were strangling the life out of the muscle car. The Firebirds sister ship the Camaro had said good-bye to Z-28, and there was talk of scrapping both the Camaro and the Firebird. Instead Pontiac overhauled the Firebird, gone were the high-powered touches like the 455 Super Duty, smaller fuel-efficient powerplants were on the horizon.

Standard 350-ci was rated at 155 hp with single exhaust. This powerplant was standard in the V-8 in all except the Trans Am models and those sold in California. California bound Firebirds, Esprits and Formulas came with a 350-ci 4-bbl V-8 rated at 170 with single exhaust. These powerplants were available only with an automatic transmission. This engine was optional in the other 49 states for all models except the Trans Am.

The 400-ci 2-bbl proved to be a poor seller. It was too big to be a fuel saver, and not powerful enough to be a performer, it was deleted for the 1975 model year. Standard in the Trans Am and optional in the Formula models was 400-ci 4-bbl V-8 rated at 185-hp, compare that to last years 225-hp. The 455-ci-powerplant was introduced late in the year. Rated at 215-hp as optional in the Trans Am only. Big cube engines were proving to be unpopular with buyers and only 857 Trans Ams were built with this platform. That is a little over 3-precent of the production total of Trans Am with the massive powerplant.

All powerplants should be painted Pontiac Silver blue, but of the same shade that was used on late built 1973 models. Oil pan was the same unit that was used in 1972 models including part number; it should be painted to match the engine block. The dipstick was listed as part number 9793342 without air conditioning and was 19-3/4 in. length. while those with air conditioning used part number 9793341 and it was 31-1/4 in. length.

1975 Engine Identification Codes

Horsepower	Codes	Transmission	Notes
		350-ci	
155	YB	Automatic	2-bbl Ex. Calf.
170	WN	Automatic	4-bbl Ex. Calf.
170	YN	Manual	4-bbl. Ex. Calf.
170	ZP	Automatic	4-bbl Calf. only
		400-ci	
185	WT	Manual	4-bbl
185	YS	Automatic	4-bbl
		455-ci V-8	
215	WX	Manual	4-speed only

1975 Short Block Part Numbers

Block	Crankshaft	Rods	Pistons	Rings	Cam Shaft
				350-ci	
498977	496413	541000	499054	489075	483555
				400-ci 4-bbl	
498978	496414	541000	499053	489139	9779067-Man. Transmission
					9779066-Automatic Transmission
				455-ci-4-bbl	
498979	496415	541000	499052	491212	9779067

THE RETURN OF THE 455 H.O.

It is incorrect for an early built 1975 Trans Am to have any other power plant except for a 400-ci 4-bbl. The 455-ci was not available at the beginning of the year. Released shortly after production began the 455-ci H.O. was made available around August 11, 1975. It was available only with a 4-speed manual transmission.

1975 V-8 Cylinder Block Casting Numbers

CID	Casting Number	Notes
350-ci	488986	
400-ci	500557	
455-ci	500813	

1976

This year would be the last year that the Firebird's lifeblood would be pumped with pure Pontiac. The line up was the same as in 1975. In an effort to get buyers to opt for smaller cube powerplants Pontiac upped the horsepower on the base 350-ci V-8. Now rated at 160 hp this two-barrel version was the standard V-8 in all models except the Trans Am or California bound cars. What was the standard engine in California? There was not one. Technically no engine was available in standard form in any car headed for California; instead the required option was the 4-bbl version of the 350-ci V-8 that rated at 165-hp. Both these powerplants were Pontiac built. Standard in the Trans Am and optional on the Formula models was the 400-ci 4-bbl rated at 185-hp.. The 455-ci returned for the last time as an option in the Trans Am and was rated at 200-hp.

All V-8 engine blocks should be painted silver blue in the same shade as in 1976. The oil pan was listed as part number 527503 for all powerplants; it too should be painted the same color as the engine block. The oil dipstick was listed as part number 9793342 without air conditioning and 9793341 with air conditioning. The unit with air conditioning is longer. Engine identification codes for all V-8 powerplants were the same as in previous years.

1976 Engine Identification Codes

Horsepower	Codes	Transmission	Notes
		350-ci	
160	YB,YR	Automatic	2-bbl Ex. Calf.
165	ZX, Y9, ZC	Automatic	4-bbl
		400-ci	
185	WT,WU	Manual	4-bbl
185	ZA,ZK	Automatic	4-bbl
		455-ci V-8	
200	WX		

1976 Short Block Part Numbers

Block	Crankshaft	Rods	Pistons		Rings	Cam Shaft
				350-ci		
498977	499863	541000	499054		489075	537441-2-bbl
						483555- 4bbl
				400-ci 4-bbl		
498978	499864	541000	499053		489139	9779067-Man. Transmission
						9779066-Automatic Transmission
				455-ci-4-bbl		
498979	496415	541000	499052		491212	9779067

1976 V-8 Cylinder Block Casting Numbers

CID	Casting Number	Notes
350-ci	488986, 500810	
400-ci	500557	
455-ci	500813	

1977

This year of invasion, no longer did a Pontiac heart beat under the hood of all Firebirds. Oldsmobile built powerplants entered the arena, much to the dismay of some Pontiac purists, and would create controversy as many thought they had a true Pontiac powerplant. And because of labeling the engine a 6.6-liter, which would also be used on the 400-ci, many buyers felt duped when they got a 403-ci Oldsmobile built power plant when they though they were getting a 400-ci Pontiac built power plant. The reason for the uproar over this was due to mind-set and legends. The Pontiac 400-ci had a long running of being a true performer, while the 403-ci Oldsmobile was just the opposite. This insight was not intended to deceive Firebird buyers, but was done to combat the every increasing government regulations on emissions. Along with increasing concerns on MPG instead of HP, smaller more efficient engine were needed, it was decided that the 400-ci powerplant would be phased out over the next five years. Also General motors were hemoglobin parts among the lines to make a better method of producing parts.

Standard V-8 in all models except the Trans Am was the all-new 5.0 liter 301-ci 2-bbl V-8 rated at 135-hp. This little power plant was good on gas mileage, as long as you didn't stand on it or do much stop and go traffic. The wimpy 135-hp was not enough power to amply push the heavy Firebird; it would take 12-14 seconds to get this car up to 60-mph from dead stop. A better contender was the optional 350-ci (5.7 Liter) 4-bbl V-8 rated a 170-hp. There was a pair of powerplants. All states except California got a Pontiac built unit, while California got an Oldsmobile built power plant. Even though they were the same displacement and rating (though torque was slightly lower in the Oldsmobile) they are drastically two different powerplants, and parts will not interchange.

Standard in the Trans Am was the L78 400-ci 4-bbl rated at 180-hp, a performance option W72 added another 20 ponies, and was the only way you could get a 4-speed manual transmission in a Trans Am. Buyers in California or High Country (Mountain regions) could not get the 400-ci power plant. Instead the 403-ci Oldsmobile built 4-bbl engine was used and only with automatic transmission and was rated at 180-hp. No performance option was available with this powerplant. All powerplants were painted the same color thwhich was now decribed as GM blue.

Two different oil pans were used. Those powerplants built by Pontiac used part number 527503 while those built by Oldsmobile used part number 555137. The dipsticks were also correlated to the engine manufacturer. Those built by Oldsmobile used part number 419242 with all applications, while those powerplants that were built by Pontiac used part number 9793342 without air conditioning and 9793341 with air conditioning.

Decals like this one with blue letter s on a white background were used at the factory for quick engine identification; they should be used on a show car only.

1977 Engine Identification Codes

Horsepower	Codes	Transmission	Notes
		301-ci	
135	WB	Manual	
135	YH, YK	Automatic	
		350-ci	
170	YB, Y9	Automatic	4-bbl Ex. Calf. (Pontiac Built)
170	,TX,TY, Q8, Q9	Automatic	4-bbl Calif. (Oldsmobile Built)
		400-ci	
185	Y6,	Automatic	4-bbl
200	WA ,YG	Manual	With W72 pkg.
200	XA	Automatic	With W72 pkg.
		403-ci 4-bbl	
180	U2, U3,VA, VB	Automatic	4-bbl (Calif. Only)

1977 Short Block Part Numbers

Block	Crankshaft	Rods	Pistons	Rings	Cam Shaft
				301-ci	
10003677	10000590	499323	10005635	547027	547868#
					10002977##
				350-ci	
498977*	499863*	541000*	499054*	489075*	526793*
555618**	231829**	554976**	231433**		562299**
				400-ci 4-bbl	
498978	499864	541000	499053	489139	549431-With W72 pkg
					549112-W/o W72 pkg.
				403-ci-4-bbl**	
556623	555479	555142	556265	556291	562299

*-Pontiac **-Oldsmobile Built #- Manual Transmission ##-Automatic Transmission

1977 V-8 Cylinder Block Casting Numbers

CID	Casting Number	Notes
350-ci	488986, 500810	
400-ci	500557	
403-ci		

THE OTHER 1977 V-8

 Due to shortages that occurred on the supply of the 301-ci 2-bbl V-8, mid-way through the year Pontiac turned to Chevrolet and began to place the 305-ci 2-bbl which was rated at 245-hp, ten more than the 301-ci; this power plant proved to be a better running platform, and simplified construction at the assembly plant as both the Firebird and Camaro both used this powerplant. It used oil pan part number 465221 the dipstick was listed as part number 3951576.

The engine codes are located in the same place as other Pontiac V-8's but are listed as CPA, CPC or CPY, these are the same codes that were used on the Camaro. The VIN stamped on the block will identify it as a Pontiac unit. It used the letter "U' in the VIN plate.

1978

The disco ball was turning on the age of muscle cars. Refugees from the muscle car wars in the 1960's and early 1970's were being pushed to the back row of the car lots. Imagine a Super Duty 455's rested in a heap of worn out parts hidden behind garages. Formula 455's tangled in multitude of grasses as it sits in a hay field, it's hood cracking in the heat of the everyday sun. Car dealers shaking their heads putting their hands up saying no they didn't want to take your trade in of a Ram Air IV Firebird on trade in for a six cylinder Gran Prix. These are all true images of they year of 1978 and engine reshuffling in the new 1978 Firebirds proved it all true.

The standard V-8 was the 305-ci Chevrolet built unit, it was nearly a carbon copy of the unit used in the later part of 1977, but it was not available in California or high country. The standard V-8 in California and High Country cars was a 350-ci V-8, which was a required option   It ,too, was built by Chevrolet. Spurred on by the *Smokie and Bandit* movie, sales for the Trans Am picked up. The standard powerplant, except in California bound cars, was the L78 400-ci 180-hp 4-bbl Pontiac built engine. The W72 option remained and it was rated at 200-hp. Neither the 400-ci nor the W72 package was available in Trans Ams that were headed for the Golden Coast. California cars were mandatory with a 403-ci Oldsmobile built power plant that was rated at 185-hp. The W72 package was available with either a 4-speed or automatic transmission, but the only way to get a 4-speed manual transmission was with the W72 option package. So no 4-speed California cars were built.

The oil pan and the dipstick that was used on 1977 305-ci V-8s was used again in 1978. The 350-ci Chevrolet built power plant used part number 465221 and the dipstick was listed as part number 3951576. The Oldsmobile built 403-ci used the same part number that it used in 1977 for both the oil pan and the dipstick. The 400-ci was the only Pontiac built power plant and it too used the same parts as it did in 1977.

1978 Engine Identification Codes

Horsepower	Codes	Transmission	Notes
		305-ci 2-bbl	
145	TH, TJ, TK 3N		N/A Calif.
		350-ci 4-bbl	
170	HR, HFHJ, HL, 3T		
		400-ci 4-bbl	
180	WC	Manual	With W72 Package
180	YA	Automatic	
180	X7	Automatic	With W72 Package
		403-ci 4-bbl	
185	VA, VB, U2, U3	Automatic	

1978 V-8 Cylinder Block Casting Numbers

CID	Casting Number	Notes
305-ci	355909	Chevrolet Built
350-ci	366245	Chevrolet Built
400-ci	500557	Pontiac Built
403-ci		Oldsmobile Built

1978 Short Block Part Numbers

Block	Crankshaft	Rods	Pistons	Rings	Cam Shaft
				305-ci	
474170	361982	3916396	364702	370409	361995
				350-ci	
6259425	3932444	3916396	6271097	14089027	3896929
				400-ci 4-bbl	
10001011	499864	541000	499053	489139	10003402-With W72 pkg
486329[1]					527471-W/o W72 pkg.
				403-ci-4-bbl	
560128	555479	555142	22510631	556291	562299

[1]- High performance

1979

As the decade drew to a close, the 301-ci V-8 returned as the standard V-8 in base Firebird and Esprit models ,only it came in two forms the standard 2-bbl rated at 140-hp and a 4-bbl version rated at 150-hp, the later of these was a credit option in the Trans Am outside of California. The 305-ci V-8 was standard in the Formula models, (the 301-ci 2-bbl was a no cost option) this two-barrel Chevrolet built power plant was rated at 145-hp. This powerplant was also a required option in California bound cars; the 301-ci V-8 was illegal, as it could not pass the tough emission standards set by the state. The Chevrolet built 350-ci V-8 remained as an option for all models except the Trans Am. It was a required option on cars sold in High Country.

All Trans Am's were standard with the 403-ci Oldsmobile 4-bbl V-8 rated at 180-hp, the 400-ci 220-hp V-8 was optional on the Trans Am only except in California, where the transmission could not pass the emission test during switching of the manual gears.

1979 Engine Identification Codes

Horsepower	Codes	Transmission	Notes
		301-ci V-8	
140	XR,XP		2-bbl
150	NA, X6, X4		4-bbl
		305-ci 2-bbl	
145	DNF,DNK, DNJ, DNZ		Req. Calif..
		350-ci 4-bbl	
170	DRJ, DRY		Req. High Country
		400-ci 4-bbl	
180	WH	Manual	N.A. Calif.
		403-ci 4-bbl	
185	QE,QJ, QK, QL, Q6, TD, TE		

1979 V-8 Cylinder Block Casting Numbers

CID	Casting Number	Notes
301-ci		
305-ci	355909	Chevrolet Built
350-ci	366245	Chevrolet Built
400-ci	500557	Pontiac Built
403-ci		Oldsmobile Built

1979 Short Block Part Numbers

Block	Crankshaft	Rods	Pistons	Rings	Cam Shaft
				301-ci	
100016651	10000590	499323	10005635	547027	527471#
					10007424##
				305-ci	
474170	361982	3916396	364702	370409	361995
				350-ci	
6259425	3932444	3916396	6271097	14089027	3896929
				400-ci 4-bbl	
486329	499864	541000	499053	489139	549431
				403-ci-4-bbl**	
556623	555479	555142	22510635	556291	562299

#- Manual Transmission ##-Automatic Transmission

1980

October 11, 1979 should be listed as the day the classic Firebird perished as any form of muscle car. This is the day that new Firebirds were officially released and gracing this news was the fact that the 400-ci powerplant was gone, as was the 403-ci and even the humble 350-ci 4-bbl. The news was sobering to all of us who associated Trans Am with big cubic inches. Sometimes size does matter.

Standard V-8 powerplant in all Firebirds (except those bound for California) was a 4-bbl version of the 301-ci Pontiac power plant that produced 150-hp. However, the 301-ci V-8 was still not rated for California emissions, thus all California bound Firebirds got the Chevrolet built 305-ci 2-bbl rated at 150-hp as their base engine.

The only bright spot of this year was the release of a turbo-charged version of the 301-ci V-8 that was optional in the Formula and Trans Am models only. Rated at 210-hp it was meant to be the wave into the new decade. However problems erupted right away for this powerplant. One was delay in production The Van Nuys plant was given the go ahead and began production in early October 1979, while production was delayed till November 1979 at the Norwood assembly plant. Another set back was when the planned release of a 4-speed manual transmission with this power plant was cancelled. All 1980 Firebird came with automatic transmission.

1980 Engine Identification Codes

Horsepower	Codes	Transmission	Notes
		301-ci V-8	
150	YN, XN		4-bbl
220	YL		Turbo
		305-ci 2-bbl	
150	CEL,CEM		Req. Calif..

1980 V-8 Cylinder Block Casting Numbers

CID	Casting Number	Notes
301-ci		
305-ci		Chevrolet Built

1980 Short Block Part Numbers

Block	Crankshaft	Rods	Pistons	Rings	Cam
			301-ci		
100016651	10000590	499323	10010447	10016047	10007
100016650*	10016646*		10013653*-RH		10012
			10013659*-LH		
			305-ci		
474170	361982	3916396	364702	370409	14044

1981

The much-awaited 4.3 liter 265-ci V-8 appeared in handful of late 1980 models and became the standard V-8 for the Formula models. Rated at 120-hp this two-barrel V-8, was optional in the base Firebird and Esprit, which were standard with the 301-ci 4-bbl V-8 that was rated at 135-hp. Trans Ams were standard with a high performance version of the 301-ci 4-bbl V-8 rated at 150-hp. This power plant was optional in all Firebirds. In was clear to see that the Trans Am had become nothing more than a thin veil wrapped around a standard Firebird.

The Turbo-Charged 301-ci V-8 rated at 200-hp was optional in the Trans Am or Formula models. For the first time the 301-ci V-8 was available in California bound cars. The last engine option was the Chevrolet built 305-ci V-8. This 4-bbl version was rated at 145-hp and was available with an automatic transmission and was the only power plant available with a 4-speed. It was optional only in the Formula and Trans Am models

1981 Engine Identification Codes

Horse power	Codes	Transmission		Notes
			265-ci V-8	
120	BA,DB, DCDH, DJ			
			301-ci V-8	
150	BD, BJ			4-bbl
200	CJ			Turbo
			305-ci	
150	DHA, DHB, DHC, DHD ,DHF, DHH, DHJ, DHK, DHU, DHZ			

1981 Short Block Part Numbers

Block	Crankshaft	Rods	Pistons		Rings	Cam Shaft
				265-ci		
10018156	10009545					
				301-ci		
100016651	10000590	499323	10010447		10016047	10007424#*
100016650*	10016646*		10013653*-RH			10012185
			10013659*-LH			
				305-ci		
14019867	361982	3916396	364702	370409	1404475	

Cylinder Head, V-8
1970

The standard 2-bbl 350-ci V-8 used a cast iron cylinder head listed as part number 478100. It used eight steel intake valves part number 9787320, and eight exhaust valves listed as part number 9792332. It used a pair of stamped steel valve covers part number 9786244- right hand and 9786245 left-hand. The covers were painted Pontiac Silver Blue to match the cylinder block in all models.

The 400-ci 2-bbl used a different set of heads listed as part number 478100. These heads were also made of cast iron and each head used eight intake valves listed as part number 9787320 and eight exhaust valves The valve covers were the same exact items used on the 350-ci set up.

Those with a 400-ci 4-bbl V-8 used three different cylinder heads, all were made from cast iron. Those without Ram Air or a manual transmission used part number 9799497, while those with a manual transmission or with the 455 H.O. used part number 9799497. Those with the Ram Air IV option used special heads listed as part number 9799498.

1970 Ram Air V-8. Note the engine identification label on the cylinder block.

1970 400-ci Valves and Valve Springs

Part	Intake	Exhaust	Notes
Except Manual Transmission H.O. or Ram Air			
Valves	478354	478348	
Springs	Inner	Outer	
	9779008	9779009	
Manual Transmission or H.O.			
Valves	9792344	9792340	
Springs	Inner	Outer	
	9781476	9779009	
		Ram Air IV	
Valves	9794021	9794019	
Springs	Inner	Outer	
	9796789	9796790	

Those with the Ram Air engines in 1970 used a chrome valve cover.

1971

All 350-ci V-8 powerplants used a cast iron cylinder head listed as part number 483713. It used eight steel intake valves with a 1.96 in. diameter head and eight 21-2 steel exhaust valves that featured a 1.66 in diameter head. These same features were used on the 400-ci 2-bbl V-8 but it used a head listed as part number 483716. Those models with a 400-ci 4-bbl used part number 481760, those with the standard 455-ci V-8 used part number 483714, while those with the 455 H.O used a special set of heads listed as part number 481758. All 4-bbl power plants used the same size of valves the intakes valves had a head diameter of 2.11 and the exhaust valves a diameter of 1.77.

1971 400/455-ci Valves and Valve Springs

Part	Intake	Exhaust	Notes
400-ci V-8			
Valves	483201*	483186*	*-2-bbl
	483211	483191	
Springs	Inner	Outer	**-Man. Trans.
	9781476**	9779009	
	9779008		
455-ci Except H.O.			
Valves	483221	483206	
Springs	Inner	Outer	
	9779008	9779009	
455-ci H.O.			
Valves	483211	483191	
Springs	Inner	Outer	
	9779008	9796790	

From 1971 on, as shown on this 1973 model all valve covers were painted, except those with special high performance packages.

1971-1972 2-bbl models used the small valve heads.

Big valves heads were used on all 4-bbl models.

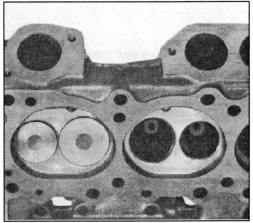

Note the unique combustion chambers on the 1971-72 455 H.O.

1972

The 350-ci V-8 used a new cylinder head listed as part number 487076. The cylinder head used on the 400-ci 2-bbl was listed as part number 487075, the 4-bbl version of the 400-ci used part number 485319. These cylinder heads used the same intake valves that were used in 1971, but the exhaust valves were restyled and used a 1.77 in diameter head for all three powerplants. However, there was a difference in the length.

All engines used the same set of painted steel covers listed as part numbers 9786244 right-hand and 9786245-left-hand. The covers should be painted the same color as the engine block.

1972 Valves and Valve Springs

Part	Intake	Exhaust	Length
350- ci			
Valves	483201	486564	4.982*
			4.971**
Springs	Inner 9779008	Outer 9779009	
400-ci 2-bbl			
Valves	483201	486564	4.982*
			4.971**
Springs	Inner 9779008	Outer 9779009	
400-ci 4-bbl/455-ci-4-bbl			
Valves	483211	486567	4.960*
			4.949**
Springs	Inner 9779008	Outer 9779009	

*-Intake **-Exhaust

1973

With the EPA enforced emission changes in mid 1973 some models built after March 15, 1973 used different heads than those built before this date. It is essential that the proper heads be used both for correctness and legality in some areas.   This is also the first year of the 455 Super Duty which used special cylinder heads using constant cross-sectioning ports, exhaust valve seat inserts, special alloy valve guides and special push rods. These were some of the best free flowing cylinder heads ever placed on an American built automobile. God bless the USA and Pontiac.

Also, due to the strict emission laws in California, the 350-ci V-8 was required to use special cylinder heads for models to be shipped to California in an effort to pass the emissions test set for by the state. Valve covers were the same units used in 1972, except the Super Duty, which used special valve covers.

1973 Cylinder Head Part Numbers

Application	Early	Late	Notes
350-ci 2-bbl	491545*	493337*	*-Manual transmission Fed.
	491544**	494336**	Automatic Calif.
		487076#	**-Automatic Fed./ Except YW
			#-YW only press in rocker studs
400-ci 2-bbl	491546	494334	
400-ci 4-bbl	488538	494332	
455-ci 4-bbl	491548	493331	Except Super Duty
455-ci 4-bbl	485214	485214	Super Duty

1973 Valves and Valve Springs

Part	Intake	Exhaust	Length	Diameter
350- ci Except code YW and 400-ci 2-bbl				
Valves	489849	489843	4.960*	1.96*
			4.949**	1.66**
Springs	Inner	Outer		
	9779008	9779009		
350-ci 2-bbl YW code				
Valves	483201	486564	4.982*	4.971**
Springs	Inner	Outer		
	9779008	9779009		
400-ci 4-bbl				
Valves	483211	489843	4.960*	2.11*
			4.949**	1.66**
Springs	Inner	Outer		
	9779008	9779009		
455-ci V-8 except Super Duty				
Valves	483221	489846	4.881*	2.11*
			4.870**	1.66**
Springs	Inner	Outer		
	9779008	9779009		

1973 455-ci Super Duty Valves and Valve Springs

Part	Intake	Exhaust	Length	Diameter
Valves	485222	493142	4.985*	2.11*
			4.969**	1.77**
Springs	Inner	Outer	Valves are swirl polished	
	493145	493144		

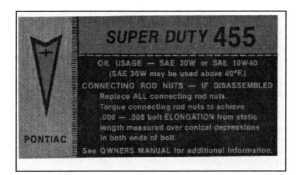

Decal used on valve covers to identify the 1973-1974 455- Super Duty. Decal courtesy of Jim Osborne Reproductions

1974

Cylinder heads were again restyled for 1974, and again this year cars sold in California required special heads to allow the Firebirds to pass the tougher state emission tests, except for the 455-ci powerplants. Valve covers were the same units used on the 1973 models, they should be painted to match the engine block. As before those headed to California required special valve covers.

1974 Cylinder Head Part Numbers

Application	Part Number	Notes
350-ci 2-bbl	494337*	*Manual Trans.
Ex. Calif.	494336**	**-Auto Trans.
350-ci 2-bbl Calif.	493337**	
350-ci 4-bbl	494336	
400-ci 2-bbl Ex. Calif.	491546	
400-ci 2-bbl Calif.	494335	
400-ci 4-bbl	494332*	
	494333**	
455-ci ex. S.D.	494331	
455-ci S.D.	485214	

1974 Valves and Valve Springs

Part	Intake	Exhaust	Length	Diameter
350-ci/400-ci 2-bbl				
Valves	489849	489843	4.960*	1.96*
			4.949**	1.66**
Springs	Inner 9779008	Outer 9779009		
400-ci 4-bbl				
Valves	483211	489843	4.960*	2.11*
			4.949**	1.66**
Springs	Inner 9779008	Outer 9779009		
455-ci 4-bbl Except Super Duty				
Valves	483221	489846	4.881*	2.11*
			4870**	1.66**
Springs	Inner 9779008	Outer 9779009		
455-ci Super Duty				
Valves	485222	493142	4.985*	2.11*
			4.969**	1.77**
Springs	Inner 493145	Outer 493144		

1975-1976

Due to ever-increasing emission standards the cylinder heads were again restyled for 1975 and the high performance heads were deleted. Valve covers were the same as they were the year before.

1975 Cylinder Head Part Numbers

Application	Part Number	Notes
350-ci Ex. Calif.	500801	
350-ci 4-bbl Calif.	497702	
400-ci Ex. Calif.	500804	
400-ci 4-bbl Calif.	500803	
455-ci	500802	

1975 Valves and Valve Springs

Part	Intake	Exhaust	Length	Diameter
350- ci				
Valves	483211	5462125#	4.960*	1.96*
		9784730##	4.949**	1.66**
Springs	Inner 9779008	Outer 9779009		
400-ci 4-bbl				
Valves	483211	5462125#	4.960*	2.11*
		9784730##	4.949**	1.66**
Springs	Inner 9779008	Outer 9779009		
455-ci V-8				
Valves	497271	9784730	4.881*	2.11*
			4.870**	1.66**
Springs	Inner 9779008	Outer 9779009	#-2-bbl #-4-bbl	

1977

Heads were again restyled for 1977, and the Oldsmobile made head for the 403-ci V-8 was added to the list.   Valve covers were listed as part numbers 10005388 left-hand and 10005387 left-hand were used on the Pontiac built powerplants, except the 400-ci with the high performance package used chrome plated covers listed as part numbers 547293 right-hand and 547294 left-hand. The 350-ci and 403-ci Oldsmobile built powerplants used painted covers that were listed as part number 22522667. All painted covers should be painted to match the engine block.

1977 Cylinder Head Part Numbers

Application	Part Number	Notes
301-ci	526384	
350-ci	500801	Pontiac built
350-ci	556281	Oldsmobile built
400-ci	500804	2.92 axle and under
400-ci	500801	2.93 axle and up
400-ci	500801	Hi. Perf.
403-ci	556282	

1977 Valves and Valve Springs

Part	Intake	Exhaust	Length	Diameter
301- ci				
Valves	527610	527602	5.0785* 4.8645**	1.72* 1.50**
Springs	3735381			
350-ci				
Valves	553396# 526102##	489843# 555456##	4.667*## 4.675**##	1.630*# 1.430**# 1.88*## 1.497**##
Springs	9779008-Inner 9779009-Outer		411226-Oldsmobile	
400-ci V-8				
Valves	526102	489843	4.864* 4.864**	2.11* 1.66**
Springs	9779008-Inner 9779009-Outer			
403- ci ##				
Valves	553402	555456	4.667* 4.675**	2.00* 1.497**
Springs	9779008-Inner 9779009-Outer		#-Pontiac ##-Oldsmobile	

1978

Was nearly a carbon copy of 1977 line up with the exception that the 350-ci Oldsmobile and 350-ci Pontiac built powerplants were deleted and replaced with the Chevrolet built 350-ci. Also the 301-ci was replaced by the Chevrolet built 305-ci V-8.   This change affected the cylinder heads, valve and valve covers.   The 400-ci power plant used the same valve covers and used the same part number it used in 1977, including the chrome covers being used on the high performance packages.   The 305-ci and the 350-ci used the same set of valve covers listed as part numbers 14025551 right-hand and14025552 left-hand. The covers should be painted the same color as the engine block, save the chrome covers..

1978 Cylinder Head Part Numbers

Application	Part Number	Notes
305-ci	14034809	
350-ci	14019821	Chevrolet built
400-ci	500804 500801*	*-High Perf.
403-ci	556282	

1978 Valves and Valve Springs

Part	Intake	Exhaust	Length	Diameter
305- ci				
Valves	14025570	14095451		
Springs	3911068-Intake		6263796-Exhaust	
350-ci				
Valves	14025572	14095451		
Springs	3911068-Intake		6263796-Exhaust	
400-ci V-8				
Valves	526102	489843	4.864* 4.864**	2.11* 1.66**
Springs	9779008-Inner 9779009-Outer			
403- ci ##				
Valves	553402	555456	4.667* 4.675**	2.00* 1.497**
Springs	9779008-Inner 9779009-Outer		#-Pontiac ##-Oldsmobile	

1979

Valve wise the cylinder heads were the same units used in 1978. All Firebirds with a 400-ci got the high performance head. The 301-ci returned and used the same part number as in 1977. The 400-ci power plant used the same valve covers and used the same part number it used in 1977, including the chrome covers being used on the high performance packages. The 305-ci and the 350-ci used the same set of as they used in 1978. The 301-ci used the same set of valve covers that were used on the non-high performance 400-ci powerplant.

1979 Cylinder Head Part Numbers

Application	Part Number	Notes
301-ci	526384	
305-ci	14034809	
350-ci	14019821	Chevrolet built
400-ci	500804	*-High Perf.
	500801*	
403-ci	556282	
305-ci	14034809	
350-ci	14019821	Chevrolet built
400-ci	500804	*-High Perf.
	500801*	

1979 Valves and Valve Springs

Part	Intake	Exhaust	Length	Diameter
301-ci				
Valves	527610	527602	5.0785*	1.72*
			4.8645**	1.50**
Springs	3735381			
305-ci				
Valves	14025570	14095451		
Springs	3911068-Intake		6263796-Exhaust	
350-ci				
Valves	14025572	14095451		
Springs	3911068-Intake		6263796-Exhaust	
400-ci V-8				
Valves	526102	489843	4.864*	2.11*
			4.864**	1.66**
Springs	9779008-Inner			
	9779009-Outer			
403-ci ##				
Valves	553402	555456	4.667*	2.00*
			4.675**	1.497**
Springs	9779008-Inner		#-Pontiac	
	9779009-Outer		##-Oldsmobile	

93

1980-1981

Big news here was the deletion of the 400-ci 350-ci and 403-ci powerplants. Both the 301-ci and 305-ci were restyled in 1980. The 301-ci used part number 10014005 and the 305-ci used part number 14034807. The latter of these was used again in 1981, but the 301-ci, was changed to part number 1001454 and the new 265-ci V-8 used part number 14034806. Though the heads were changed the valve covers used the same part numbers as in previous years (the 267-ci used the same covers as the 301-ci) with one exception and that was the right-hand cover on Turbo charged models, which used part number 10009620. This had a special shape to fit the Turbo-charger.

Cylinder Head Casting Numbers			
Casting Number	Carb Type	Model Years	Notes
12	4-bbl	1970	400-ci H.O.
614	4-bbl	1970	400-ci Ram Air IV
11	2-bbl	1970	350/400-ci
96	4-bbl	1970	400-ci 4-bbl
01	All	1977-1981	301-ci V-8
65	All	1980-1981	265-ci
367450	All	1978-1979	305-ci
14022301	All	1980-1981	305-ci
94	2-bbl	1971-1971	350-ci
11	2-bbl	1970	350-ci
4X	4-bbl	1973-1976	400-ci/ 455-ci
6X	4-bbl	1977-1979	400-ci/ 455-ci
554717	4-bbl	1977-1979	403-ci
66	4-bbl	1971	400-ci
97, 91	4-bbl	1971	400-ci H.O.
6H (16 On center exhaust ports)	4-bbl	1973-1974	455-ci S.D.

Air Cleaner, Standard
1970-1972

Only one air cleaner was used on the 350-ci 2-bbl V-8 listed as part number 6485785, it is unique to the Firebird line, and other models will not properly fit. This same unit was also used on the 400-ci 2-bbl powerplants. All except the Trans Am models and Formulas without Ram Air used part number 6486117. The two-barrel V-8 powerplants continued to use the same air cleaners that were used on the 1970 models. Like wise the standard air cleaner used on cars with a 400-ci 4-bbl, ex Trans Am or those with Ram air, also used the same part number as it used the year before. The 400-ci H.O. for 1971-72 used a special listed as part number 6486812 .All air cleaners should be painted 60-degree gloss black. Trans Am air cleaners are discussed in the Ram Air section of this chapter.

An example of a air cleaner decal used on 1970 models. Decal courtesy of Jim Osborne reproductions.

1973-1974

All air cleaners were drastically restyled for 1973. The twin snorkel design was replaced with a single snorkel design that featured a cold air inlet. That consisted of a black flexible duct hose (part number 489909) that attached the end of the snorkel with an adapter part number 497082 and routed up towards the front of the car. A diaphragm part number 6487372bbl and 6488214-4-bbl was used on the snorkel of the air cleaner to either shut the valve on cold start up allowing the engine to use warm air and then open at a specified temperature to allow cold air into the engine.

The standard Trans Am air cleaner assembly looked much like the standard unit that was used on the other 4-bbl models, with the exception that it had a provision on top of it that allowed shaker type non-functional hood scoop. The following air cleaners were used.

1973-1974 Air Cleaner Part Numbers

Usage	Carb type	Part Number	Notes
350/400-ci	2-bbl	6487591	
400/455-ci	4-bbl	6488273	Ex Ram
Trans AM	4-bbl	6488273	Air.

1975

A heavy-duty air cleaner was again used on all the 2-bbl V-8 powerplants. It was listed as part number 8994382, and was actually phased into production on late 1974 models. As in the year before it continued to use a cold air inlet, as did the unit used on the 4-bbl platforms. All 4-bbl v-8s used part number 8994002, except the Tran Am. The Tran Am used part number 8995334 with the 400-ci 4-bbl and part number 8994006 with the 455-ci powerplant.

Air cleaner decal used on 1972-1973 Trans Am's Decal courtesy of Jim Osborne Reproductions.

Air cleaner decal used on 175 Trans Am's with 455-ci Decal courtesy of Jim Osborne Reproductions

1976

The two-barrel 350-ci V-8 used part number 8995192 while the 350-ci 4-bbl used part number 8995231. As before cold air inlet system was used. The 400-ci V-8 V-8, except for Trans Am used part number 8995354. The Tran Am models used part number 8995235 with all powerplants.

1977

There were two different air cleaner assemblies used on the 301-ci Pontiac built V-8. Those with round shaped carburetor opening used part number 8995537, while those with a D-shaped opening used part number 8996184. The Pontiac built 350-ci and the 400-ci V-8 used the same air cleaner assembly listed as part number 8995543, except Tran Am models. Those with the Oldsmobile built 350 or 403-ci used part number 8996089 except on the Trans Am models. Both these air cleaners were made exclusively for the Firebird line and air cleaners from other model lines, even with the same cubic displacement, will not fit.

1978 air cleaner assembly, note placement of decal.

Trans Am model used special air cleaner assemblies and they too were grouped by the engine manufacture. Those with the 400-ci Pontiac built V-8 used part number 8995542, while those in California used the Oldsmobile built 403-ci V-8 listed as part number 8996090.

1978

The 305-ci V-8 used part number 8996427, which is the same assembly used on all 305ci V-8 in 1977-1978 Pontiac models. The 350-ci Chevrolet built V-8 used part number 8995520, unlike the 305-ci powerplant this air cleaner used only in the Firebird line, other Pontiac models will not fit. The 400-ci powerplant used a host of air cleaners depending on the model and whether or not the performance package option was ordered.

Formulas with a 400-ci V-8 used part number 8997019 without the performance package and part number 8997016 with it. Trans Am models required a special set of air cleaners listed as part number 8997020 without the performance package and part number 8997017 with the package. The 403-ci Formula used part number 8996089 while the Trans Am used the same part number it used the year before.

1979

The 301-ci 2-bbl used part number 8996749 a different air cleaner assembly than the 4-bbl version part number 8996748, and the Trans Am used part number 8997681, which it used up till the end of the 1980 model year. The 305-ci equipped models used part number 8996708, and the 350-ci V-8 part number 8997352. The Formula with a 400-ci V-8 used part number 8997017 and part number 8996089 with the 403-ci V-8. The Tran Am with a 403-ci V-8 used part number 8996090, and part number 8997017 with the 400-ci powerplant.

1980-1981

The 301-ci V-8 except in Trans Am with the shaker hood or performance package option used part number 8997678. When ordered with the performance package but without the shaker hood option part number 8997050 was used. With the shaker hood hood option part number 8997679 was used. With the 305-ci V-8 without the shaker hood scoop part number 8997056 was used with the shaker hood scoop the part number was changed to 8997680.

The year of 1981 brought new part numbers The 4.3 liter V-8 used part number 25040182, unless it was exported to Canada where part number 25040184 was used. The 301-ci V-8 used part number 25040184 with the shaker hood and 25040185 with a closed loop and without the shaker hood. The 305-ci without the shaker hood used part number 25040287 with the shaker hood; part number 25040668 was used unless it was exported to Canada where part number 25041408 was used, without the shaker hood part number 25040700 was used on cars exported to Canada.

Trans Am came standard with a shaker hood scoops.

1979 Air Cleaner assembly, note the snorkel position and the route of the air inlet duct.

Air Cleaner, Ram Air
1970-1974

There were basically tw Ram Air designs. Those used on the Formula models and those used on the Trans Am. Both worked the same way to increase horsepower. The inlets were at a high-pressure area for a slight supercharged effect, and the fact that the engine breathed cool outside air instead of warm under hood air.

The Formula used a simple design that consisted of a special air cleaner that featured longer and wider snorkels that were mated to the hood scoops baffle on the under side of the hood via a rubber boot. This forced air from the hood scoops directly into the carburetor, this basic design remained until 1973.

1970-1974 Formula Ram Air Part Numbers

Model	Air Cleaner	Boot	Adapter
1970-71 Ram Air III	6486684	481433	N/A
1970 Ram Air IV	6486474	481433	N/A
1971-1972 455- H.O.	6486474	481433	N/A
1973-1974*	6488275	481433	N/A

The other Ram Air set up was the Shaker hood scoop. Set ups were used on the Trasn Am models, but there are exceptions like the Formulas with the 455-ci Super Duty in 1973 and 1974. There was a change in the design of the lower ductwork in 1973 and the solenoid that valve controlled the flapper on the scoop and a duct door on the bottom of the scoop that mated with the air cleaner assembly.

1970-1974 Shaker Hood Scoop Ram Air Part Numbers

Model	Air Cleaner	Seal	Scoop
1970 Ram Air III	6486668	481697	481689
1970 Ram Air IV	6486669	481697	481689
1971-72	6486686	481697	481689
1973-1974	6488274	490996	491982

Typical 1970-1972 Style Shaker hood setup, 1970 T/A is shown.

A rare sight! The 1973 455-ci Super Duty with shaker ood scoop.

Side view of the 1977 shaker hood scoop, note the callout decal

1976-1981 Shaker Hood Scoop Part Numbers

Model	Air Cleaner	Seal	Scoop
1975-400-ci	8994002	490996	491982
1975- 455-ci	8994006	490996	491982
1976	8995235	490996	491982
1977- 400-ci	8995542	481697	10010211
1977-1979 403-ci	8996090	527230	10010210
1978	8997017	527230	10010211
1979 301-ci	8997681	527230	10010209
1979 400-ci	8997017	527230	10010211
1980 301-ci	8997679	527230	10012062
1980 305-ci	8997680	527230	10010221
1981 301-ci	25040184 25041408*	10012875	10013722
1981 305-ci	25040668 25041408*	10012875	10010221

Before photo original 1977 shaker hood scoop.

Next remove the scoop, and then remove the seal that is used between the scoop and the scoop. You may have to use a small putty knife to remove the glue that is left behind.

Begin by removing all hoses that are attached to the air cleaner, but first note their location and their route. Then remove the retaining ring that holds the Air cleaner and scoop together.

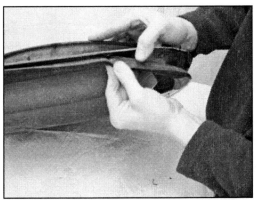

Next remove the seal on the scoop, it is held in place with small plastic screws. Pull the seal out away from the screws.

100

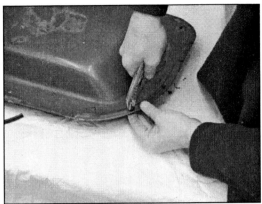

Use pillars to remove the plastic screws. Gently pull out with a twisting motion.

Spray the air cleaner assembly down with engine degreaser, use a brush and steel wool then rinse with clear water. Allow to dry to wipe down with wax and grease remover.

Next sand the air cleaner base down with 400 grit wet or dry sandpaper sand till a smooth surface is obtained.

Wipe down and again with wax and grease remove and then tack wipe. Then apply two to three coats of semi-gloss black paint. Aerosol cans work better for this than a paint gun.

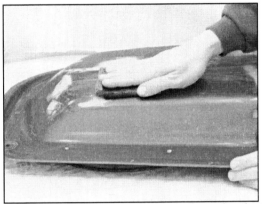

Use glazing putty to fill small nicks in the surface the wet sand with #400 sand paper, till smooth.

Wipe the scoop down with wax and grease remove then tack wipe. Apply two coats of primer allow to dry sand then wipe down again with wax and grease remover and apply the top coat.

Begin the new hood to scoop seal at the center rear edge of the scoop. It will be highlighted with two closely grouped mounting holes. Carefully press the plastic mounting screws down into the hole and work around the scoop.

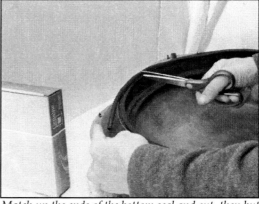

Match up the ends of the bottom seal and cut, then but ends together.

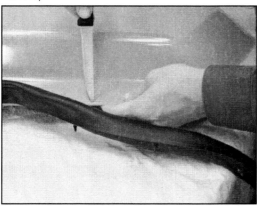

You may have to slightly enlarge the mounting holes, but only a slight amount, check the fit, then if needs be enlarge the hole more. But don't enlarge it too much or you will have to use a sealer to hold it in place.

There was no set location for the hood scoop callouts. They are usually place short of the rear edge of the scoops sides. Trial fit the decals to find the proper look.

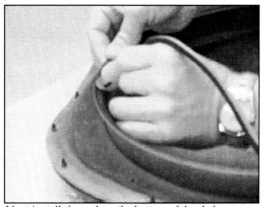

Next install the seal on the bottom of the shaker scoop, firmly press the seal down into the groove. Make sure the groove is clean.

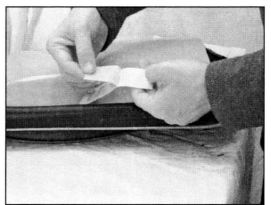

Peel back the backing off the decal and position into place on the scoop.

Gently, but with steady pressure rub the decal with a clean soft cloth. This will help the decal adhere to the surface better.

Carefully pull the protective top label away from the decal , pulling sometimes at a right angle, making sure the decal stays in place.

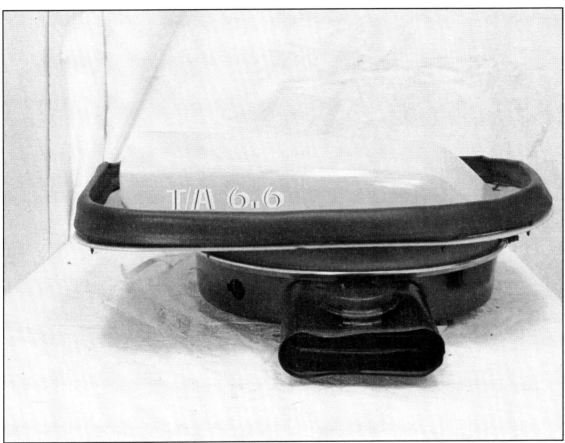

Our restored shaker hoodscoop with it's bright Mayan Red top coat.

Carburetor, Standard 2-bbl

1970-1971

A Rochester 2GV series two-barrel carburetor was standard on the 350-ci 2-bbl and 400-ci 2-bbl powerplants. The carburetor part number was stamped on a horizontal section of the float bowl, near the fuel inlet nut. This part number can be used for identification of the carburetor. Besides engine size factors that may affect carburetor usage are transmission, and emission controls. For example: in certain cases a different carburetor was used on cars going to California than other parts of the country. Air conditioning may also affect usage. For correctness and reliability of usage the proper carburetor should be used.

Carburetor identification number can be found here (white arrow), while the build date cab be found in code (black arrow).

Rochester 2GV 2-bbl Carburetor Identification Numbers						
Engine	Transmission	Air Conditioning	California	Federal	Part Number	Notes
1970						
350-ci	Manual	With/Without	No	Yes	7040071	Without E.E.S
350-ci	Automatic	With/Without	No	Yes	7040062	Without E.E.S
350-ci	Automatic	With/Without	No	Yes	7040076	High Altitude
350-ci	Manual	With/Without	No	Yes	7040471	With E.E.S
350-ci	Automatic	With/Without	Yes	No	7040463	With E.E.S.
400-ci	Manual	With/Without	No	Yes	7040066	Without E.E.S
400-ci	Automatic	With/Without	No	Yes	7040060	Without E.E.S
400-ci	Automatic	With/Without	No	Yes	7040064	High Altitude
400-ci	Manual	With/Without	Yes	No	7040466	With E.E.S
400-ci	Automatic	With/Without	Yes	No	7040461	With E.E.S
1971						
350-ci	Manual	With/Without	All	All	7041171	
350-ci	Automatic	With/Without	All	All	7041063	
350-ci	Automatic	With/Without			7041072	High Altitude
400-ci	Automatic	Without	All	All	7041060	
400-ci	Automatic	With/Without			7041070	High Altitude

1972

The 350-ci powerplants used two different makes of carburetor, dependent on the transmission type. Those models with a manual transmission used a Carter WGD 2-bbl, while the Rochester 2GV unit was used on all other applications with a two-barrel carburetor.

The number 488062, which is stamped into the base of the body, can identify the Carter WGD unit. Several different Rochesters were used according to engine size and transmission type.

1973

All new Rochester 2GC models two-barrel carburetors greeted the 1973 2-bbl powerplants. Decoding was the same as before and in the same location. California and high altitude cars required special carburetors.

1974

Were similar in design to the 1973 units, with a few exceptions. The carburetors were recalibrated to meet 1974 EPA specifications, also a side window was added to the float needle seat, and the vacuum break diaphragm, plunger stem, pump shaft and lever assembly have a Teflon coating added. Decoding was the same as before and in the same location. California and high altitude cars required special carburetors.

Rochester 2GV 2-bbl Carburetor Identification Numbers 1972-1974						
Engine	Transmission	Air Conditioning	California	Federal	Part Number	Notes
1972						
350-ci	Automatic	With/Without	No	Yes	7042062	
400-ci	Automatic	With/Without	No	Yes	7042060	
400-ci	Automatic	With/Without	Yes	No	7042061	
1973						
350-ci	Automatic	With/Without	No	Yes	7043062	
350-ci	Automatic	With/Without	Yes	No	7043063	
350-ci	Manual	With/Without	Yes	Yes	7043071	
350-ci	Automatic	With/Without	No	Yes	7043072	High Altitude
400-ci	Automatic	With/Without	No	Yes	7043060	
400-ci	Automatic	With/Without	Yes	No	7043061	
400-ci	Automatic	With/Without	No	Yes	7043070	High Altitude
1974						
350-ci	Manual	With/Without	No	Yes	7043071	
350-ci	Automatic	With/Without	No	Yes	7043062	
350-ci	Automatic	With/Without	No	Yes	7043072	High Altitude
350-ci	Automatic	With/Without	Yes	No	7044063	
350-ci	Automatic	With/Without	No	Yes	7044066	
400-ci	Automatic	With/Without	Yes	No	7044067	
400-ci	Automatic	With/Without	No	Yes	7043070	High Altitude

1975

Were similar in design to the 1974 units, but were equipped with dual vacuum break choke units, that improved warm-up. Also a large hole was drilled in the air horn, which leads from inside the air horn to a vapor dome located in the air horn casting above the float bowl. Also vapor can purge ports are located in the throttle body casting.

1976

Only one two-barrel Rochester model carburetor was used stamped with identification number 17056162 it was used on all 350-ci V-8's with an automatic transmission.

1977

With the introduction of the 305-ci V-8, which replaced the 350-ci 2-bbl, the Rochester 2-bbl carburetor was revamped to fit this powerplant. Be aware that there was change in carburetors, and early models used different carburetors than the later built models. The change of this date is not known. Also note that those models with air conditioning required a special carburetor.

Rochester 2GV 2-bbl Carburetor Identification Numbers 1975-1977						
Engine	Transmission	Air Conditioning	California	Federal	Part Number	Notes
1975						
350-ci	Automatic	With/Without	No	Yes	7045171	
1976						
350-ci	Automatic	With/Without	No	Yes	17056162	
1977						
305-ci	All	Without			17057112	1-st Type
305-ci	All	With			17057114	1-st Type
305-ci	All	Without			17057192	2-nd design
305-ci	All	With			17057194	2-nd design
350-ci	Automatic	Without			17057374	
350-ci	Automatic	With			17057375	

1978-1979

The 305-ci V-8 continued to use a Rochester 2-bbl carburetor both years. California cars in 1978 required special units, as did those models with air conditioning. For 1979 the 305-ci V-8 was available only in California models.

1980-1981

The Firebird model use a 2-bbl carburetor. Either year was the standard 231-ci six cylinders, which is not covered in this guide.

Rochester 2GV 2-bbl Carburetor Identification Numbers 1978-1979						
Engine	Transmission	Air Conditioning	California	Federal	Part Number	Notes
1978						
305-ci	Automatic	Without	Yes	No	17058108	
305-ci	Automatic	With	Yes	No	17058414	
305-ci	Automatic	Without	No	Yes	17058112	
305-ci	Manual	Without	Yes	Yes	17058111	
305-ci	Automatic	With	No	Yes	17058114	
305-ci	Automatic	With	No	Yes	17058121	
1979						
305-ci	Automatic	Without	Yes	No	17059434	
305-ci	Automatic	With	Yes	No	17059436	

Carburetor, 4-bbl-H.O.

1970

Only one power plant, the 400-ci V-8, used a Rochester Quardajet 4-bbl carburetor. However, transmission type and engine output greatly affected their usage. Also those cars being shipped to California required special carburetors.

The carburetor is identified by its part number, which is stamped on a vertical surface of the float bowl, near the secondary throttle lever. The carburetor should have natural finish.

1971

Again the Rochester Quardajet 4-bbl carburetor was used on both the 400-ci and 455-ci powerplants. And those with the Ram Air package required special carburetors. Due to modifications to engines California cars no longer required special carburetors. Identification and finish are the same as in the previous year.

The Rochester Q-jet 4-bbl was used on a host of powerplants.

1972

Very few changes occurred in the design of the Rochester Quardajet 4-bbl carburetor, as engine size, out put and transmission type still affected their usage. However, California emissions did not. Identification and finish are the same as in the previous year.

1973

Carburetors were recalibrated to meet 1973 EPA standards, and those used on the 455-ci Super duty and H.O. options have a triple venturi set-up in the primary bores for improved metering control, thus avoiding a lag when the car is suddenly under full throttle. Transmission continued to affect the carburetor's usage and while no special carburetors were used on cars with California emission, those going to high country (mountain areas) did require a special carburetor. Super Duty also required special carburetors. All used a Rochester Quardajet unit. Identification and finish are the same as in the previous year. Late in the year the Super Duty Carburetors were revamped and the primary venturi bore was increased to 1-7/32 –in diameter. There is no date known of this change.

1974

Carburetors were recalibrated to meet 1974 EPA standards, and new line of carburetors appeared that were used on the 350-ci Firebirds. The primary throttle lever was revised to provide separate holes for the attachment of the down shift lever, in cars with an automatic transmission, and for installation of a dual throttle return spring. Some California cars required special carburetors again this year. All carburetors were Rochester Quardajets. Identification and finish are the same as in the previous year.

Rochester Quardajet 4-bbl Carburetor Identification Numbers 1970-1974

Engine	Transmission	Air Conditioning	California	Federal	Part Number	Notes
1970						
400-ci	Manual	With/Without	No	Yes	7040263	Without Ram Air
400-ci	Automatic	With/Without	No	Yes	7040264	Without Ram Air
400-ci	Automatic	With/Without	Yes	No	7040564	Without Ram Air
400-ci	Manual	With/Without	Yes	No	7040563	Without Ram Air
400-ci	Manual	With/Without	No	Yes	7040273	With Ram Air
400-ci	Automatic	With/Without	No	Yes	7040270	With Ram Air
400-ci	Manual	With/Without	Yes	No	7040573	With Ram Air
400-ci	Automatic	With/Without	Yes	No	7040570	With Ram Air
1971						
400-ci	Manual	With/Without	Yes	Yes	7041263	Without Ram Air
400-ci	Automatic	With/Without	Yes	Yes	7041264	Without Ram Air
400/455-ci	Automatic	With/Without	Yes	Yes	7041271	High Altitude
455-ci	Automatic	With/Without	Yes	Yes	7041262	Without Ram Air
455-ci	Manual	With/Without	Yes	Yes	7041267	H.O. Without Ram Air
455-ci	Automatic	With/Without	Yes	Yes	7041268	H.O Without Ram Air
455-ci	Manual	With/Without	Yes	Yes	7041273	With Ram Air
455-ci	Automatic	With/Without	Yes	Yes	7041270	With Ram Air
1972						
400-ci	Manual	With/Without	Yes	Yes	7042263	
400-ci	Automatic	With/Without	Yes	Yes	7042264	
455-ci	Automatic	With/Without	Yes	Yes	7042262	Except H.O.
455-ci	Manual	With/Without	Yes	Yes	7042273	H.O.
455-ci	Automatic	With/Without	Yes	Yes	7042270	H.O.
1973						
400-ci	Manual	With/Without	Yes	Yes	7043263	
400-ci	Automatic	With/Without	Yes	Yes	7044264	
400-ci	Automatic	With/Without	Yes	Yes	7043274	High Altitude
455-ci	Manual	With/Without	Yes	Yes	7043265	Ex S.D.
455-ci	Automatic	With/Without	Yes	Yes	7043262	Ex S.D.
455-ci	Automatic	With/Without	Yes	Yes	7043272	High Altitude
455-ci	Manual	With/Without	Yes	Yes	7043273	Super Duty (Early)
455-ci	Automatic	With/Without	Yes	Yes	7043270	Super Duty (Early)
455-ci	Manual	With/Without	Yes	Yes	7044273	Super Duty (Late)
455-ci	Automatic	With/Without	Yes	Yes	7044270	Super Duty (Late)
1974						
350-ci	Manual	With/Without	No	Yes	7044269	
350-ci	Automatic	With/Without	No	Yes	7044268	
400-ci	Manual	With/Without	No	Yes	7044263	
400-ci	Automatic	With/Without	Yes	Yes	7044266	
400-ci	Automatic	With/Without	Yes	Yes	7044274	High Altitude
455-ci	Automatic	With/Without	Yes	Yes	7044262	
455-ci	Automatic	With/Without	Yes	Yes	7044272	High Altitude
455-ci	Manual	With/Without	Yes	Yes	7044274	Super Duty
455-ci	Automatic	With/Without	Yes	Yes	7044270	Super Duty

1975

Carburetors were recalibrated to meet 1975 EPA standards. To ease the serviceability, alphabetical code letters were added to the air horn, float bowl and throttle body at the external tube locations to help in identifying air, vacuum, and fuel hose routes under the hood. All models used a Rochester model M4MC Quardajet, except for those in high altitude conditions, which used a model M4MCA, which used a special barometric pressure-sensitive aneroid, which is sensitive to altitude changes. It automatically expands or contracts to lower or raise the metering rod. Special Carburetors were also used on California car with a 350-ci or 400-ci V-8. Identification and finish are the same as in the previous year.

1976

A Rochester 4-bbl carburetor was used on all applications. California cars all used special carburetors. Identification and finish are the same as in the previous year.

1977

Rochester 4-bbl carburetors were again used on all applications. Some California cars used special carburetors. Also rear axle ratios affected the carburetors in Firebirds with the 400-ci powerplant. Identification and finish are the same as in the previous year.

1978

Rochester 4-bbl carburetors were again used on all applications. As before some California cars used special carburetors. The performance package on the 400-ci powerplant used a special carburetor. Also be aware that there was a change in design on carburetors on Firebirds with the 400-ci (Code YA) powerplant.

1979

Last of the big cube engines used a Rochester 4-bbl carburetor. Once again special carburetors were used in high altitude conditions.

1980-1981

Smaller engines required smaller Rochester 4-bbl carburetors. Special carburetors were used with the Turbocharger and the performance package on the 301-ci V-8. Making matters even more confusing was the fact that different carburetors were used in Export conditions in 1981.

An example of a casting date code on an intake manifold. The letter is month, next two digits are day, last digit is year. This would be Nov. 30, 1968 and would be incorrect for any model in this guide.

Rochester Quardajet 4-bbl Carburetor Identification Numbers 1975-1981						
Engine	Transmission	Air Conditioning	California	Federal	Part Number	Notes
1975						
350-ci	Manual	With/Without	No	Yes	7045269	
350-ci	Automatic	With/Without	No	Yes	7045268	
350-ci	Automatic	With/Without	Yes	No	7045569	
400-ci	Manual	With/Without	No	Yes	7045263	
400-ci	Automatic	With/Without	Yes	No	7045564	
455-ci	Manual	With/Without	No	Yes	7045262	
1976						
350-ci	Automatic	With/Without	Yes	No	17045668	
400/455-ci	Manual	With/Without	No	Yes	17056263	
400-ci	Automatic	With/Without	No	Yes	17056274	
400-ci	Automatic	With/Without	Yes	No	17056564	
1977						
350-ci	Automatic	With/Without	No	Yes	17057262	Pontiac Built
350-ci	Automatic	Without	Yes	No	17057550	Oldsmobile built
350-ci	Automatic	With	Yes	No	17057553	Oldsmobile built
350-ci	Automatic	With/Without	No	Yes	17057258	Oldsmobile built High Altitude
400-ci	Automatic	With/Without		Yes	17057266	With 3.23 axle
400-ci	Automatic	With/Without		Yes	17057274	With 2.41 axle
403-ci	Automatic	Without	Yes	No	17057550	
403-ci	Automatic	With	Yes	No	17057553	
1978						
350-ci	Automatic	Without	No	Yes	17058202	Chevrolet Built
350-ci	Automatic	With	No	Yes	17058204	Chevrolet Built
350-ci	Manual	Without		Yes	17058203	Chevrolet built
350-ci/403-ci	Automatic	With/Without	Yes	No	17058553	Chevrolet Built
350-ci	Automatic	Without		Yes	17058582	Chevrolet Built
350-ci	Automatic	With		Yes	17058584	Chevrolet Built
400-ci	Manual	With/Without		Yes	17058263	
400-ci		With/Without		Yes	17058266	Code X7
400-ci	Automatic	With/Without		Yes	17058276	Code YA 1st design
400-ci	Automatic	With/Without		Yes	17058278	Code YU
1979						
301-ci	Manual	With/Without	No	Yes	17059271	
301-ci	Automatic	With/Without	No	Yes	17059272	
350-ci	Automatic	Without			17059582	
350-ci	Automatic	With			17059584	
400-ci	Manual	With/Without	No	Yes	17059263	
403-ci	Automatic	Without	No	Yes	17059250	
403-ci	Automatic	With	No	Yes	17059253	
1980						
301-ci	Automatic				17080272	Except W72
301-ci	Automatic				17080027	With W72
301-ci	Automatic				17080274	Turbo
305	Automatic				17080517	
1981						
301-ci	Automatic				17081270	With closed loop
301-ci	Automatic				17081273	Turbo
301-ci	Automatic		Export	Canada	17081276	Turbo
305-ci	Manual	Without			17081203	
305-ci	Manual	With			17081207	
305-ci	Automatic				17059321	
305-ci	Automatic	Without	Export	Canada	17081284	
305-ci	Automatic	With	Export	Canada	17081285	

Intake Manifold

All intakes were painted the same shade as block, note that there was a changed to a darker blue shade after March 15,1973. Also approximately 700 engines before this date were also painted with the darker blue shade. The casting date on the intake manifold is one of the most important features on the unit. Care must be used to ensure that the proper casting date is used. The casting date usually appears in the same

1970-1981

general location that the casting number was, located near the waterneck or on a runner. The casting date breaks down the same as the engine block, and uses the same codes. To be proper the casting date must be BEFORE the assembly date for your Firebird. Typically the date should be any where from two to six weeks before the assembly date.

Intake Manifold Part Numbers 1970-1978

Carburetor	Part Number	Notes
		1970
2-bbl	9799067	350-ci/400-ci
4-bbl	9799068	Except Ram Air IV
	9799084	Ram Air IV
		1971
2-bbl	481732	
4-bbl	481733	Except High Output
4-bbl	483674	High Output (use with 9796395 cross over)
		1972
2-bbl	485911	
4-bbl	485912	Except High Out Put
4-bbl	488945	High Output
		1973
2-bbl	492318	Manual transmission (Before March 15, 1973)- 350-ci
2-bbl	492319	Automatic Transmission (Before March 15, 1973) Except Calif.
2-bbl	494410	Manual transmission (After March 15, 1973) 350-ci
2-bbl	494412	Automatic Transmission (After March 15, 1973) Except Calf.
2-bbl	492318	Automatic transmission (Before March 15, 1973) California 350-ci only
2-bbl	494410	Automatic transmission (After March 15, 1973) California 350-ci Only
4-bbl	492706	Except Super Duty (Before March 15, 1973)
4-bbl	496295	Except Super Duty (After March 15, 1973)
4-bbl	492743	455-ci Super Duty (Before March 15, 1973)
4-bbl	494419	455-ci Super Duty (After March 15, 1973)
		1974
2-bbl	495100	350/400-ci
4-bbl	495102	Except Super Duty
4-bbl	495103	Super Duty
		1975-1976
2-bbl	496143	
4-bbl	495102	
		1977
2-bbl	6269796	305-ci
4-bbl	495102	350-ci/ 400-co Pontiac built
4-bbl	556752	403-ci or 350-ci Oldsmobile built
		1978
2-bbl	6269796	305-ci
4-bbl	10003396	400-ci Pontiac built
4-bbl	561998	403-ci
4-bbl	14057062	350-ci

Intake Manifold Part Numbers 1979-1981

Carburetor	Part Number	Notes
		1979
2-bbl	1000517	301-ci 2-bbl
4-bbl		301-ci 4-bbl
4-bbl	14057056	305-ci
		1980
2-bbl	1000517	301-ci 2-bbl
4-bbl	1009966	301-ci 4-bbl
4-bbl	14057056	305-ci
4-bbl	10013115	With Turbocharger
		1974
2-bbl	495100	350/400-ci
4-bbl	495102	Except Super Duty
4-bbl	495103	Super Duty
		1981
2-bbl	10013290	4.3 liter
4-bbl	10013291	301-ci
4-bbl	14057054	305-ci with closed loop
4-bbl	10013296	301-ci Turbocharger

1980-1981

Turbo Charger

Listed as an option on the 301-ci V-8 both years was a turbocharger. This option was good for 50-more ponies over the standard 4-bbl set up. The turbocharger technology was to improve performance, while maintaining a good fuel economy. Its design was to provide power on demand. As the throttle was opened more air-fuel mixture would flow into the combustion chamber. As this increased mixture is burned a larger volume of higher energy exhaust gas enters through the turbocharger turbine housing. Then some of this energy is used to increase the speed of the turbine wheel, which is connected by a shaft to the compressor wheel; the increase in the compressor allows it to compress the fuel-air mixture that it receives from the carburetor and then delivers it to the intake manifold. The resulting higher pressure allows a heavier mixture to enter the combustion chamber resulting in more power. The boost is controlled to a maximum amount by a wastegate, which allows a portion of the exhaust gas to bypass the turbine wheel. An actuator assembly that sensed when the pressure crosses the compressors controls the wastegate. If the pressure were too high the gate would open, and allow the gases to pass by.

Turbo Charger Part Numbers

Part	Part Number	Notes
Turbocharger	10013383	1980
	10018807	1981
Actuator	10013385	1980
	10018606	1981
	10013385	1981-Canada
Plenum	10009267	1980
	10017613	1981
Bracket	10010040	1980–81
Turbo Support		
Bracket	10012930	1980
Plenum Support	10016633	1981
Regulator	10010090	1980
Power Enrich		1981- Canada
Compressor	10013386	1980-81
Housing		
Elbow	10013387	1980-81
Elbow	10013389	1980-81
Turbine		
Housing		
Turbine Inlet	10012205	1980
Pipe	10018718	1981
Turbine Outlet	10012206	1980
Pipe	10018719	1981
By Pass hose	10017731	1980-81

Exhaust Systems

All Firebird models used cast iron exhaust manifolds. They should have a fresh cast appearance; painting them with high temp cast iron gray paint can duplicate this. To get the best finish you should start with a clean surface. First clean the manifold with a stiff wire brush, wear gloves and eye protection when doing this procedure to avoid injuries. For manifolds that are very rusty they may have to be bead blasted, then using compressed air thoroughly blow clean, being sure to get into all the crevasses. Then apply a thin coat of the paint, allow to dry for 1-2 hours then apply second coat. Allow to dry for 24 hours. Bake the part at 400-degrees for 1-hour, unless you're looking for a divorce do not use the oven in the kitchen, it is best that you have a separate oven for the curing method. If this is not possible allow the heat of the engine to cure the paint. The finish may not have as much durability as the baking process but it will cure.

Two exhaust systems were used with the V-8 engines-single and dual. The single exhaust system was standard on all models except the Formula or the Trans Am which came standard with dual exhaust. The mufflers were welded to the exhaust pipes when the car came from the factory, and this should be duplicated; clamps are acceptable for correctness.

The pipe and muffler hangers were a "rubber block" type, which is made up of a rubber block placed in stamped metal bracket, which bolts to the underbody. For correctness these types of supports should be used. Unlike its big sister the GTO, the Firebird did not use twin mufflers with dual exhaust set up, instead a single tri-flow muffler was used each year. This muffler was mounted transversally near the rear axle. The tailpipes were welded to the muffler assembly originally, and exited at the back of the car.

1970-1981

E.P.A. regulation and noise laws placed a strangle hold on a true dual exhaust system in 1975, with the additional of a catalytic converter. This little piece of hardware was placed between the exhaust manifold and the muffler. Its purpose was to reduce the hydrocarbons and carbon monoxide, and required the use of unleaded fuel only. To most car buffs at the time, this piece of hardware was an annoying nuisance, and was quickly discarded, and a straight through piece of pipe took its place. Back then this operation added horsepower, today due to some emission laws this can be illegal. With the addition of the catalytic converter only a single cross over pipe was routed from the exhaust manifolds to the converter, thus only a single exhaust system was used. Some models did use twin tailpipes, to simulate the dual exhaust system. But no true dual exhaust systems were installed on a factory Firebird for 1975. This set up was slightly on the 1978 400-ci equipped models as two resonators are added behind the single catalytic converter, with separate tail pipes, again this only give the manifestation of dual exhaust as only a single cross over pipe was exited from the engine. A similar design was used on both the 400 and 403-ci models in 1979. Again in 1980 on the 301-ci 4-bbl , turbocharger and 305-ci V-8, although it was only standard on the turbocharged models.

Casting numbers can be used to identify exhaust manifolds. They should be painted cast iron gray to duplicate the fresh cast look.

Exhaust Manifold Part Numbers-1970 Firebird

	350-ci 2-bbl	400-ci 2-bbl	400-ci 4-bbl	400-ci H.O.	400-ci Ram Air IV
L.H.	480602	480602	480602	478140	478141
R.H.	9799720	9799720	9799720	9799720	9799721

Exhaust Manifold Part Numbers-1971 Firebird

	350-ci 2-bbl	400-ci 2-bbl	400-ci 4-bbl	455-ci 4-bbl	455-ci H.O.
L.H.	483608	483608	483608	483608	478141
R.H.	9796992	9796992	9796992	9796992	9799721

Exhaust Manifold Part Numbers-1972 Firebird

	350-ci 2-bbl	400-ci 2-bbl	400-ci 4-bbl	455-ci 4-bbl	455-ci H.O.
L.H.	483608	483608	483608	483608	478141
R.H.	9796992	9796992	9796992	9796992	9799721

Exhaust Manifold Part Numbers-1973 Firebird

	350-ci 2-bbl	400-ci 2-bbl	400-ci 4-bbl	455-ci 4-bbl	455-ci S.D.
L.H.	483608	483608	483608	483608	490803
R.H.	9796992	9796992	9796992	9796992	490802

Exhaust Manifold Part Numbers-1974 Firebird

	350-ci 2-bbl	400-ci 2-bbl	400-ci 4-bbl	455-ci 4-bbl	455-ci S.D.
L.H.	483608	483608	483608	483608	490803
R.H.	9796992	9796992	9796992	9796992	490802

Exhaust Manifold Part Numbers-1975 Firebird

	350-ci 2-bbl	350-ci 4-bbl	400-ci 4-bbl	455-ci 4-bbl
L.H.	10002755	10002755	10002755	10002755
R.H.	9495986	9495986	9495986	9495986

Exhaust Manifold Part Numbers-1976 Firebird

	350-ci 2-bbl	350-ci 4-bbl	400-ci 4-bbl	455-ci 4-bbl
L.H.	10002755	10002755	10002755	10002755
R.H.	495986	495986	495986	495986

Exhaust Manifold Part Numbers-1977 Firebird

	301-ci 2-bbl	350-ci 4-bbl (Pontiac)	350-ci 4-bbl (Oldsmobile)	400-ci 4-bbl	403-ci 4-bbl
L.H.	10014846	10002755	14067365	10002755	14067365
R.H.	526031	495986	49586	495986	49586

Exhaust Manifold Part Numbers-1978 Firebird

	305-ci 2-bbl	350-ci 4-bbl	400-ci 4-bbl	403-ci 4-bbl
L.H.	14067365	14067365	10002755	14067365
R.H.	346222	346222	495986	49586

Exhaust Manifold Part Numbers-1979 Firebird

	301-ci	305-ci 2-bbl	350-ci 4-bbl	400-ci 4-bbl	403-ci 4-bbl
L.H.	10014846	14067365	14067365	10002755	14067365
R.H.	526031	346222	346222	495986	49586

Exhaust Manifold Part Numbers-1980 Firebird

	301-ci 4-bbl	301-ci Turbo	305-ci 4-bbl
L.H.	10014846	10014846	14007400
R.H.	526031	10014526	346222

Exhaust Manifold Part Numbers-1981 Firebird

	4.3 Liter	301-ci 4-bbl	301-ci Turbo	305-ci 4-bbl	305-ci Export
L.H.	10013735	10013735	10013737	14007400	745994
R.H.	10013737	10013737	10014526	346222	346222

VEHICLE EMISSION CONTROL INFORMATION — GM — PC

PONTIAC MOTOR DIV.   GENERAL MOTORS CORP.

DISTRIBUTOR SETTING: 9 B.T.D.C. AT IDLE
DWELL: 30°   SPARK PLUG GAP .035

IDLE SPEED SETTING	WITHOUT MIXTURE SCREW CAPS		WITH MIXTURE SCREW CAPS
	CARB. SCREW	MIX. SCREWS	CARB. SCREW
AUTO. TRANS. (IN DRIVE)	675 RPM	650 RPM	650 RPM
MANUAL TRANS.	1050 RPM	950 RPM	950 RPM

MAKE ADJUSTMENTS WITH ENGINE AT NORMAL OPERATING TEMPERATURE, DISTRIBUTOR HOSE OFF, AIR CLEANER ON, AND AIR CONDITIONING OFF.
IF CARB. MIXTURE SCREWS HAVE CAPS TO PREVENT ADJUSTMENTS, OMIT STEPS 3 AND 4.
1. DISCONNECT DISTRIBUTOR VACUUM HOSE PLUG HOSE LEADING TO CARBURETOR.
2. ADJUST CARBURETOR SPEED SCREW FOR PROPER SPEED.
3. ADJUST MIXTURE SCREWS TO OBTAIN BEST LEAN SETTING AT THIS SPEED.
4. ADJUST MIXTURE SCREWS EQUALLY (CLOCKWISE) TO REDUCE IDLE RPM TO PROPER SPEED.
5. WITH TRANS. IN NEUTRAL SET FAST IDLE SCREW TO 2000 RPM ON TOP STEP OF FAST IDLE CAM.
6. RECONNECT DISTRIBUTOR VACUUM HOSE.

(SEE SERVICE MANUAL FOR ADDITIONAL INSTRUCTIONS)   PART NO. 482340

Emission decal for 1970 400-ci except Ram Air IV. Decal Courtesy of Jim Osborn Reproductions.

PH 400 CU. IN. 4 BBL. CARB. — VEHICLE EMISSION CONTROL INFORMATION — GM

PONTIAC MOTOR DIVISION   GENERAL MOTORS CORP.

CCS EXHAUST EMISSION CONTROL	AUTOMATIC TRANSMISSION
DWELL	30°
TIMING (B.T.D.C. @ R.P.M.)	12° @ 700
SPARK PLUG GAP	.035
CARBURETOR SCREW (R.P.M.)	700 (IN PARK)
FAST IDLE SCREW (R.P.M.)	1700 (IN PARK)

MAKE ADJUSTMENTS WITH ENGINE AT NORMAL OPERATING TEMPERATURE, CHOKE OPEN, AND AIR CONDITIONING OFF. PLUG DISCONNECTED VACUUM FITTINGS. SET PARKING BRAKE AND BLOCK DRIVE WHEELS.
1. DISCONNECT CARBURETOR HOSE FROM VAPOR CANISTER.
2. DISCONNECT DISTRIBUTOR VACUUM HOSE. PLUG HOSE LEADING TO CARBURETOR.
3. SET DWELL AND TIMING AT SPECIFIED R.P.M.
4. ADJUST CARBURETOR SPEED SCREW TO SPECIFIED R.P.M.
5. WITH TRANSMISSION IN PARK (OR NEUTRAL) SET FAST IDLE TO SPECIFIED R.P.M. ON TOP STEP OF CAM.
6. RECONNECT DISTRIBUTOR AND CANISTER HOSES.

IDLE MIXTURE PRESET AT FACTORY DO NOT REMOVE CAPS

(SEE SERVICE MANUAL FOR ADDITIONAL INFORMATION)

Emission decal for 1971 400-ci with automatic transmission. Decal courtesy of Jim Osborne Reproductions.

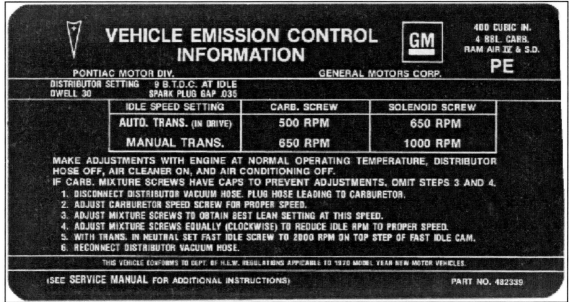

VEHICLE EMISSION CONTROL INFORMATION — GM — 400 CUBIC IN. 4 BBL. CARB. RAM AIR IV & S.D. — PE

PONTIAC MOTOR DIV.   GENERAL MOTORS CORP.

DISTRIBUTOR SETTING   9 B.T.D.C. AT IDLE
DWELL 30   SPARK PLUG GAP .035

IDLE SPEED SETTING	CARB. SCREW	SOLENOID SCREW
AUTO. TRANS. (IN DRIVE)	500 RPM	650 RPM
MANUAL TRANS.	650 RPM	1000 RPM

MAKE ADJUSTMENTS WITH ENGINE AT NORMAL OPERATING TEMPERATURE, DISTRIBUTOR HOSE OFF, AIR CLEANER ON, AND AIR CONDITIONING OFF.
IF CARB. MIXTURE SCREWS HAVE CAPS TO PREVENT ADJUSTMENTS, OMIT STEPS 3 AND 4.
1. DISCONNECT DISTRIBUTOR VACUUM HOSE. PLUG HOSE LEADING TO CARBURETOR.
2. ADJUST CARBURETOR SPEED SCREW FOR PROPER SPEED.
3. ADJUST MIXTURE SCREWS TO OBTAIN BEST LEAN SETTING AT THIS SPEED.
4. ADJUST MIXTURE SCREWS EQUALLY (CLOCKWISE) TO REDUCE IDLE RPM TO PROPER SPEED.
5. WITH TRANS. IN NEUTRAL SET FAST IDLE SCREW TO 2000 RPM ON TOP STEP OF FAST IDLE CAM.
6. RECONNECT DISTRIBUTOR VACUUM HOSE.

THIS VEHICLE CONFORMS TO DEPT. OF H.E.W. REGULATIONS APPLICABLE TO 1970 MODEL YEAR NEW MOTOR VEHICLES.

(SEE SERVICE MANUAL FOR ADDITIONAL INSTRUCTIONS)   PART NO. 482339

Emission decal for 1970 400-c Ram Air IV. Decal courtesy of Jim Osborne Reproductions

CAUTION

THIS COOLING SYSTEM PROTECTED TO ___ °F.

GM PERMANENT TYPE ANTI-FREEZE-COOLANT

DATE INSTALLED _____

This type of label was used also on the support wall. was hand written in at the factory. It was used from 1970-1973.

Later style models those after 1973 used this anti-freeze label.

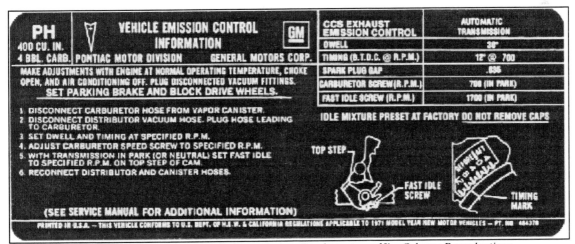

PN 455 CU. IN. 4 BBL. H.O.

VEHICLE EMISSION CONTROL INFORMATION
PONTIAC MOTOR DIVISION   GENERAL MOTORS CORP.

MAKE ADJUSTMENTS WITH ENGINE AT NORMAL OPERATING TEMPERATURE, CHOKE OPEN, AND AIR CONDITIONING OFF. PLUG DISCONNECTED VACUUM FITTINGS.
SET PARKING BRAKE AND BLOCK DRIVE WHEELS

1. DISCONNECT CARBURETOR HOSE FROM VAPOR CANISTER.
2. DISCONNECT DISTRIBUTOR VACUUM HOSE, PLUG HOSE LEADING TO CARBURETOR. DISCONNECT THROTTLE SOLENOID WIRE.
3. SET DWELL AND TIMING AT SPECIFIED R.P.M.
4. ADJUST CARBURETOR SPEED SCREW TO SPECIFIED R.P.M.
5. RECONNECT SOLENOID WIRE, MANUALLY EXTEND SOLENOID SCREW AND ADJUST TO SPECIFIED R.P.M.
6. SET FAST IDLE TO SPECIFIED R.P.M. ON TOP STEP OF CAM.
7. RECONNECT DISTRIBUTOR AND CANISTER HOSES.

(SEE SERVICE MANUAL FOR ADDITIONAL INFORMATION.)

PRINTED IN U.S.A. — THIS VEHICLE CONFORMS TO U.S. DEPT. OF H.E.W. & CALIFORNIA REGULATIONS APPLICABLE TO 1971 MODEL YEAR NEW MOTOR VEHICLES — PT. NO. 484674

CCS EXHAUST EMISSION CONTROL	AUTO. TRANSMISSION
DWELL	30
TIMING (B.T.D.C. @ R.P.M.)	12 @ 600
SPARK PLUG GAP	.035
CARBURETOR SCREW (R.P.M.)	700 (IN PARK)
FAST IDLE SCREW (R.P.M.)	1700 (IN PARK)

IDLE MIXTURE PRESET AT FACTORY DO NOT REMOVE CAPS

Emission decal for 1971 455-ci H.O. with automatic transmission. Decal courtesy of Jim Osborne Reproductions

PM 455 CU. IN. 4 BBL. H.O.

VEHICLE EMISSION CONTROL INFORMATION
PONTIAC MOTOR DIVISION   GENERAL MOTORS CORP.

MAKE ADJUSTMENTS WITH ENGINE AT NORMAL OPERATING TEMPERATURE, CHOKE OPEN AND AIR CONDITIONING OFF. PLUG DISCONNECTED VACUUM FITTINGS.
SET PARKING BRAKE AND BLOCK DRIVE WHEELS.

1. DISCONNECT CARBURETOR HOSE FROM VAPOR CANISTER.
2. DISCONNECT DISTRIBUTOR VACUUM HOSE, PLUG HOSE LEADING TO CARBURETOR. DISCONNECT THROTTLE SOLENOID WIRE.
3. SET DWELL AND TIMING AT SPECIFIED R.P.M.
4. ADJUST CARBURETOR SPEED SCREW TO SPECIFIED R.P.M.
5. RECONNECT SOLENOID WIRE, MANUALLY EXTEND SOLENOID SCREW AND ADJUST TO SPECIFIED R.P.M.
6. WITH TRANS. IN PARK (OR NEUTRAL), SET FAST IDLE TO SPECIFIED R.P.M. ON TOP SET OF CAM.
7. RECONNECT DISTRIBUTOR AND CANISTER HOSES.

(SEE SERVICE MANUAL FOR ADDITIONAL INFORMATION)

PRINTED IN U.S.A. — THIS VEHICLE CONFORMS TO U.S. DEPT. OF H.E.W. & CALIFORNIA REGULATIONS APPLICABLE TO 1971 MODEL YEAR NEW MOTOR VEHICLES - PT. NO. 484382

CCS EXHAUST EMISSION CONTROL	MANUAL TRANSMISSION
DWELL	30°
TIMING (°B.T.D.C. @ R.P.M.)	12° @ 600
SPARK PLUG GAP	.035
CARBURETOR SCREW (R.P.M.)	600
FAST IDLE SCREW (R.P.M.)	1700
SOLENOID SCREW (R.P.M.)	1800

IDLE MIXTURE PRESET AT FACTORY. DO NOT REMOVE CAPS.

Emission decal for 1971 455-ci H.O. with manual transmission. Decal courtesy of Jim Osborne Reproductions

PH 400 CU. IN. 4 BBL. CARB.

VEHICLE EMISSION CONTROL INFORMATION
PONTIAC MOTOR DIVISION   GENERAL MOTORS CORP.

MAKE ADJUSTMENTS WITH ENGINE AT NORMAL OPERATING TEMPERATURE, CHOKE OPEN, AND AIR CONDITIONING OFF. PLUG DISCONNECTED VACUUM FITTINGS.
SET PARKING BRAKE AND BLOCK DRIVE WHEELS.

1. DISCONNECT CARBURETOR HOSE FROM VAPOR CANISTER.
2. DISCONNECT DISTRIBUTOR VACUUM HOSE, PLUG HOSE LEADING TO CARBURETOR.
3. SET DWELL AND TIMING AT SPECIFIED R.P.M.
4. ADJUST CARBURETOR SPEED SCREW TO SPECIFIED R.P.M.
5. WITH TRANSMISSION IN PARK (OR NEUTRAL) SET FAST IDLE TO SPECIFIED R.P.M. ON TOP STEP OF CAM.
6. RECONNECT DISTRIBUTOR AND CANISTER HOSES.

(SEE SERVICE MANUAL FOR ADDITIONAL INFORMATION)

PRINTED IN U.S.A. — THIS VEHICLE CONFORMS TO U.S. DEPT. OF H.E.W. & CALIFORNIA REGULATIONS APPLICABLE TO 1971 MODEL YEAR NEW MOTOR VEHICLES — PT. NO. 484379

CCS EXHAUST EMISSION CONTROL	AUTOMATIC TRANSMISSION
DWELL	30°
TIMING (B.T.D.C. @ R.P.M.)	12° @ 700
SPARK PLUG GAP	.035
CARBURETOR SCREW (R.P.M.)	700 (IN PARK)
FAST IDLE SCREW (R.P.M.)	1700 (IN PARK)

IDLE MIXTURE PRESET AT FACTORY DO NOT REMOVE CAPS

Emission decal for 1971 400-ci with automatic transmission. Decal courtesy of Jim Osborne Reproductions

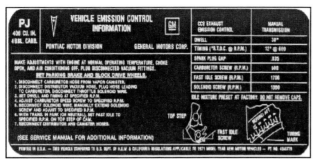

Emission decal for 1971 400-ci with manual transmission. Decal courtesy of Jim Osborne Reproductions.

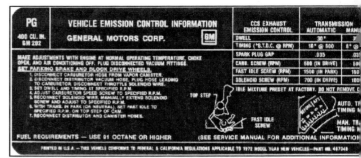

Emission decal for 1972 400-ci. Decal courtesy of Jim Osborne Reproductions.

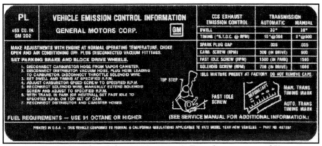

Emission decal for 1972 455-ci. Decal courtesy of Jim Osborne Reproductions.

Emission decal for 1973 455-ci with manual transmission except S.D. Decal courtesy of Jim Osborne Reproductions.

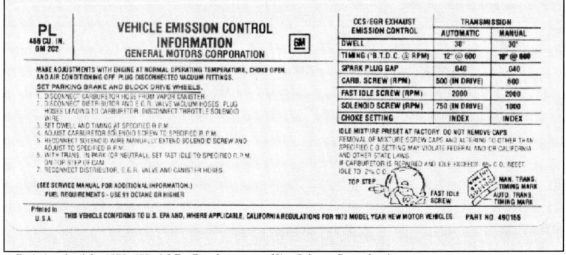

Emission decal for 1973 455-ci S.D. Decal courtesy of Jim Osborne Reproductions

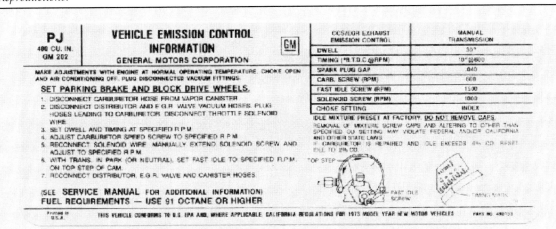

Emission decal for 1973 455-ci with automatic transmission except S.D. Decal courtesy of Jim Osborne Reproductions.

Emission decal for 1973 400-ci with manual transmission Decal courtesy of Jim Osborne Reproductions

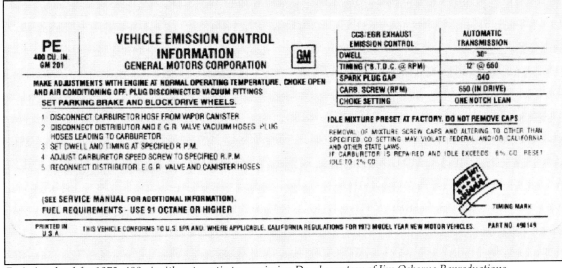

Emission decal for 1973 400-ci with automatic transmission Decal courtesy of Jim Osborne Reproductions

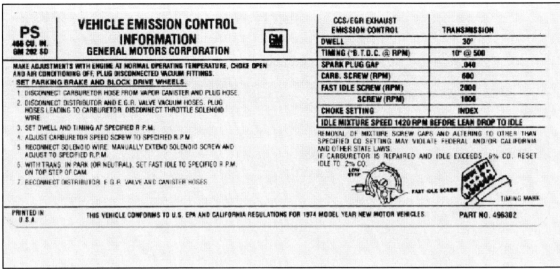

Emission decal for 1974 455-ci S.D with manual transmission. Decal courtesy of Jim Osborne Reproductions

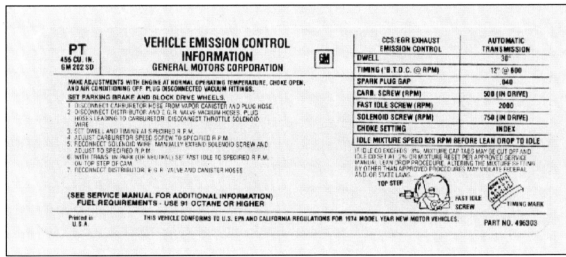

Emission decal for 1974 455-ci S.D with automatic transmission. Decal courtesy of Jim Osborne Reproductions

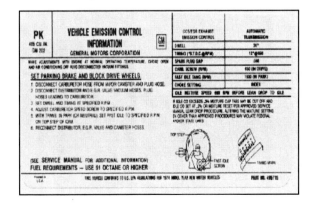

Emission decal for 1974 455-ci with automatic transmission except S.D. transmission. Decal courtesy of Jim Osborne Reproductions.

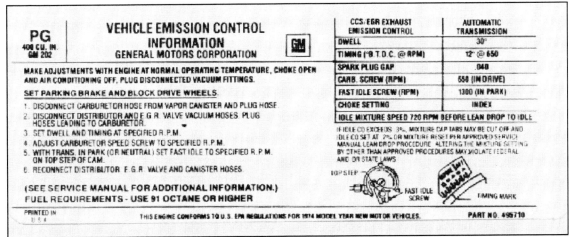

Emission decal for 1974 400-ci with manual transmission except Ram Air. Decal courtesy of Jim Osborne Reproductions.

Emission decal for 1974 400-ci with automatic transmission except Ram Air. Decal courtesy of Jim Osborne Reproductions.

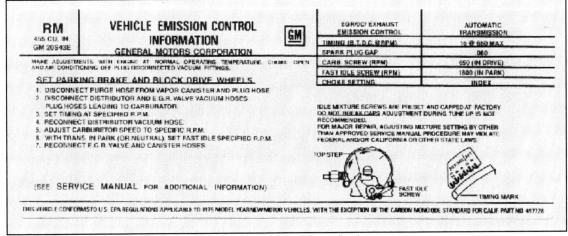

Emission decal for 1974 400-ci with automatic transmission and Ram Air. Decal courtesy of Jim Osborne Reproductions.

Emission decal for 1975 455-ci. Decal courtesy of Jim Osborne Reproductions

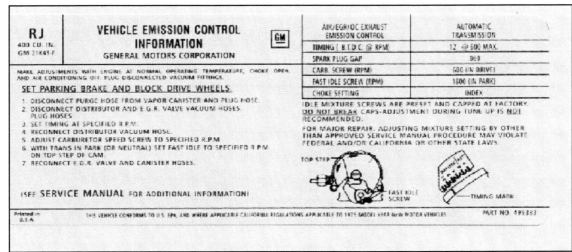

Emission decal for 1975 400-ci. Decal courtesy of Jim Osborne Reproductions.

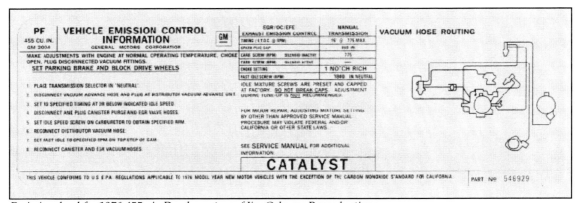

Emission decal for 1976 455-ci. Decal courtesy of Jim Osborne Reproductions.

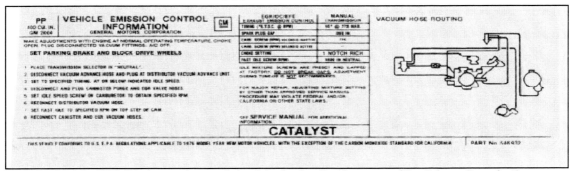

Emission decal for 1976 400-ci manual transmission federal only. Decal courtesy of Jim Osborne Reproductions.

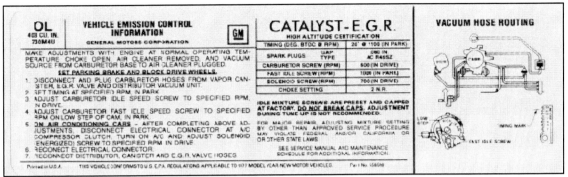

Emission decal for 1977 403-ci high altitude. Decal courtesy of Jim Osborne Reproductions.

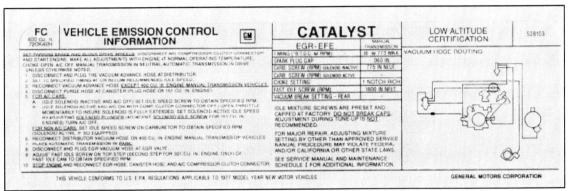

Emission decal for 1977 400-ci with manual transmission. Decal courtesy of Jim Osborne Reproductions

Emission decal for 1977 403-ci California. Decal courtesy of Jim Osborne Reproductions

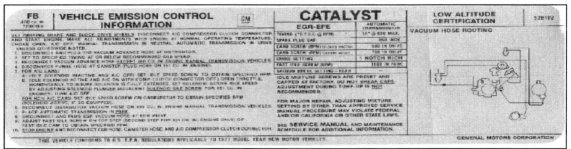

Emission decal for 1977 400-ci high performance. Decal courtesy of Jim Osborne Reproductions.

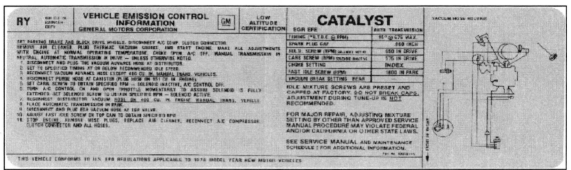

Emission decal for 1978 400-ci automatic, has a silver background. Decal courtesy of Jim Osborne Reproductions

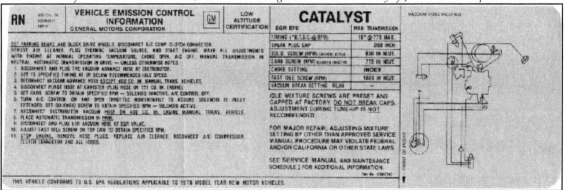

Emission decal for 1978 400-ci manual transmission, has a silver background. Decal courtesy of Jim Osborne Reproductions.

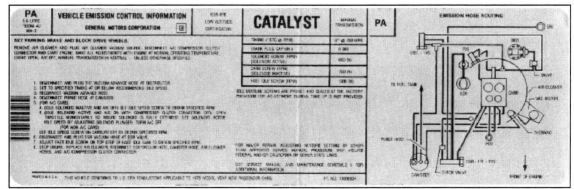

Emission decal for 1979 6.6 Liter with manual transmission, has a silver background. Decal courtesy of Jim Osborne Reproductions.

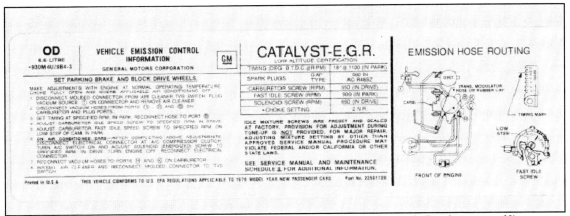

Emission decal for 1979 6.6 Liter with automatic transmission, has a silver background. Decal courtesy of Jim Osborne Reproductions.

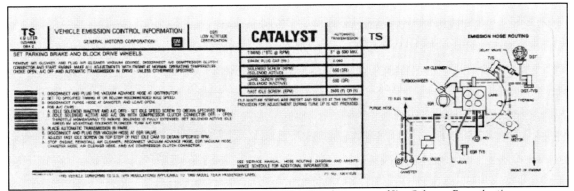

Emission decal for 1980 301-ci Turbo, has color hose diagram. Decal courtesy of Jim Osborne Reproductions

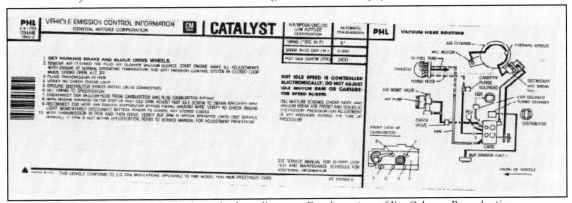

Emission decal for 1981 301-ci Turbo, has color hose diagram. Decal courtesy of Jim Osborne Reproductions

There was no set location for the tune-up "emissions " label. It was only to appear on the radiator support wall. A common location is shown.

This type of label was used also on the support wall. The information was hand written in at the factory. It was used from 1970-1973.

Late models used this type of anti-freeze decal.

126

Body and Sheet Metal

Exterior Finish

There is a big difference in the quality of paint then (1970-1981), especially the early 1970-1974 models, and now. The quality of the paint has greatly improved. Modern day paint is much deeper and richer in color and has a higher gloss than the original finish. The main reason for this is the care that is placed into painting a classic car today, while when it was new the paint was quickly applied, and even runs can be seen. Now I am not suggesting that you haphazardly apply your paint to your car to duplicate the factory look. That is one area that would not get you any points at a car show; in fact it would get you a deduction in points. The purpose of a restoration is not to look just like it came from the factory, but to look like it came from the factory, if they were building only a classic, and took care and time to hand assemble each part. Which would mean a flawless paint job. So when applying your paint take extra care. A quality paint job can make the difference between the best of show and going home empty handed.

For all 12 years Firebird were painted with acrylic lacquer paint, with two exceptions. The urethane bumpers and body parts were painted with an enamel base NOT lacquer base. This special endura paint features a film that responds to impact without cracking or splitting. If regular acrylic lacquer finish is used without first sealing, the finish will not hold and will crack. The important things to remember when painting these types of parts is that it requires a tri-coat primer sealer (part number 1051214) prior to the application of the paint. And second, you cannot spot repair a panel, due to variations in paint materials, and the entire panel must be sealed with the tri-coat primer before the endura color coat and clear topcoat. Also beware that in some later models the paint was a water based acrylic enamel, which can be determined by the letter "W' stamped on to the body tag next to the pint code. Those cars with lacquer based have the letter "L" stamped into the tag, which can be used for identification.

Cars as old as your classic Firebird may have seen more than one paint job, and possibly some other color than the original was used. The original color can be determined by a pair of codes that appear on the body tag that is attached to the firewall (see chapter 1 for more details on locating and decoding this tag.)

1970 Exterior Color Codes

Code	Color Name	Du Pont	Ditzler	Rinshed-Mason
10	Polar White	5040-L	8631	A-1802
14	Palladium Silver	5032-L	2059	A-2108
19	Starlight Black	99-L	9300	A-946
25	Bermuda Blue	5123-L	2165	A-2261
26	Lucerne Blue	5190-L	2213	A-262
28	Atoll Blue	5124-L	2166	A-2264
34	Mint Turquoise	5119-L	2168	A-2265
43	Keylime Green	5126-L	2170	A-2266
45	Palisade Green	5122-L	2171	A-2268
47	Verdoro Green	5195-LH	2095	A-2210
48	Pepper Green	5116-L	2173	A-2269
50	Sierra Yellow	5121-L	2175	A-2270D
51	Goldenrod Yellow	5026-LH	2094	A-2119
53	Coronado Gold	5073-L	23211	A-2091F
55	Baja Gold	5120-L	2178	A-2271D
58	Granada Gold	5117-L	2179	A-2272
60	Orbit Orange	5210-L	2257	107B770
63	Palomino Copper	2125-L	2183	A-2275
65	Carousel Red	5021-LM	2084	A-211R
67	Castilian Bronze	5076-LH	23215	A-2276G
75	Cardinal Red	5118-LH	2189	A-2278F
78	Burgundy	5063-LH	50700	A-2107M

1971 Exterior Color Codes

Code	Color Name	Du Pont	Ditzler	Rinshed-Mason
11	Cameo White	5338-L	2058	A-2080
13	Nordic Silver	5032-L	2327	A-2438
16	Blue Stone Gray	5324-L	2161	A-2472
19	Starlight Black	99-L	9300	A-946
24	Adriatic Blue	5270-L	2328	A-2439
26	Lucerne Blue	5190-L	2213	A-262
29	Regency Blue	5327-L	2330	A-2441
39	Aquarius Green	5277-L	2331	A-2442
42	Limekist Green	5274-L	2333	A2444G
43	Tropical Lime	5322-LH	2334	A-2445D
49	Laurentian Green	5273-L	2337	A-2448
53	Quetzal Gold	5280-LH	2339	A-2449F
55	Baja Gold	5120-L	2178	A-2271D
59	Aztec Gold	5328-LM	2359	A-2450G
61	Sandalwood	5325-L	2181	A-2273
62	Canyon Copper	5281-LH	2340	A-2451G
66	Bronzini Gold	5343-LH	2367	A-2480G
67	Castilian Bronze	5076-LH	23215	A-2276G
75	Cardinal Red	5118-LH	2189	A-2278F
78	Rosewood	5275-L	2350	A-2461

1972 Exterior Color Codes

Code	Color Name	Du Pont	Ditzler	Rinshed-Mason
11	Cameo White	5338-L	2058	A-2080
14	Revere Silver	5426-L	2429	A-2541
18	Antique Pewter	5427-L	2430	A2542
19	Starlight Black	99-L	9300	A-946
24	Adriatic Blue	5270-L	2328	A-2439
26	Lucerne Blue	5190-L	2213	A-262
28	Cumberland Blue	5124-L	2166	A-2264
36	Julep Green	5436-L	2433	A-2546D
43	Springfield Green	5428-L	2435	A-2548
48	Wilderness Green	5429-L	2439	A-2552
50	Brittany Beige	5431-L	2441	A-2554
53	Quetzal Gold	5280-LH	2339	A-2449F
54	Arizona Gold	5432-L	2442	A-2556D
55	Shadow Gold	5433-L	2443	A-2557
56	Monarch Yellow	5443-L	2444	A-2558G
57	Brasilia Gold	5439-L	2445	A-2559
62	Spice Beige	5437-L	2447	A-2561
63	Anaconda Gold	5434-L	2448	A-2562D
65	Sundance Orange	5435-L	2450	A-2564D
69	Cinnamon Bronze	5438-L	2452	A-2566
75	Cardinal Red	5118-LH	2189	A-2278F

1973 Exterior Color Codes

Code	Color Name	Du Pont	Ditzler	Rinshed-Mason
11	Cameo White	5338-L	2058	A-2080
19	Starlight Black	99-L	9300	A-946
24	Porcelain Blue	5437-L	2523	A-2623
26	Regatta Blue	5478-L	2524	A-2624
29	Admiralty Blue	5474-L	2526	A-2626
42	Verdant Green	5489-L	2528	A-2628
44	Slate Green	5475-L	2529	A-2689
46	Golden Olive	5479-L	2530	A-2631D
48	Brewster Green	5480-L	2531	A-2632
51	Sunlight Yellow	5484-L	2533	A-2634G
56	Desert Sand	5481-L	2537	A-2638
60	Valencia Gold	5490-L	2538	A-2639D
64	Ascot Silver	5476-L	2541	A2643
66	Burnished Umber	5482-L	2542	A-2645
68	Burma Brown	5483-L	2543	A-2647D
69	Cinnamon Bronze	5438-L	2452	A-2566
74	Florentine Red	5477-L	2545	A-2649F
75	Buccaneer Red	5485-L	2546	A-2650F
75	Cardinal Red	5118-LH	2189	A-2278F
81	Mesa Tan	5491-L	2549	A-2563
97	Navajo Orange	5552-L	2555	A-2659

1974 Exterior Color Codes

Code	Color Name	Du Pont	Ditzler	Rinshed-Mason
11	Cameo White	5338-L	2058	A-2080
19	Starlight Black	99-L	9300	A-946
24	Porcelain Blue	5437-L	2523	A-2623
26	Regatta Blue	5478-L	2524	A-2624
29	Admiralty Blue	5474-L	2526	A-2626
36	Gulfmist Aqua	42805-L	2640	2702
40	Ferniest Green	42800-L	2641	2703
44	Lakemist Green	42802-L	2642	2704
46	Limefire Green	42806-L	2643	2705
49	Poinemist Green	42803-L	2645	2707
50	Camel Beige	42807-L	2646	2708
51	Sunstrom Yellow	42809-LM	2677	2709G
53	Denver Gold	42876-LM	2649	2710G
55	Colonial Gold	42808-L	2650	2711
59	Crestwood Brown	42875-L	2367	2480G
64	Ascot Silver	5476-L	2541	A2643
66	Fire Coal Bronze	42801-LH	2553	2714G
69	Shadowmist Brown	42804-L	5656	2716
74	Honduras Maroon	42810-LM	2658	2718F
75	Buccaneer Red	5485-L	2546	A-2650F

1975 Exterior Color Codes

Code	Color Name	Du Pont	Ditzler	Rinshed-Mason
11	Cameo White	5338-L	2058	A-2080
13	Sterling Silver	43537-L	2518	A-2618
15	Graystone	43450-L	2742	A-2793
19	Starlight Black	99-L	9300	A-946
24	Arctic Blue	43451-L	2745	A2798
26	Bimini Blue	43452-L	2746	A2799
29	Stellar Blue	43453-L	2748	A2802
31	Gray	43538-L	2751	A2877
39	Burgundy	43539-LM	2786	A2878M
44	Lakemist Green	42802-L	2642	2704
45	Augusta Green	43460-LH	2750	A-2804G
49	Alpine Green	43454-LH	2752	A2805
50	Camel Beige	42807-L	2646	2708
50	Carmel Beige	42807-L	2646	A2708
51	Sunstrom Yellow	42809-LM	2677	2709G
55	Sandstone	43455-L	A2808	A2643
58	Ginger Brown	43461-LH	2757	A2810
59	Oxford Brown	43456-L	2758	A-2811D
63	Copper Mist	43457-LH	2759	A-2812D
64	Persimmon	43458-LH	2760	A2813F
66	Fire Coal Bronze	42801-LH	2553	2714G
72	Roman Red	5498-LM	2544	A26484F
74	Honduras Maroon	42810-LM	2658	2718F
75	Buccaneer Red	5485-L	2546	A-2650F
80	Tampico Orange	5568-LM	2548	A2652F

1976 Exterior Color Codes

Code	Color Name	Du Pont	Ditzler	Rinshed-Mason
11	Cameo White	5338-L	2058	A-2080
13	Sterling Silver	43537-L	2518	A-2618
16	Medium Gray	44146-L	2862	A2928
19	Starlight Black	99-L	9300	A-946
28	Athena Blue	4414-L	2772	A-2801
35	Polaris Blue	44130-LH	2863	A2930D
36	Firethorn Red	43953-LM	2811	A-2916F
37	Cordovan Maroon	44131-LM	2864	A-2931G
40	Mealtime Green	44137-LH	2866	A-2933D
49	Alpine Green	43454-LH	2752	A2805
50	Bavarian Cream	2867	44132-L	A-2935
51	Goldenrod Yellow	44139-LH	2094	A-2936D
55	Anniversary Gold	44167-LM	2861	A-2992D
57	Cream Gold	44178-L	2884	A-2996
65	Buckskin Tan	44159-L	2829	A-2939
67	Durango Bronze	44138-L	2871	A-2941
72	Roman Red	5498-LM	2544	A26484F
78	Carousel Red	44140-LM	2084	A-2942R

1977 Exterior Color Codes

Code	Color Name	Du Pont	Ditzler	Rinshed-Mason
11	Cameo White	5338-L	2058	A-2080
13	Sterling Silver	44716-L	2953	A-8680
15	Gray	44146-L	2862	A2928
19	Starlight Black	99-L	9300	A-946
21	Lombard Blue	44133-L	2815	A2929
22	Glacier Blue	44717-L	2955	A-8682
29	Nautilus Blue	44718-L	2959	A-8885
32	Royal Lime	44771-LH	2960	A-8686F
36	Firethorn Red	43953-LM	2811	A-2916F
38	Aquamarine	44714-L	2961	A-8687
44	Bahia Green	44719-LH	2964	A-8690
48	Berkshire Green	44720-LH	2965	A8691
50	Cream Gold	44178-L	2884	A-2996
51	Goldenrod Yellow	44139-LH	2094	A-2936D
61	Mojave Tan	44713-L	2869	A-2999
63	Buckskin Tan	44722-L	2970	A-8695D
64	Fiesta Orange	44790-LH	2968	A-8696R
69	Brentwood Brown	44721-LH	2972	A-8698F
72	Roman Red	5498-LM	2544	A26484F
75	Buccaneer Red	5485-LM	2546	A-2650F
78	Mandarin Orange	44715-LH	2976	A-8702F

1978 Exterior Color Codes

Code	Color Name	Du Pont	Ditzler	Rinshed-Mason
11	Cameo White	5338-L	2058	A-2080
15	Platinum	45177	3076	A-9369
16	Gray	45188	3077	A-9370
19	Starlight Black	99-L	9300	A-946
21	Dresden Blue	45178	3078	A-9371
22	Glacier Blue	44717-L	2955	A-8682
24	Martinique Blue	45185	3079	A-9372D
29	Nautilus Blue	44718-L	2959	A-8885
44	Seafoam green	45179	3081	A-9374
45	Mayfair Green	45192	3082	A-9375
48	Berkshire Green	44720-LH	2965	A8691
50	Special Edition Gold	45278	3071	A-9572D
51	Sundance Yellow	45186	3084	A-9377F
55	Accent Gold	44856	82352	
56	Burnished Gold	45190	3086	A-9379
58	Accent Blue	4855	15109	
61	Desert Sand	45180	3088	A-9381
63	Laredo Brown	45181	3090	A-9383D
67	Ember Mist	45183	3091	A-9384F
69	Chesterfield Brown	45182	3092	A-9385G
75	Mayan Red	45187	3095	A-9388F
77	Carmine Poly	45184	3096	A-9389F
79	Claret	45189	3098	A9391F
85	Medium Blue Irid			A8776

1979 Exterior Color Codes

Code	Color Name	Du Pont	Ditzler	Rinshed-Mason
11	White	5338-L	2058	A-2080
15	Silver Irid	45177	3076	A-9369
16	Gray	45188	3077	A-9370
19	Starlight Black	99-L	9300	A-946
21	Pastel Blue	45800	3119	A-9800
22	Light Blue Irid	44717-L	2955	A-8682
24	Bright Blue Irid	45807	3120	A-9801
29	Dark Blue Irid	45801	3121	A-9802G
40	Pastel Green	45802	3122	A-9803
44	Medium Green Irid	45803	3123	A-9805D
50	Gold Irid (Special Order)	45278	3071	A-9572D
51	Bright Yellow	45186	3084	A-9377F
56	Med. Gold	45190	3086	
61	Medium Beige	45804	3124	A9809
63	Camel Irid	45806	3125	A-9811D
69	Dark Brown Irid	45805	3126	A-9813G
75	Red	45187	3095	A-9388F
77	Carmine Irid	45184	3096	A-9389F
79	Dark Carmine Irid	45189	3098	A9391F
80	Red (Special Order)	45831	72326	A-9761R
85	Medium Blue Irid	44724	2280	A8776

1980 Exterior Color Codes

Code	Color Name	Du Pont	Ditzler	Rinshed-Mason
11	White	5338-L	2058	A-2080
15	Silver Irid	45177	3076	A-9369
16	Gray	45188	3077	A-9370
19	Starlight Black	99-L	9300	A-946
21	Light Blue	B8006	3205	A11400
22	Medium Blue	B8020	3206	A11401
24	Bright Blue Irid	B8013	3217	A11402
29	Dark Blue Irid	B8007	3207	A11403D
37	Accent Yellow	B8025	3224	A11433
40	Lime Green	B8011	3218	A11404
44	Dark Green Irid	B8008	3208	A11406
51	Bright Yellow	B8019	3219	A11409
56	Yellow	B8024	3225	A11435
57	Gold Poly	B8014	3215	A11410D
59	Beige	45205	3087	A9380
63	Light Camel	B8018	3210	A11412
67	Dark Brown	B8016	3226	A11413
69	Medium Camel	B8017	3211	A11415D
72	Red	44770	2973	A8699F
75	Claret	B8009	3220	A11416
76	Dark Claret	B8010	3212	A11417F
77	Cinnabar	B8001	3213	A11418R
79	Red Orange	B8002	3221	A11419
80	Rust	B8015	3222	A11420
84	Charcoal	B8012	3223	A11421
85	Vapor Gray	B8005	3214	A11422

1981 Exterior Color Codes

Code	Color Name	Du Pont	Ditzler	Acme
09	Red	45187	3095	25404Q
11	White	5338-L	2058	5644
16	Silver Metallic	B8140	3308	31314
19	Starlight Black	99-L	9300	A-946
20	Bright Blue Metallic	B8110	3309	31033
21	Light Blue Metallic	B8141	3310	31311
29	Dark Blue Irid	B8007	3207	A11403D
51	Bright Yellow	B8019	3219	30413
54	Gold Metallic	B8116	3322	31046
56	Yellow	B8114	3324	31048
57	Orange Metallic	B8113	3325	31049
67	Dark Brown Metallic	B8142	3328	31313
75	Bright Red	B8115	3332	31056
77	Dark Maroon Metallic	B8109	3333	31057
84	Dark Charcoal Metallic	B8012	3223	30473

Front End Sheet Metal

1970-1972

Standard hood for all models except the Formula and the Trans Am was a single outer panel with a rugged inner panel reinforcement listed as part number 478940. The Formula hood featured twin hood scoops that were molded into the hood; two types were used. Those without the Ram Air option used a hood with scoops that were blocked off and was listed as part number 480172 while those with Ram air used part 479677 which featured functional hood scoops.

Trans Am's used a special hood with a cut out in the center of the shaker hood scoop. The hood was listed as part number 481845.

All four hoods used the same set of hinges, listed as part number 9790524 right–hand and 9790525- left-hand, and springs were listed as part number 3848272 and fit either side. The hinges and springs should be painted semi-gloss black, such as under hood black. Some were left natural.

Listed as part number 9721788 the hood latch should have natural appearance.

1970 Trans Am used a special hood that featured a cutout for the shaker hood scoop.

While the hood part numbers remained the same the hinges did not and were changed in 1971 to part numbers 3990431 right-hand and 3990432- left-hand. The hood spring was changed to part number 3907626. The hood latch was also restyled and given part number 9857248, although the hood latch release lever remained the same listed as part number 478663.

Trans Am models came with color decal stripes on the hood. They were available in either white for blue colored cars or blue for white colored cars. Though the stripes look similar they differ between 1970 and 1971. Also engine callouts were used on the sides of the hood scoops.

1970 — 1972 Trans Am Hood Stripes

Color	Part Number
	1970
White	481969
Blue	481970
	1971-1972
White	483712
Blue	483713

1970 — 1971 Engine Callout Decals

Callout	Part Number	Notes
	1970	
Ram Air	9794721*	Used with Ram Air III
	9794722**	
	9794723***	
Ram Air IV	9789041*	Used with Ram Air IV
	9789042**	
	9789043***	
	1971	
Ram Air	484257*	Used with 400-ci Ram Air
	484258**	
	484273***	
455 HO	484323*	With 455 HO
	484324**	

*-White **-Black ***-Red

1972 Tran Am hood stripe.

The 1971 Trans Am with the 455 HO powerplant used these decals as engine callouts. White cars with blue stripes would use the white lettering.

Note the correct finish under the hood. Originally the hood was painted gloss black underneath and then painted the body color. Overlap and overspray were common on the underside of the hood. While later models (after 1972) have tendency to be painted solid semi-gloss black.

Front fenders for all Firebirds except Tran Ams in 1970 used part numbers 478612 right-hand and 478613- left-hand. These were changed to part numbers 483512 right-hand and 483513-left-hand in 1971 and were listed as part numbers 9793816-right-hand and 9793817-left-hand, and again in 1972 as part numbers 492991 right-hand and 492992 left-hand. The Trans Am used special fenders that allowed wider tires to be used plus featured air extractors on the sides behind the wheel openings. Only one pair of fenders, part numbers 480898 right hand and 480899 left-hand were used through the three-year run. Likewise, the air extractors part numbers 480796 right-hand and 480797 left-hand remained the same.

The Firebird nameplate was used on the front fenders of all firebird models except the Trans Am. The nameplate was listed as part numbers 481544 in 1970 and 483951 in 1971 and 1972. Those in 1970 with a V-8 except the Formula or Tran Am models used an engine call out (350- part number 481541 and 400- part number 480181). Formula models used the Formula 400 callouts, part number 481545 below the Firebird name. For 1971 three different nameplates were used, those with a 350-ci powerplant used part number 483949. It read "Formula 350" while those with the 400 used part number 483948 and the rare birds were with a 455-ci powerplant which used part number 483950, read Formula 455. In 1972 the Formula nameplates were used again but the part numbers were changed to: Formula 350- 487745 Formula 400- 487744 and Formula 455-487776.

Before removing the hood mark the hinge locations with a permanent marker. This will ease the installation later. Hoods are heavy have a friend help hold it on the other side.

The Formula name was used under the Firebird nameplate on the fenders of the 1970 models.

The Trans Am fender decal. Blue colored decals were used on white cars and white was used on blue colored cars, as shown.

1971 Firebirds featured louvers listed as part numbers 483915-right-hand and 483916-left-hand

Trans Am did not used any nameplates; instead they used a colored decal. Either blue part number 546290 with white cars or white part number 481961 with blue colored cars was used.

Black colored body side moldings were available as an option (RPO B84) on all Firebirds except the Tran Ams, though they are most likely to appear on Esprit models. They were listed as part number 480641-right–hand and 480642 left-hand. These parts were revamped in 1974 and a single part (part number 488141) fit either side.

Chrome wheel trim was used around the front wheel opening of all Firebirds except Trans Ams. They were listed as part numbers 481536 right –hand and 481537 left-hand, all three years.

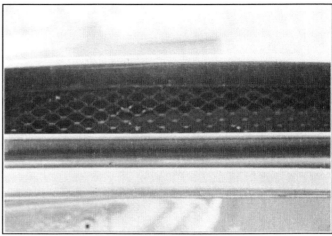

A close up of hood scoop inserts used on 1970-1972 Formula models, with Ram Air.

Typical 1972 Fender nameplate mountings.

The Formula nameplate was used by itself from 1971-1975. The 1972-1975 style is shown here. On a very rare 1973 model with the 455 Super Duty. The Firebird emblem part number 1735919 was used on all 1972-1973 Firebirds except Trans Ams.

1973-1975

Standard hood for all models except the Formula 400/455 and the Trans Am was a single outer panel with rugged inner panel reinforcement, listed as part number 500085 all three years. The Formula 350 used the same hood as the standard models but those with the 400-ci or 455-ci used a fiberglass hood with twin non-functional hood scoops that was listed as part number 490660. Those models with Ram Air used part number 490661 which included functional hood scoops. The exception was those models with the Super Duty 455 powerplant. When it was ordered the package included the Shaker hood part number 500154 that was used on all Trans Ams, regardless of the power train. Hinges for all hoods were listed as part number 3990432 right-hand and 3990433 left-hand. The hood springs were listed as part number 14034133 and were used with all hoods.

The inner portions of the fender should be painted semi-gloss black as shown.

The famous 'Screaming Chicken" first appeared on the hood of the 1973 Trans Ams. However, this symbol, based on the legendary Phoenix, which rose from the ashes, the bird of fire was not standard affair on the Trans Am. It was listed as option RPO WW7, it looked much like the smaller bird decal that was standard and used only on the nose of the car. The colorful birds were used according to the exterior color of the car.

1973-1975 Trans Am Hood Decals

Exterior Color	Decal Color	Part Numbers Standard (1)	WW7
White or Blue	Lt Blue/Dk Blue	493370	493364
Green	Green**	493371	493365
Red	Lt. Orange/Dk Orange	493372	493366
Silver	Red/charcoal*	Not used	500666

*-1975 only **- Not used in 1975 (1) 1973 only

Engine callouts corresponded with the color of the Firebird decal. For 1973-1974 only the 455-ci equipped Trans Ams and those Formulas and Trans Ams with the 455 Super Duty used the decals. In 1975 those Trans Ams with the 400-ci, or 455-ci H.O. used the decals. Those 1973-1974 Formula 400/455 except those with the 455 S.D. powerplant, and with ram air used "RAM AIR" decals on the sides of the hood scoops. White colored decals were used on dark colored cars and black colored decals were used on light colored cars.

When the optional WW7 decal was used the standard 1973 nose decal was deleted.

The hood latch was the same part that was used on the 1972 models and was used up till 1975, and with all hoods.

All Firebirds except the Trans Am models used the same set of fenders that were used on 1972 models. The Tran Am models used special fenders part numbers 492993 right-hand and 42994 left-hand that featured provisions for air extractors, which used the same exact part numbers as before. Only the base Firebird and Esprit models used the Firebird nameplate listed as part number 486904 all three years.

For the Formula models these nameplates were used: Formula 350- 487745, Formula 400-487744, and Formula 455-487776. It is incorrect for the Formula nameplate to be used with the Firebird name. These models were Formula models, not Firebird Formulas, as in 1970.

Trans Am continued to use a decal name plate, but the decal design was changed and those from earlier models will not properly fit. The lettering style was bolder and featured a stenciled looked. The decals came in the same colors as the Firebird decal.

1973-1975 Trans Am Fender Decals

Exterior Color	Decal Color	Part Number
White or Blue	Lt Blue/Dk Blue	493369
Green	Green**	493370
Red	Lt. Orange/Dk Orange	493371
Silver	Red/charcoal*	500670

*-1975 only **- Not used in 1975

Black colored body side moldings were available as an option (RPO B84) on all Firebirds except the Tran Ams, though they are most likely to appear on Esprit models. They were listed as part number 480641-right –hand and 480642 left-hand. These parts were revamped in 1974 and a single part (part number 488141) fit either side.

Chrome wheel trim was used around the front wheel opening of all Firebirds except Trans Ams. They were listed as part numbers 481536 right –hand and 481537 left-hand, all three years.

An example of the 1973-1975 Trans Am fender decal, shown is the orange colored decal that was used on red colored cars.

Hood callouts used on the 1973-1974 455 S.D. This one is on a rare 1973 Formula 455.

The 400 callouts were used on 1975 models. Note this car is without the optional WW7 decals

1976

Very few changes occurred in 1976, the same hoods that were used before were used again with one exception. The Formula models lost their fiberglass twin snorkel hood. The hood was completely restyled and made of metal. It was listed as part number 499976 and featured twin non-functional hood scoops only. Functional hoodscoops were no longer available. Hinges and hood springs were the same units that were used in 1975.

The optional RPO WW7 screaming chickens were again optional and were revamped a little. Again the colors of the birds were regulated to body color. An important item to remember is that the 50th Anniversary edition Trans Ams used special gold and black decals, while the regular non-S.E. models that were painted black used an orange and gold bird decal. However, due to problems in the bubbling of the decal gold color birds were replaced with charcoal colored birds, this information was taken from a 1976 Dealer Technical Bulletin # 76-T-4 dated 11/25/75. Either a gold bird or charcoal bird would be correct. This does not apply to the Special Edition Trans Am's these all used gold color birds. At the beginning of February 1976 the gold bird again appeared in production. Likewise, the engine callout that was used on the sides of the shaker hoodscoop were also color keyed to the exterior of the car. Only 400 or 455 decals were used. It is believed that the gold color callouts were used even when a charcoal colored bird was used. Those on the 50th Anniversary S.E. models used special gold decals with German-style script numbers.

1976 Trans Am Hood Decals

Exterior Color	Decal Color	Part Numbers
Silver	Red/Charcoal	500666
Except Silver	Yellow/Orange/gold	527047
Black*	Yellow/Orange/gold /black	547163
Black**	Gold	547045

*- Except S.E. **- 50 the S.E.

1976 Trans Am Callout Decals

Exterior Color	Decal Color	Part Number
	400-ci	
Silver	Red/Charcoal	500669
Except Silver	Yellow/Orange/gold	
Black*	Gold	527048
Black**	Gold	547503
	455-ci	
Silver	Red/Charcoal	526256
Except Silver	Yellow/Orange/gold	
Black*	·Gold	527047
Black**	Gold	547502

Front fenders were also restyled for the 1976 models, and other models years will not fit. All models except Trans Ams used part numbers 546936 right-hand and 546937 left-hand, the Trans Am used special fenders listed as part numbers 546938 right-hand and 546939 left-hand, that featured side air exactors that were listed as part numbers 480796 right-hand and 480797 left-hand. The Firebird nameplate part number 486904 was used on all models except Trans Am. The Trans Am models continued to use decals for the nameplates and as before the colorful decals were color-keyed to the exterior of the car. Likewise, the Formula

models also used a decal, which was placed just below the Firebird nameplate on the fender. It came in blue, red, orange or charcoal.

Trans Am with the 50th Anniversary S.E. package used a special Gold lettering with a triple stripe, and a medallion decal part number 547505 just below the Trans Am name.

1976 Trans Am Fender Decals

Exterior Color	Decal Color	Part Numbers
White or Silver	Red/Charcoal	500670
Firethorn, Red or Yellow	Yellow/Orange/gold	500671
Black*	Yellow/Orange/gold /black	500672
Black**	Gold	547501

*- Except S.E. **- 50 the S.E.

1976 Formula Fender Decals

Decal Color	Part Numbers
Blue	255076
Red	255077
Charcoal	525079
Orange	525078

The 1976 50th Anniversary Special Edition package (RPO Y84) used special decal on the front fenders.

1977-1979

There were drastic changes in the front-end design of the 1977 Firebird; along with it were changes in the hood. The hood was flatter with less design creases and detail. Three different hoods were used. The standard hood was used on all models except the Formula and the Trans Am, it was listed as part number 10011150, and it would remained the standard hood till the end of the 1979 model year. The Formula's hood was down graded in styling. Listed as part number 10012180 it only featured simulated hood scoops ornaments, part numbers 525920-right-hand and 52591 left-hand. The Trans Am still featured a cutout for the center shaker scoop, it was listed as part number 10011151, and technically the Trans Am was not standard with the shaker hood and scoop. Listed as option code RPO T48 the shaker hood was not standard but optional on the highest of the Firebirds, it is unclear if any were built without the hood, but it was possible. While the hoods were restyled the hood hinges and springs were not. Latch part number 9857248 was also the same unit used in the 1976 models.

Engine callouts were again placed on the sides of the scoop. Those models with the 403-ci V-8 or the 400-ci without Ram Air used decals that read "T/A 6.6 Liter", while those models with the 400-ci V-8 and Ram Air used decals that read "6.6 Liter", this applied only to the 1977 models. Those 1977 models with the Special Edition package known back then as a Bandit package on the street, so named so because of the movie *Smokie and the Bandit* used special gold German style lettering.

For 1978 and 1979 the hood callouts were restyled a little. Those models with the 403-ci used decals that read "6.6 Liter" while those with the 400-ci powerplant read "T/A 6.6 Liter". As in years past the decals were color-keyed to the exterior of the car. The 10th Anniversary Special Edition model used charcoal colored callouts.

The Screaming Chicken hood decal remained optional, except with the special edition packages where it was a no cost option. As before the colorful birds were color keyed to the exterior color of the car, with a couple of exceptions. Those with the Special edition packages (RPO Y82 and RPO Y84) used gold colored birds. The 10th Anniversary Edition, in 1979 used a larger charcoal colored bird.

1977 Trans Am Hood Decals

Exterior Color	Decal Color	Part Numbers
White or Silver	Red/Charcoal	500666
Black Gold, Brown, Red	Yellow/Orange/gold	527047
Black*	Yellow/Orange/gold/black	547163
Black**	Gold	547045

*- Except S.E.   ** S.E. packages

1978 Trans Am Hood Decals

Exterior Color	Decal Color	Part Numbers
Blue	Lt. Blue/Medium Blue	10003739
Black	Gold/Yellow/Orange/Black	547163
White, Silver	Red/Charcoal	500666
Red, Yellow, Brown	Yellow/Orange/gold	527047
Black**	Gold/Black	547045
Gold**	Lt Gold/Dk. Gold	10002974

1979 Trans Am Hood Decals

Exterior Color	Decal Color	Part Numbers
Red, Yellow, Brown, Gold Black	Lt. Orange/Dk. Orange/Red/Gold	10006160
Silver	Silver/Red	10006161
Silver**	Lt. Charcoal	10006163

1977-1979 Trans Am Callout Decals

Exterior Color	Decal Color
	6.6 Liter
White, Silver* Black**, Red ** Silver **	Charcoal/Red
Black*, Yellow*, Brown* Red*	Gold/Yellow
Black#*	Gold
Brown,** Copper**, Black#** Yellow**	Mustard /Dk. Brown
	T/A 6.6 Liter
White, Silver* Black, Red Silver **	Charcoal/Red
Black, Yellow, Brown, Red*	Gold/Yellow
Black#	Gold

*1977-78 only **1979 #- Black Special Edition

Fenders were also restyled to match the new front end. As in years past two different sets were used; all but the Trans Am used part numbers 526147 right hand and 526148 left-hand, while the Trans Am models used part numbers 526149 right – hand and 526150 left-hand, both of which featured air extractors, which used the same part numbers as in 1976.

The Firebird nameplate was listed as part number 486904 all three years and was used on all Firebirds except the Trans Am models. The Esprit nameplate as it was in 1976 was placed below the Firebird name. The 1976-early 1979 models used part number 525451 which included nuts and lugs. The later 1979 models used a stick on type nameplate listed as part number 10009181. It is incorrect for a 1977-1978 model to have the stick on type nameplate.

Formula models used a Formula Decal placed below the Firebird nameplate, only if the optional striping was not ordered. The Decals were available in Charcoal, Blue, Aqua, Red or Gold. These decals were used only on the 1977-78 models. In 1979 the Firebird nameplate was deleted from the fenders of the Formula models and the Formula decals, without the W50 appearance package, were of a three tone color that was color keyed to the exterior color of the car.

The Trans Am models used colorful decals all three years, and as before the decals were color-keyed to the exterior color of the car. Note that the wingtips of the 10th Anniversary Special Edition model in 1979 were placed on the top edges of the fenders and were charcoal and red. Also there is a unique tidbit of information for 1979 models being shipped to Japan, which used a different nameplate than other models. The lettering was different, and was available only in blue.

1977-1978 Formula Fender Decals

Decal Color	Part Numbers
Blue	547424
Red	547426
Charcoal	547423
Aqua	547425
Gold	547428

1977-1978 Formula Fender Decals

Decal Color	Part Numbers
Red/Orange/Dk. Red	10006122
3 Shades of Gold	10006123
3 Shades of Blue	10006124

1977 Trans Am Fender Decals

Exterior Color	Decal Color	Part Numbers
White, Silver	Charcoal/Red	500670
Black, Yellow, Brown, Red	Gold/Yellow Orange/Black	500671
Black*	Gold	547501

*- S.E. models

1978-1979 Trans Am Fender Decals

Exterior Color	Decal Color	Part Numbers
White, Silver	Charcoal/Red	500670
Black, Yellow, Brown, Red	Gold/Yellow Orange/Black	500671
Blue	Blue	1003737** 1003738***
Black*	Gold	547501

*- S.E. models **- Except Japan export ***- Japan export

1977 Trans Am with Special Edition (Bandit) package.

1977-Early 1979 used an Esprit nameplate that bolted on. Later 1979 models used one that stuck on.

Listed as part number 10009246 this decal was used on the 10th Anniversary Special Edition models, and placed just below the Trans Am name on the front fenders. This car is incorrectly painted black.

A special larger hood appliqué was used on the 10th Anniversary Special Edition model. Notice how the tips of the wings flow over onto the tops of the front fenders.

Regular hood appliqué for 1979 Trans Am models.

An example of the 1979 Trans Am Fender Decals.

Some Trans Am Models used this hood callout decal, but only with the 400-ci V-8.

1980-1981

Though it may appear that the Trans Am was greatly restyled it was not. However this was the first year that the Trans Am's famous shaker hoodscoop look was no longer part of the package. In fact the standard hood on Trans Ams was the same flat hood that was used on all other Firebirds except those with the Turbo-charged 301-ci or the Formula models. Listed as part number 10011150, it was the same hood used on the 1979 base Firebird models. The Formula model used the same hood that it used in 1979 with the twin-simulated hoodscoops. All part numbers were the same including the air scoop ornaments.

The shaker style hood was optional (RPOT48) but only with the 305-ci or conventional 301-ci V-8. The new hood was part number 10014554 which featured an off center hood blister, it was used only on those models with the Turbo-charged V-8. A special ornament part number 10009232 was used on the blister. The hinges, springs and latch were all the same part that was used on the 1979 models.

Hood callouts came in two forms. Those with the 301-ci V-8 non-turbocharged which read "T/A 4.9" and those with the Turbocharged V-8 that read "TURBO 4.9". No callouts were used on the sides of the scoop (if so ordered) with the 305-ci V-8 in 1980. In 1981 this changed and those with the 305-ci used a callout that read (5.0 Liter). Be aware that there was a change in the callout decals on the 1981 models. For correctness the proper decals should be used. The difference is a slight difference in the shade of color on gold and orange colored decals. Also note that the while the Turbo 4.9 callout and Turbo hood was used on the Formula in 1981 when the Turbo 301-ci V-8 was ordered, the callouts are different, in their color tone.

Bird decals were also different if used with the Turbo hood. The bird was smaller and faced to the left, instead of the right as with the conventional powerplants. There was also a design change on the birds on the 1981 models. Like the callouts, the early models used decals that were lighter in color than the darker later models. The turbocharged vehicles with a bird decal also featured a separate flame decal that emitted from the bird's mouth and draped across the hood blister.

1980 Trans Am Hood Decals

Decal Color	Non Turbo	Turbo Bird	Turbo Flame
Charcoal	10006161	10011815* 10013459**	10013061
Red	10011783		10013059
Gold	10011810	10011814	10013058
Blue	10011811		10013060
Burgundy	10011813	10011762	
Bronze	10011791	10011784	

1981 Trans Am Hood Decals

Decal Color	Non Turbo		Turbo Bird		Notes
	Early	Late	Early	Late	
Gold	10016939	10018990	10016944	10018989	10016949-Flame* 10018988-Flame **
Orange	10016938		10016943		10016949-Flame* 10018989-Flame **
Charcoal	10016940		10016945		
Black			10019167		
Blue	10016941		10016946		10016951-Flame
Red	10016942		10016947		10016952-Flame

*-Except Special Edition. **- Special Edition used Charcoal and red / Charcoal, Red, Black and Blue were not changed.

Fenders were the same units as in 1979 for all models. The Firebird nameplates also used the same part numbers and were used on all models except the Trans Am models. The Esprit script was used below the Firebird nameplate on the front fenders and was the stick on type, the same part numbers as late 1979 models were used. On Formula models without the appearance package decals the models name was used on the front fenders just below the firebird nameplate. Decals of either three shades of blue, gold or red were used. In 1981 the Formula decal was revamped and came in gold, charcoal or orange. The orange and gold decals were changed to a darker tone midway through the model year.

Trans Am used only the decal on the front fenders and it was available in gold, red, bronze or burgundy. On cars with the Pace Car package the Indianapolis Motor Speedway decal was used below the Trans Am name; it was listed as part number 10013066. As with other models the Trans Am name was changed during 1981. When gold or orange lettering is used the later style is darker in color. It is essential for correctness that the proper shading be use.

Typical hood decal dimensions. The bird must be centered on the hood. Dimensions are from the 1978 models, Other years are similar.

Front end Trans Am decal location for 1977-1978 models.

1977-1978 front fender decal location dimensions

Grille and Front Bumper
1970-1972

The same two sets of grilles were used both years. All models except Formula or Trans Ams with the 400-ci or 455-ci powerplants used an argent silver set of grilles that were listed as part number 478512 right-hand and 478513 left-hand. Those models with a 400-ci or 455-ci powerplant used a black colored grille listed as part numbers 479690 right – hand and 479691 left-hand.

All 1970 Firebirds, except Trans Am used the Pontiac nameplate part number 481547 on the left-hand grille. In 1971 this was changed to part number 483933. Callouts were used on all models except the Trans Am models or Formula 455 models. Those with the 350 used part number 483944, while those with the 400 used part number 483945 and was placed below the Pontiac nameplate.

All but the Trans Am models used argent silver painted grille assemblies listed as part numbers 485264 right-hand and 485265 left-hand, while those on the Trans Am only were painted black and were listed as part number 485575 right -hand and 485576 left-hand. The Pontiac nameplate were listed as part number 487732 and was used on the left-hand grille of all models including the Trans Ams. Callouts were used below the nameplate on the base and Esprit models if ordered with a 350-ci (part number 487706) or a 400-ci (part number 487707).

1970 grille used no nameplate

1973

Over all design of the grille assemblies was the same as in the previous years. However, new grille units were used. All except the Trans Am models or those with the Sports Option package (read Formula) used argent silver grilles listed as part numbers 488965 right-hand and 488966-left-hand. The Formula and Trans Am models used a black accented grille listed as part numbers 491194 right-hand and 491195 left-hand. The Pontiac nameplate was listed as part number 487735 and was used on the left-hand side grille on all models. Callouts were used on the cars with the 350-ci (part number 491125) or the 400-ci (part number 491119). No callouts were used on cars with the 455-ci powerplant.

1972 Grille, for Trans Ams. The Pontiac logo should not be used.

1974-1975

The front end was given a face-lift with a sharper angled nosed and smaller grille assemblies with multiple vertical bar inserts instead of a crosshatch pattern as in previous years. The 1975 grille had vertical bars.

As before two different grille assemblies were used. All but the Trans Am and Formula models used part numbers 485546 right-hand and 485547-left-hand in 1974 and 496286 right-hand and 496287 left-hand in 1975 they were painted argent silver. Those used on the Trans Ams and Formula models were listed as part numbers 485552 right-hand and 485553-left-hand for 1974 and 496284 right-hand and 4926285 left-hand for 1975 these grilles are accented in flat black. The Pontiac nameplate was listed as part number 495108 both years and place on the left-hand grille of all models including Trans Ams. Callouts were not used on the grilles.

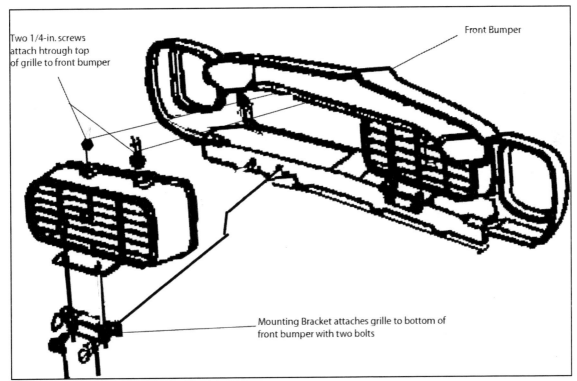

Two 1/4-in. screws attach htrough top of grille to front bumper

Front Bumper

Mounting Bracket attaches grille to bottom of front bumper with two bolts

Typical 1970-1974 Grille mounting.

153

1976 Trans Am grille Special Anniversary Edition

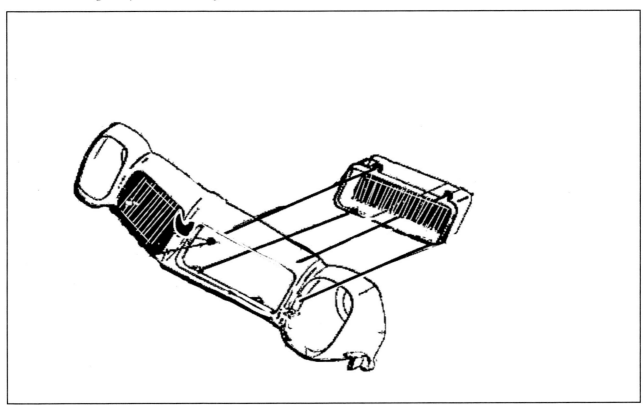

Typical grille mounting for 1974-1976 models.

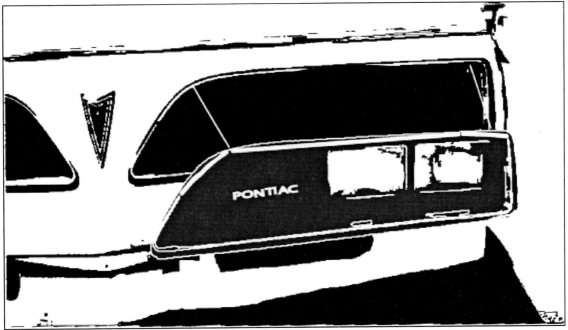

1977-1978 Grilles bolt are mounted front the outside of the bumper.

1976

Two different grilles were again used in 1976. All Firebird, including the Trans Am and Formula, except the 50th Anniversary Special Edition Trans Am models used part numbers 498835 right–hand and 498836 left-hand. The Golden Anniversary Special Edition model used special grille inserts with a honeycomb texture. They were listed as part numbers 546943 right-hand and 546944 left-hand and the frame was highlighted in gold.

The Pontiac nameplate was listed as part number 498834 and was used on the left-hand grille of all models, including the Special Edition models.

1977 Firebird Grilles

Model	Color	Part Number
Firebird	Silver	526089-RH
Esprit*		526090-LH
Skybird#	Blue	549228-RH
		549929-LH
Trans Am		526087-RH
Formula	Black	526088-LH
Trans AM S.E.	Gold	548054-RH
		548055-LH

* Except with Skybird (RPOW60) package
\#- RPOW60 pkg. option on Esprit models

1977-1978

Again the Firebird was given a much needed face-lift, the nose was given a more pronounced "bird look" with a predominate center beak. The dual headlamp design was dropped and quad headlamps returned to the Firebird. Several different grilles were used each year according to the model. Special models like Skybird, Red Bird and others required special body colored grilles. Today these grilles can be impossible to find and usually a regular grille is just painted to match.

1978 Firebird Grilles

Model	Color	Part Number
Firebird	Silver	549365-RH
Esprit*		549366-LH
Skybird#	Blue	549950-RH
		549951-LH
Redbird##	Red	10005499-RH
		10005450-LH
Trans Am		549946-RH
Formula	Black	549947-LH
Trans AM S.E.	Gold	549948 RH
		549949-LH

* Except with Skybird or Redbird packages
\#- RPOW60 pkg. option on Esprit models
\#\#-RPO W68 Redbird package

1979-1981

The front end of the 1979 Firebird looked heavier, but was more aerodynamic than before. The front bumper dominated to the front end and the grilles were smaller and placed down low on the car. The idea behind this was to pick up airflow at low pressure point on the car, near the road surface, which would help in cooling, which it did at highway speed, but temperature would rise in heavy slow moving traffic. Only one set of grille inserts were used through out the three-year run. All models used part numbers 10010503 right hand and 10010504 left-hand. They were painted black when used on the Trans Am and Formula models. No nameplates were used on the grilles.

Front Bumpers

1970-1972

It appeared that the Firebird had no front bumper instead it was a development of the 1969 design. The bumper actually was the entire front nose on the car and was painted body color. The bumper was listed as part number 477705 for all three years and all models. The Trans Am models featured a bird decal on top of the bumper in the center. Two types were used, a white and black bird for blue colored cars and a blue and black bird for white colored cars.

1973

The basic design of the earlier models (1970-1972) was carried over to the 1973 model year. However a new bumper part number 488410 featured a safety mandate reinforcement. This bumper was also body colored. The standard bird decal on the Trans Am was restyled and was more colorful. It came in blue, green or orange and was used according to the exterior color of the car. If the optional hood bird RPO WW7 was used then this decal was deleted. See hood section of this chapter for more details on this decal.

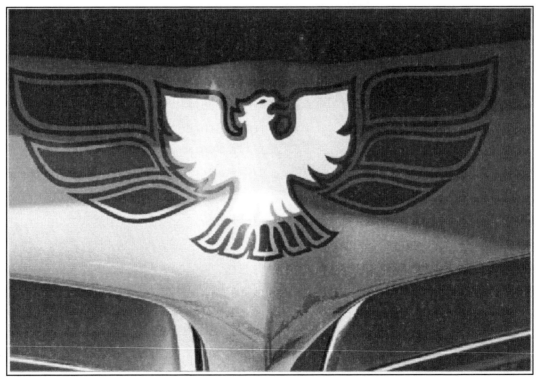

The blue colored decal was listed as part number 481953; the white bird (shown) was listed as part number 493350

1974

With the restyle of the front end the bumper was also restyled. The bumper was a black horizontal unit that was behind the urethane body colored material. Two different bumpers were used California and Maryland used part number 495461 while the other 48 states used part number 491937. Unlike the previous years the bumper was not the entire front end but was the lower portion that graduated into the front of the car due to the body color paint. A Bird medallion part number 492106 was placed in the center of the front end between the grilles.

1975

There was slight improvement over the 1974 models with more braces added. The bumper bar was listed as part number 498472, as before a bird medallion was placed in between the grilles on the front end. It was listed as part number 494476.

1976

The front bumper was listed as part number 499500 and should be painted to match the car, as in 1974-1975 it was on the lower portion of the front of the car. A small bird emblem part number 494476 was used on the front of the car in between the grilles of all models. The model name was carried on the top portion of the nose of the car on the driver's side. Several colors were used, according to the exterior color of the car.

1976 Firebird Front End Nameplates

Model	Color	Part Number
Formula	Red	525077
	Blue	525076
	Charcoal	525079
	Dark Gold	547421
Trans Am	Charcoal/Red	525470
	Gold/Yellow	527044
Trans Am S.E.	Gold	547499
Firebird Esprit	Emblem	494776

1977-1978

The front bumper on the 1977 and 1978 models is strange, as there really is no bumper. There is a reinforcement part number 525761 that hides behind the front urethane shell listed as part number 547092, which was painted to match the body that doubles for the front bumper, but there is no actual separate bumper bar. The Pontiac medallion part number 499724 was placed in the center of the front end between the grilles of all models in 1977 and all but the those 1978 models except, Esprits with the Redbird package, or the Special Edition Trans Am models. The Redbird package and the Special Edition Trans Am package used part number 10003679, which has a gold color, instead of the standard red. Decals of the model names were used on the front end of certain models on the driver's side.

1977 Firebird Front End Nameplates

Model	Color	Part Number
Formula	Red	547325
	Blue	547323
	Charcoal	547322
	Dark Gold	547421
Trans Am	Charcoal/Red	525470
	Gold/Yellow	527044
Trans Am S.E.	Gold	547499
Skybird	Blue	549892

1978 Firebird Front End Nameplates

Model	Color	Part Number
Redbird	Red	10005498

1979-1981

The front bumper on the 1979 to 1981 models was the same all three years and was the same design construction as the 1977-78 models. It consisted of a reinforcement part number 10005812 and absorber part number 10005782 and outer shell nose cone listed as part number 10004629. A red colored Pontiac crest medallion part number 499724 was used on all models except Trans Ams with the Special Edition packages and the Esprits with the Redbird or Yellowbird packages. These models used a gold colored medallion listed as part number 1003679.

Decal nameplates were used on the front end on the driver's side of Trans Am and Formula models.

1979 Firebird Front End Nameplates

Model	Color	Part Number
Formula	Red	10006118
	Blue	10006120
	Gold	11006119
Trans Am	Blue	10006143
	Red	10006144
	Charcoal	10006145
	Gold	10006146
Esprit w/W73 (Pontiac)	Gold	10006029
Redbird	Gold	10005498

1980 Firebird Front End Nameplates

Model	Color	Part Number
Formula	Red	10011611
	Gold	10011612
	Blue	10111620
Yellowbird		10011782
Yellowbird (Pontiac)	Gold	10011613

1981 Firebird Front End Nameplates

Model	Color	Part Number
Formula	Orange	10016776*
		10019000**
	Gold	10016796*
		10018999*
	Blue	1006120
	Charcoal	10016802
Esprit w/W73 (Pontiac)	Gold	10011613
Esprit w/o W73 (Pontiac)	Silver	10011613
Yellowbird		10011782

*- Early **-Late   Early lighter in color

1976 Center header panel decal

1976 Trans Am header decal with Special Edition package.

1977 Trans Am grille with Special Edition package, note how the frame is painted gold.

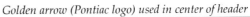

Golden arrow (Pontiac logo) used in center of header

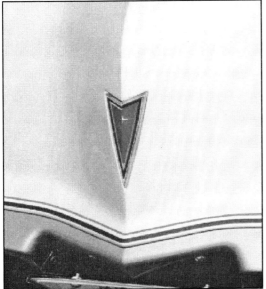

Red arrow (Pontiac logo) medallion used on 1978-1981 Firebirds except those with S.E. or appearance packages.

159

1979 Trans Am Front end decals

1979 Formula front-end decals, note the Pontiac name was originally part of this decal.

Door and Door Hinges

1970-1981

All doors are of one style, an open style for all 12 years that this book covers. In fact there is a great deal of interchange available, as doors from 1970-1981 will fit all models. However, they have to be changed with the inner door panels and handles which will most likely be incorrect. The following doors were used

1970-1981 Firebird Door Part Numbers

Model Year	Driver Side	Passengers Side
1970	9804221	9804220
1971	9863007	9863006
1972-1974	9681673	9681672
1975-1981	20162369	20162368

Hinge assembly remained constant through out the run of this guide. The upper hinges were unique to each side of the car and are listed as part numbers 1706370 right-hand and 1706371 left-hand. The bottom hinge part number 9816926 will fit either side.

Lock assemblies were listed as part number 1748553 right-hand and 1748554 left-hand for all years. They should have a natural appearance. The inside door handle was listed as part numbers 9836342 right-hand and 9836343 left-hand for 1970-1974. In an effort to save money the door handles were restyled for 1975 and now share the same handle that were used on all Ventura II models. These handles were listed as part numbers 1747336 right-hand and 20347099 left-hand.

Outer door handles, used the flush mount design all 12 years. Those models with custom trim used a colored tape insert. The tape inserts were color keyed to the exterior color of the car.

The window crank handle was used in all models except those with power windows. In 1970-1974 part number 8732962 was used, it fit either side and had a clear knob. Part number 20037597 was used from 1975-1980 it too, had a clear knob. Some Firebirds in 1981 used part number 20348200 which featured a black knob. Part number 20037597 became the replacement part for all 1970-1974 models in 1975.

The window regulators with manual windows were listed according to the interior type. Those with custom trim used a different regulator than those with the standard trim. Regulators with standard trim have a 7/8-in. long spindle. Those with power windows also used a different set of window regulators and have a provision for the power motor, but they do not differ between trim styles.

1970-1981 Firebird Window Regulator Part Numbers

Model Year	Driver Side	Passengers Side
	Manual Windows	
1970-1972	9806079*	9806078*
190-1972	9833311**	9833310**
1973-1981	20041529 (1)	20041528 (1)
	Power Windows	
1970-1972	9723313	9723312
1973-1981	20041549 (1)	20041548 (1)
	Power Window Motor	
1970-1971	5045588	5045587
1972-1979	4996678	4996680
1980-1981	1697345	22048341

*-Standard Trim **-Custom Trim (1) Replacement part for 1970-1972 models

Beginning in 1979-1981 those models with 4-wheel disc brakes used this insert in the door handles. It was available in red, blue, charcoal or gold lettering. This was a separate decal and was used over the body color tape insert.

1970-1974 Style of inner door handle.

Cars with custom trim or special packages used body color tape inside the outside door handle.

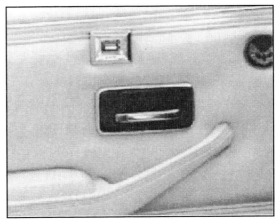

1975-1981 style of inner door handle.

Outside Mirror-Standard
1970-1981

Unlike other Pontiacs the 1970-1972 Firebird came standard with a body colored racing mirror on the driver's side only. Listed as part number 9865801 it was used on all models, the outer case was painted to match the upper portion of the door. In 1973, although it is hardly ever seen a chrome plated manual control mirror was standard. It was listed as part number 9814436; it remained standard till the end of 1981. This mirror could fit either side of the car, but was only installed by the dealer on the passenger's side. More common was the racing mirror. The left-hand unit was listed as part number 9606231 and was remote controlled. The matching right-hand unit part number 20154908 was manually controlled. Both units were painted to match the upper portion of the door; they too were available till the end of the 1981 model year.

Certain models used stripes around the mirror. These included the 1976-1979 Black Special Edition Trans Ams which used gold colored stripes. The 1977-1980 Esprit with Skybird package used blue stripes. The 1978 Trans Am Gold Special Edition models used dark gold stripes. The 1979 Trans Am with the 10th Anniversary Package used Charcoal stripes. The 1979 Formula models used red, gold or blue colored stripes. The gold and blue stripes were used again in 1980 on the Formula models. The 1980 Esprit with the Yellowbird package used gold stripes, and the 1981 Formula models with the W50 appearance group package, used blue, orange or black colored stripes. The 1980 Trans Am with the pace car package, used charcoal stripes.

1972 sport mirror

Some mirrors like this 1977 model have dual pin stripes on them.

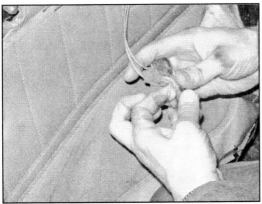

The control handle for the remote control mirror is held in place with a natural appearing clip. This clip must be removed and retained to remove the sport mirror.

To remove the doors support door with a floor jack and then remove the hinge bolts. First mark the location of the hinges with a pen

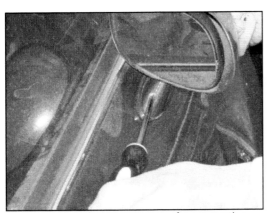

To remove the side mirror unscrew from mounting bracket.

Once the retaining screws are removed, the 1979-1981 grille just slides out of the front bumper.

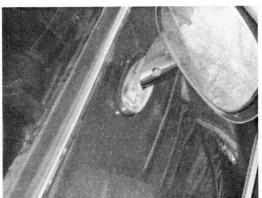

The mirror bracket on the door has a natural appearance.

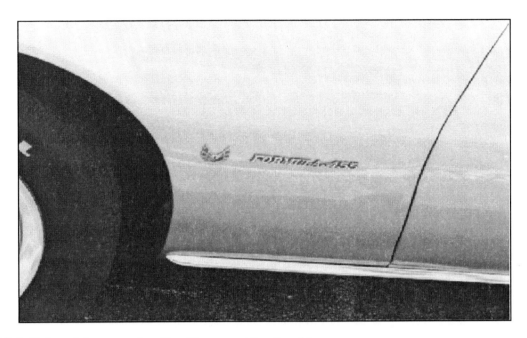

All firebirds used the same rocker sill moldings except Esprit models

Rocker Panels and Moldings

The rocker panel consisted of a two-part design. The part numbers were listed as 1680401 right-hand and 1680402 left-hand for the outer and 9820060 right-hand and 9820061 left-hand for all 12 years. The outer moldings depend on the model and model year.

For all 12 years two different molding were used. All but the Trans Am and Esprit models used a narrow molding listed as part number 481546 both years and it fit either side. The Esprit model used a wider (3.00 in.) molding that was unique to each side of the car; they were listed as part numbers 481539 right-hand and 481540 left-hand.

Roof and Drip Moldings
1970-1981

A total of four different roof assemblies were used throughout the 12 year run. The 1970-1973 models used part number 9668359, while the 1974 model used part number 9739600. In 1975 the rear window wrapped around the sides and a new panel was required. It was listed as part number 20212998, in 1976 the hatch roof option (RPO CC1) became available ;no new roof was made, the standard roof was converted to fit the Hurst built glass panels.

In 1978 the Hurst hatch was phased out after several production problems with T-top roof panels not sealing well and leaking. With this came the Fisher built, panels along with it a new part listed as part number 20176800 to accommodate the glass panels. Both the Fisher and the Hurst panels were used in 1978 models. The Fisher panels were larger extending more rearward and more towards the center. They had the feeling that they were built with the car, while the smaller Hurst built hatches had a feeling of an add on feature.

The Fisher built panels had black finished outer trim, while most (but not all) of the Hurst built hatches had bright trim. Also the center section in between the panel is wider on those with Hurst hatches. Of the two those with the Hurst hatch is more desirable. From 1979 on only the Fisher built hatch was used. Note that the 10th Anniversary Edition Trans Am in 1979 and the Pace car Editions in 1980 used silver colored lifted glass panels.

Windshield Molding Part Numbers

Model Year	Upper	Sides	Lower
1970-1972	9808500	9841148-RH	9841146 RH*
		9841149-LH	9841147-LH*
1973-1981	9739207#	9868730-RH#	3062231-RH
		9868731-LH#	3062232-LH
		With Revel moldings (Black)	
1976-81	3064183	3064186- RH	3062231-RH
		3064187- LH	3062232-LH

* Plastic corner moldings #-Replacement part number for 1970-1972 models.

Roof Molding Part Numbers

Scalp	Lace (Door meets Roof)
20092658 RH	20136316 RH
1652949 LH*	20136317 LH

Rear Window Molding Part Numbers

Upper	Sides		Lower
		1970-1974	
9690565	9854740 RH*		9690566 RH
	9854741 LH*		9690567 LH
		1975-1981	
9738198	9738210-RH		9738212
	9738211-LH		

Rear Quarter Panel And Moldings
1970-1981

The rear quarter panel was dependent on model year. If a vinyl top or two-tone was ordered, than a quarter belt moldings were used. Part numbers were listed as 9841310 right-hand and 9841311 left-hand for 1970-1974 models, for 1975-1981 models part numbers 1659548 right-hand and 1659549 left-hand were used. The wheel well opening trim was listed as part numbers 8704037 right-hand and 8704038 left-hand all 12 years. However, wheel trim moldings were not used on Trans Am models.

The Esprit model script part number 9828627 was used on the rear roof sail panels from 1970-1975. Beginning in 1976 a Firebird decal was placed on the sail panels of certain models, these birds came in a variety of colors that were used according to the package options on the car and the exterior color.

A gold color bird decal part number 547497 was used on the Special Edition Black Trans Ams. A blue colored bird was used on Esprits with the 1977-1978 Skybird package, it was listed as part number 549568, and a red color bird was used with the 1978-1979 Redbird packages. The Red bird decal was listed as part number 10002976, and was special design, with a softer appearing design. The 1979-1980 Firebirds all came with a decal that was color-coded to the exterior color of the car.

Note, there were changes in the color of orange and gold colored birds on the 1981 models the earlier models are lighter in color. For correctness the proper decal must be used. The colors of blue, charcoal and red colored birds were not changed.

1978 Gold bird decal used with special edition models

Red/orange bird used with black, red and yellow cars.

Charcoal colored sail panel bird.

Trunk Lid and Rear End Panel

The trunk lid used part number 9819030 all 12 years, with or without a spoiler, for all body styles. Likewise only one set of strap-hinges were used and listed as part numbers 9723492 right-hand and 9723493 left-hand. Two torque rods were used. Part number 9868539 was used on the left-hand side of all models; it was color-coded with green paint. The torque rod on the right-hand side was determined by whether or not a rear spoiler was used. Those without a rear spoiler used part number 9868538, it was color coded with red paint. Since the rear spoiler added weight to the deck lid a stiffer rated torque rod part number 9868539 was required, it was color coded with yellow paint.

1970-1973
The rear end panel supported the tail lamps, and trunk lock mechanism. The 1970-1973 models used the same panel listed as part number 9869602 and featured a fiberglass finishing panel part number 9851259 that was held in place with four attaching studs and nuts.

The Pontiac name was spelled out in individual letters across the center of the rear end panel each year. The 1970 originally used different letters than the 1971-1973 models, which became the replacement in 1975.

1970 Rear End Panel Lettering

P	9812717	O	9812718
N	9812719	T	9812720
I	9812721	A	9812722
C	9812723		

1971-1973 Rear End Panel Lettering

P	9855976	O	9855977
N	9855978	T	9855979
I	9855980	A	9855981
C	9855982		

A Firebird medallion part number 20193825 was used on the trunk lid on the rearward edge in the center, but was used only on models without a rear spoiler. Likewise a "400" callout part number 9808505 was used on the right hand side of the deck lid, but only on models with the 400 powerplant and no rear spoiler, this callout was used only on the 1970 models.

The Trans Am name was placed across the rear face of the rear spoiler. For 1970-1972 either white was used on the blue colored cars, or on white colored cars were used. For 1973 the name TRANS AM was spelled out and now the color choices were blue part number 493375 for white colored cars, green part number 493374 for green cars and orange part number 493373 for red colored cars.

1976-1978 models, except Trans Ams with a rear spoiler, used this decal. Shown is the white colored bird used on blue colored cars. Blue and orange were also available

1970 Rear end panel lettering.

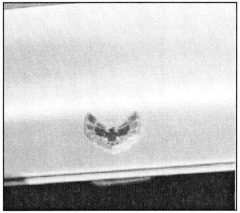

Firebird medallion used from 1970-1981, see text for usage.

1974-1976

The Firebird medallion was placed in the center rear edge of the trunk lid on all Firebird models without a rear spoiler. When the rear spoiler was ordered on any other model except Trans Am, the Firebird medallion was deleted and a Firebird decal was added to the rear face of the spoiler in the center. A total of three different colors were used; blue part number 493370, green 493371 and orange part number 493372. The Trans Am name was offered in the same colors as the 1973 model and used the same part numbers.

For 1975 the Firebird medallion was used again, but was used with or without the rear spoiler. The Pontiac nameplate part number 1728933 was placed on the right-hand side of the trunk lid's face. The Trans Am nameplate continued to be a decal that was placed on the rear face of the rear spoiler. Color choices now were orange, blue and charcoal.

For 1976 all except Trans Am or Esprit with appearance package used a Firebird medallion on the trunk lid, part number was the same as before. The Pontiac nameplate was used on the far right hand side of the deck lid and was listed as part number 1728933.

On Formula models the Formula name was a decal and placed above the Pontiac nameplate. This decal came in blue, red or charcoal; color usage was regulated by exterior color of the car.

1976 Formula Trunk Lid Decals-Without Spoiler

Color	Part Number	Exterior Colors
Blue	525076	White, or blue cars
Red	525077	Red or Yellow, Orange cars
Charcoal	525079	Silver cars

Formulas with a rear spoiler used a different decal than those without the spoiler. They were offered in the same colors as those without the spoiler, but the part numbers were different. The Pontiac nameplate was changed to a decal that matched the color of the Formula decal.

1976 Formula Trunk Lid Decals-With Spoiler

Color	Part Number	Exterior Colors
Blue	525084	White, or blue cars
Red	525085	Red or Yellow, Orange cars
Brown	525086	Brown cars
Charcoal	825087	Silver cars

Pontiac Name Decal

Color	Part Number	Exterior Colors
Blue	525097	White, or blue cars
Red	525095	Red or Yellow, Orange cars
Brown	525098	Brown cars
Charcoal	525099	Silver cars

A bird decal was used on the rear face of all cars with a rear spoiler, except the Trans Am models. These birds were offered in blue, brown, charcoal or red. These birds measured 7.22 in wide. The Trans Am name was still a decal, it was offered in charcoal or gold. Those early models used bright gold while later models used matte gold. It is important that the proper shade be used. These do not apply to those 2,590 Trans Am built with the RPO Y82 Special Edition package. These models used special gold decals (part number 547500) with German style lettering. The Pontiac name decal in gold and black part number 547498 was used on the right-hand side of the rear face of the spoiler. The Pontiac name decal was also used here with other Trans Ams in gold or charcoal. Like the Trans Am decal, early models used bright gold while later models used matte gold.

1977-1978

A bird medallion, or decal was used on the trunk lid as in previous years for all models except Trans Am or Formula models. The Pontiac nameplate part number 1728933 was used on the far right-hand side of the trunk lid of the base Firebird and Esprit models unless the Skybird appearance package was ordered along with a rear spoiler. If the Skybird package was ordered without a rear spoiler than the medallion was removed and the Skybird name was placed in the center, which was part of the stripes on the car. If the rear spoiler was ordered with the package, then an unique bird decal part number 10000417 was used in the center rear face of the spoiler. On the right-hand side of the spoiler face was the Skybird Pontiac decal listed as part number 549892.

Formula models without a rear spoiler used a small bird decal in the center rear face of the trunk lid. The Pontiac nameplate was removed and replaced by a "Formula Pontiac" decal. That came in a ray of colors that color-sorted according to the exterior color of the car. When the rear spoiler was ordered the small bird decal was replaced with a larger bird decal and placed on the rear face of the spoiler. The Formula Pontiac decal was also changed and placed on the spoiler. But some used separate decals for the Formula name and used the standard Pontiac decal.

1977-1978 Formula Trunk Lid Decals-Without Spoiler

Color	Part Number	Exterior Colors
Blue	525076	White ,or blue cars
Red	525077	Red or Yellow, Orange cars
Charcoal	525079	Silver cars

1977-1978 Formula Trunk Lid Decals-With Spoiler

Color	Part Number	Notes
Blue	547329	With Pontiac Name
Red	547331	With Pontiac Name
Green	547332	With Pontiac Name
Charcoal	547328	With Pontiac Name
Gold	547422	With Pontiac Name
Blue	547424	Without Pontiac Name
Red	547426	Without Pontiac Name
Aqua	547425	Without Pontiac Name
Charcoal	547423	Without Pontiac Name
Gold	547428	Without Pontiac Name

Pontiac Name Decal

Color	Part Number
Blue	525097
Red	525095
Brown	525098
Charcoal	525099
Gold	527043

1976-1978 Trans Am trunk lid decal with Special Edition package.

Example of the trunk lid lettering used on the 10th Anniversary Edition Trans Am in 1979, note the special decal to the right.

Standard Trans Am Rear spoiler lettering.

Trans Am continued to use decals for nameplates on the rear face of the spoiler. Colors and part numbers were the same as they were in 1976, except that all gold color is matte gold, save those black Special Edition models which used the same gold and lettering that was used in 1976. As before the Pontiac name decal was used on the spoiler.

1979

As in previous years the base Firebird and Esprit models and Formulas without the rear spoiler used a Firebird crest medallion, part number 20193825. The Pontiac name was a decal placed on the right-hand side of the trunk lid. A bird decal was used when a spoiler was ordered on a car, except with the Trans Am. Those models with the Redbird package were the same as in 1978, which consisted of a gold colored decal that read Redbird and was placed in the center of the trunk's rear face or on the right-hand side if the rear spoiler was ordered.

Formula models used a Formula Pontiac decal on the rear spoiler. It came in red, gold or blue. Trans Am continued to use decals on the rear spoiler, three distinct styles were used. Those used on the Standard Trans Am without the Special Edition package came in gold or light argent, they were actually multiple colored but they are the dominant colors. Those with the Special edition package used smaller charcoal color lettering part number 10002966 and this is followed by a special 10th Anniversary decal listed as part number 1009245, and is placed on the rear face of the spoiler.

1980-1981

Trans Ams continued to use decals on the rear spoiler. Two types were used: those without the 301-ci Turbo-charged power-plant used decals that read Trans Am, those with this powerplant used decals that read Turbo Trans Am. Likewise the Formulas with the turbo motor used decals that read Formula Turbo. Without this powerplant Formulas used decals that read Formula.

Color Choices were red, gold, bronze and burgundy for the Trans Am models. Gold, burgundy, charcoal and bronze for the Turbo Trans Ams. Formula lettering was in gold. The yellow bird decals were in yellow gold. For 1981 the names were the same, but the color choices varied slightly. Those

171

Trans Ams without the turbocharged powerplant used TRANS AM name. It came gold, orange, charcoal blue and red colors. These same colors were offered with the Turbo motor, but the decal read " TURBO TRANS AM". There was a change in the gold and orange colors mid way through the year. The later styles are darker in color.

Formula models without the turbo charged 301-ci engines used Formula decals while those with the turbocharger used "Turbo Formula" decals. They were offered in gold, orange blue and charcoal. Like the Trans Am decals both sets of these decals had changed to darker shades on the gold and orange color decals.

Glass Part Numbers

Model	Clear	Tinted	Notes:
Windshield			
1970-1979	3062233#	3062234#	* Early 1970 Used ball type mirror
	3062235*	3062236*	#- Without Antenna
1980-1981	9841588#	1735277#	
	9841588	9841589	
Door Glass			
1970-1981	9864176- R.H.	9864178- R.H.	
	9864177- L.H.	9864179- L.H.	
Back Glass			
1970-1974	8775901	8775902	**- with electric defroster
		9821093**	
1975-1981	9733868	9733869	
		20213672**	

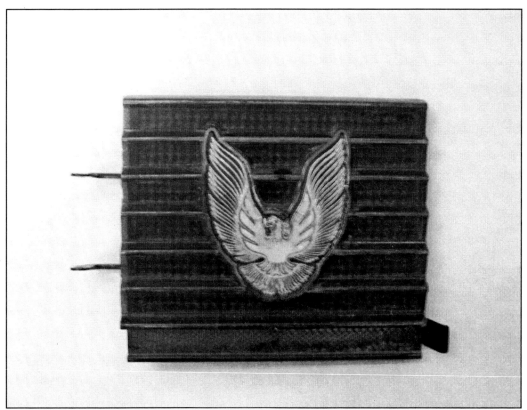

1979-1981 Firebirds or Trans Ams with the standard trim used this rare center panel in the tail lamps.

Spoilers
1970-1981

The most incorrect thing about most Firebirds today is the addition of a rear spoiler, when that car did not come with it originally. Standard only on the Trans Am all 12 years, it was optional on all other models, but most Formulas had the optional blade type spoiler.

The rear spoiler consisted of three different parts the middle spoiler that attached to the trunk lid, and the extension that were attached to the top of the rear quarter panels, and completed the full width look at the rear of the car. The center spoiler unit was listed as part number 480161 all 12 years. While the center unit remained the same two different sets of extensions were used. The 1970-1974 models used part numbers 480159 right-hand and 480160 left-hand. The 1975-1981 models used part numbers 493687 right-hand and 493688 left-hand. The spoiler was usually painted the same color as the rest of the body, and decorated with stripes. See Sport Stripes section of this chapter for more details.

While the rear spoiler was optional on all Firebird models, the front spoiler was used and standard only on the Trans Am models, except those exported to Japan, where only the center section was used. The spoiler consisted of a center spoiler and outer wheel flares on the front wheel well openings. Originally these items were molded in color that matched the car's exterior color. Some early (1970-1974) Tran Ams originally used plastic front valances that allowed the spoiler to be mounted, those with a steel valance required a special mounting kit listed as part number 486036.

Beginning in 1976 the spoiler was molded in silver and had to be painted to match the car's exterior color. For 1979-1981 the front spoiler was change to a urethane plastic and has to be painted to match the car but in a urethane finish.

Thought it is not part of the front spoiler, small flares were added to the front edge of the rear wheel well openings to act as spoilers there. Unfortunately all this dress was just that, as they had no benefit at highway speeds except to look fast.

Front fender flares gave the spoiler a full width appearance, shown are those on a 1979 model.

The center rear spoiler was listed as part number 480161 all 12 years.

Front Spoiler and Wheel Flare Part Numbers						
Color	Spoiler	Front Flares		Rear Flares		Notes
		Right-Hand	Left-Hand	Right-Hand	Left-Hand	
1970-1975						
White	481629	483889	483890	483887	483888	
Blue	482007	482011	482012	482049	482050	1970-1972 only
Red	494195	489751	489752	489740	489741	1973-75 only
Blue	494194	494306	494307	494308	494309	1974 only
Dark Blue	496808	496804	496805	496798	496799	1975 Only
Silver	498401	498399	498400	498404	498405	1975 only
Green	494196	489752	489753	489742	489743	1973 only
1976-1978						
Paint to match	10005779	526825	526825	526829	526830	
1979-1981						
	10006809	10006865	10006866	10006833	10006834	Except Japan Export
Fender flares where not used on Japan export models nor was rear spoiler						

Rear Bumpers

1970-1973

Unlike the front bumpers the rear bumpers were brightly plated chrome. Though they are very similar, the 1973 unit is slightly different than the 1970-1972 unit listed as part number 9799744. The 1973 unit part number 484947, is an impact type bar, which simply meant that it is heavier. The 1973 bar became the replacement bar for the 1970-1972 models in 1974. There are also differences in the brackets, all brackets should be painted flat black.

1974-1975

In 1974 the rear bumper was painted to match the exterior color of the car. The outer urethane shell, which was the actual bumper, was backed up by a flat black reinforcement, which was attached to the body by brackets. The bumper was listed as part number 492015 in 1974 and part number 499737 in 1975.

174

A close up of the front spoiler on a 1970 Trans Am. Not the flat black appearance of the mounting bolts,and the sloppy fit, which is typical of original cars.

Rear wheel flares were standard with Trans Am models except those being exported to Japan

1976-1978

Due to federal mandates the bumper had to be restyled, to pass the crash test an absorber part number 549509 had to be installed between the outer shell part number 526899, which was still painted to match the body, and the reinforcement bar part number 549510 that was held to the body by brackets.

1979-1981

Basically the same set up that was used in 1976-78 but restyled parts. The reinforcement bar was deleted and replaced with a slimmer bumper bar part number 10003955 and was covered by a restyled outer shell part number 10004176 that was again painted to match the lower portion of the car. In between the bumper and the outer shell was a restyled absorber part number 10004243. Mounting brackets were deleted and supports on the back of the bumper bar were used to secure the bumper assembly to the car.

Sport Stripes
1970-1972

Basically there was one stripe treatment that was used on the Trans Am models. These stripes came in either white for blue colored cars or the more common blue stripes for white cars. The blue stripes should have a fade out pattern at the edges like the originals. The blue stripes should have a solid black border. The white and blue stripes were originally a single layer, many reproductions are of a layer type and that is incorrect. The stripe kits consisted of three-part design: hood, roof, and trunk lid and were positioned on the centerline of the car. It is incorrect for these stripes to be painted on. All stripes were decal type. It is strongly recommended that you have a professional shop do the installation of these stripes, as it easy to stretch the film.

1970-1972 Trans Am Stripes

Color	Hood	Roof	Trunk
White	481969*	481962*	481965
	483712	483883	
Blue	481970	481963	481964

8-1970 only

Sport stripes were available on the 1972 Firebird, except the Trans Am models. These stripes ran along the bottom portion of the car on the same axis as the rear side marker lamp from the rear edge of the front wheel well opening to the end of the car. They were available in White, Black or Red. Listed as option RPO D98 they were made of vinyl.

1970-1972 Trans Am came with a single stripe that was routed down the middle of the car.

Two distinct styles were used. Blue stripes with white cars and white and black stripes with blue cars.

1973

Two or three-tone accent stripes were optional (RPO D98) on all models. The stripes were decal type and were routed along the upper design of the body sides from the front of the front fender to just shy of the rear edge of the door. A total of four colors were offered, the color choice depended on the exterior color of the car. The stripe was one long unit originally and not two separate units, but was unique to each side of the car.

1973 Accent Stripes

Colors	Part Number
Blue/Black	493166 RH
	493167 LH
Yellow/Green/Black	493168 RH
	493169 LH
Red/Orange/Brown	493170 RH
	493171 LH
Black/Orange	493172 RH
	493173 LH

1974-1975

Accent stripes were again optional and took the same route as they used in 1973, and featured a black background. Unlike the 1973 version these stripes were two separate units; one for the fender and one for the door, and like the 1973 units they were unique to each side of the car. A total of three colors were used.

1974-1975 Accent Stripes

Color	Fender	Door
Orange/Black	495605-RH	491058 RH
	495606 LH	491059 LH
Green/Black	495607-RH	495609 RH
	495608 LH	495610 LH
Blue/Black	491050-RH	495611 RH
	491051 LH	495612 LH

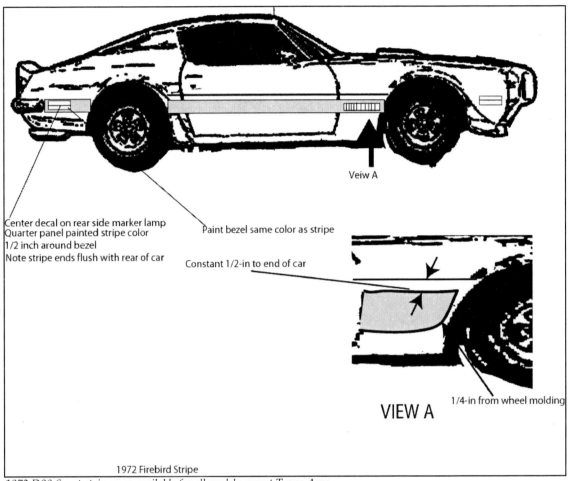

Center decal on rear side marker lamp
Quarter panel painted stripe color
1/2 inch around bezel
Note stripe ends flush with rear of car

Paint bezel same color as stripe

Constant 1/2-in to end of car

Veiw A

1/4-in from wheel molding

VIEW A

1972 Firebird Stripe

1972 D98 Sport stripe was available for all models except Trans Ams

1976-1978

Stripes went crazy in 1976, as separate option for all models, except those with appearance packages. That used the same route as in 1975, but instead of ending at the door the stripes went up and over the roof of the car. Like the 1975, the stripes were separate items and came in a triple shade with a black edge. These stripes were mostly seen on the Formula models but were available on all models including Trans Am. They were listed as option RPO D98, and were offered in seven different shades, with the exterior color of the car determining the usage. The color or availability of the stripe can be determined by the code on the Fisher body tag.

1976 Trans Am with Special Edition package used dual gold pin stripe on the trunk, this route would again be repeated on the later Black S. E. models

178

1976-1978 D98 Accent Stripes

Color	Fender		Door	Roof
Blue	525257 RH		525267 RH	525277
	525258 LH		525268-LH	
Silver/White	525259- RH		525269 RH	525278
/Charcoal	525260 LH		525270-LH	
Red	525261- RH		525271 RH	525279
	525262 LH		525272-LH	
Brown	525265- RH		525275 RH	525281
	525266 LH		525276-LH	

Color	Option Code
Blue	24A
Silver/White /Charcoal	13A
Red	78A
Brown	64A

Stripes were also available as part of package option like the RPO W50 appearance package on the Formula models. This package greatly dressed up the Formula and gave it that road racer look. It consisted of pin stripes in a two-tone shade that were routed along the front bumper and the lower body sides and around the rear bumper to the other side of the car, the Formula name in a racing stripe just continued the stripe across the door. The stripe was the same color as the rest of the pin striping.   There were also stripes on forward edges of the hood scoops that match the same color as the sides.

1976 Formula W-50 Appearance Group Stripes

Front Bumper	Front Fender Front	Front Fender Rear	Formula Door Decal	Rear Quarter	Rear Bumper
Blue					
525171-RH 525167 525172- LH			525195		525219-Upper 525215-Lower
Charcoal Red					
525177- LH 525170 525178- LH			525198		525222- RH Upper 525223- RH Upper 525217- Lower
Red					
525173- RH 525168 525174- LH			525196		525220-RH- Upper 525221-LH Upper 525216-Lower

The most popular stripe package was the one used on the RPO Y82 Special Edition Trans Am. As part of 50th Anniversary of Pontiac special gold color pin stripes were placed on a black Trans Am. The stripes are unique by the fact they are double pin stripes. The wrapped around the lower edges of the car across the front spoiler, the wheel well opening and fender flares and the rear bumper plus around the hood scoop opening behind the scoop and over the roof and the deck lid.   They were also wrapped around the tail lamps, the grille openings and the forward edge of the fender scoops. There were also gold stripes around the front and rear windows. This is one of the high-decorated cars of the year.

Gold pin striping was also placed around the wheel openings and outer edges of the fender flares. Shown is a 1977 model. The striping remained the same for 1976-1978.

Gold pin striping was used around the grille openings with the black Special Edition package, shown is a 1977 model.

Note the dual pin stripes on the hood around the scoop opening.

Note the gold pin stripes around the fender scoop opening and the top edges of the hood and door.

Close up of scoop with Special Edition package. 1977 models are shown.

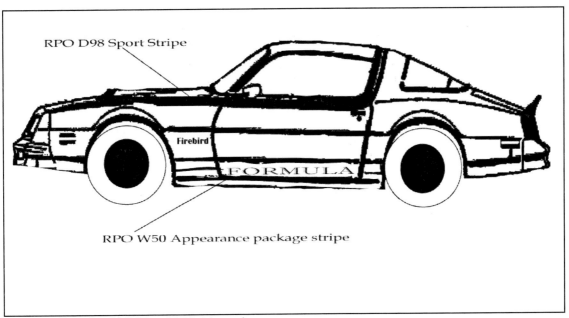

1976-1978 Formula with W50 and D98 stripe packages.

1977-1978 Formula W-50 Appearance Group Stripes					
Front Bumper	**Front Fender Front**	**Front Fender Rear**	**Formula Door Decal**	**Rear Quarter**	**Rear Bumper**
Blue					
525171-RH 525167 525172- LH	549994- RH 549995 -LH	1000003- RH 1000004- LH	525195	Front 10000011- RH 10000012- LH Rear 10000019- RH 10000020- LH	525219-Upper 525215-Lower
Charcoal Red					
525177- LH 525170 525178- LH	549998- RH 549999 -LH	1000009- RH 1000010- LH	525198	Front 10000015- RH 10000016- LH Rear 10000024- RH 10000025- LH	525222- RH Upper 525223- RH Upper 525217- Lower
Red					
525173- RH 525168 525174- LH	549996- RH 549997 -LH	1000005- RH 1000006- LH	525196	Front 10000013- RH 10000014- LH Rear 10000021- RH 10000022- LH	525220-RH- Upper 525221-LH Upper 525216-Lower

181

The stripe package return for 1977 and 1978, and basically had the same pattern as before and many part numbers were the same. The Formula W50 package used wider side stripes. And the Special Edition package returned on a limited number of Trans Am models.

A new stripe pattern was also used on those 1977-1978 Esprits with the W60 Skybird and the 1978 RPO W68 Redbird packages.

The Skybird package consisted of blue colored pin stripes that wrapped around the center hood peak and then across the back of the hood and the top of the front fenders, around the top of the door, behind the side mirror, up the rear roof pillar where a Skybird decal was placed. Then the stripe across up on the roof just above the door, down the windshield pillar another blue pin stripe was wrapped around the back window. A blue pin stripe was also wrapped around the car across the bumpers and the lower sides of the car. While blue pinstripes were used else where on the car, red colored pinstripes were used around the tail lamps and the bottom edge of the rear spoiler if it was ordered. The 1978 Redbird package RPO W68 used the same pattern as the Skybird blue but the stripes were gold, and the paint was darker red below the pinstripes on the body, this includes the lower portions of the bumpers and doors.

1979 RPOD98 Sport Stripe

1979-1981

The RPO D98 Accent stripes were restyled and rerouted. They consisted of a multiple colored format that ran along the top design line of the car from tip of front fender to the rear of the quarter panel. The stripes were of a three-part design. And when the stripes were ordered the standard bird medallion on the rear roof pillars was replaced with color coordinated bird decal.

These stripes were available for most models, but were not available with appearance package.

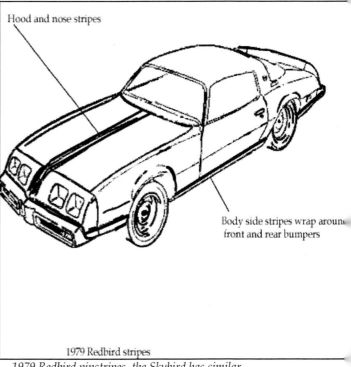

1979 Redbird pinstripes, the Skybird has similar routes.

1979-1981 D98 Accent Stripes

Color	Fender	Door	Quarter Panel	Bird Decal Color	Part Number
Argent/Red	10007847-RH	10007848-RH	10007850-RH	Silver	1006139
	10007846-LH	10007849-LH	10007851-LH		
Blue/Gold	10007839-RH	10007841-RH	10007843-RH	Blue	1006140
	10007840-LH	10007842-LH	10007844-LH		
Red /Gold	10007832-RH	10007834-RH	10007836-RH	Red	1006141
	10007833-LH	10007835-LH	10007837-LH		
Gold/Ochre	10007853-RH	10007855-RH	10007857-RH	Gold	1006138
	10007854-LH	10007856-LH	10007858-LH		

1979 D98 Accent Stripe Color Break Down				
Main Colors	**1st Color**	**2nd color**	**3rd Color**	**4th Color**
Argent/Red	Dark Silver	Medium Silver	Light Siver	Red
Blue/Gold	Dark Blue	Medium Blue	Light Blue	Gold
Red /Gold	Dark Orange	Red	Dark Red	Gold
Gold/Ochre	Dark Gold	Medium Gold	Light Gold	Dark Ochre

The Formula appearance group W50 looked much like that of previous years. It included two tone stripes that were routed along the lower portion of the bumpers and the sides of the car. The Formula name decal was used on the bottom portion of the doors. Do not confuse this with the appearance package option W66, which was similar to the RPO W50, but did have the Formula graphics on the doors, and instead used the Formula name on the front fenders below the Firebird nameplate. Nor were there any stripe accents on the hoodscoops.

Also the pinstripe around the bottom portion of the car was one color. They came in red, blue or gold. This package was not available with a rear spoiler, and the Formula name decal was placed below the tail lamp on the right-hand side. A decal that read "4-wheel Disc" was placed on the rear roof pillar below the bird decal, but only with the standard trim, with custom trim the decal was used on the door handles.

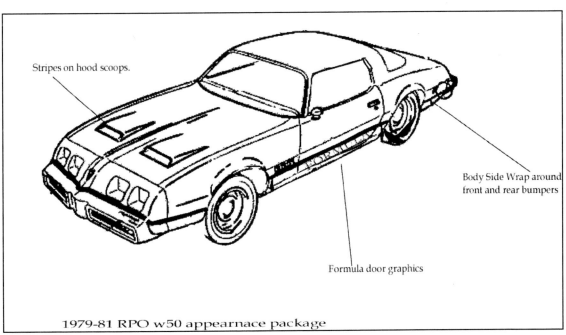

Stripes on hood scoops.

Body Side Wrap around front and rear bumpers

Formula door graphics

1979-81 RPO w50 appearnace package

1979 Formula with W50 appearance package.

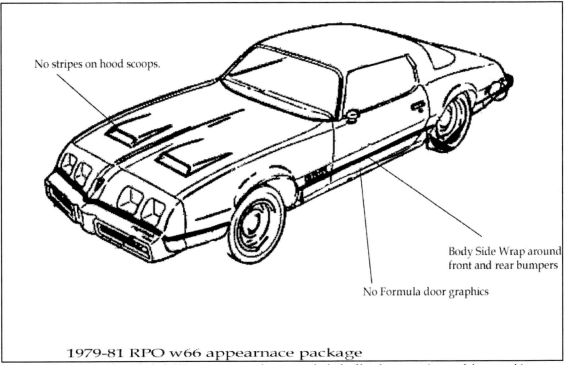

No stripes on hood scoops.

Body Side Wrap around front and rear bumpers

No Formula door graphics

1979-81 RPO w66 appearnace package

The lesser know Formula with the W66 appearance package, note the lack of hood scoop stripes and door graphics.

The Skybird package was deleted but the Redbird appearance package with its gold color pin stripes continued. The scheme was pretty much the same as before with only modifications done to enhance the new front and rear ends.

The 10th Anniversary Special Edition Trans Am used a more sedate striping scheme that wrapped charcoal colored stripes around the lower portion of the car, around the air extractors, the tail end and around hatch roof panels.

1980

There were very few changes in 1980 The RPO D98 accent stripes were the same as those on both the W50 and W66 Formula packages. The position for the 4-wheel disc brake decal was moved backward just under the back window where it wraps around the side of the car, if so equipped and only with

the standard trim. The decal was offered in charcoal or white. The red bird package was cancelled and replaced with the RPO W73 Yellowbird package, which used the same striping scheme as the 1979 Redbird, and like the redbird package used gold colored stripes. The black Y84 Special Edition used the same gold stripe scheme that was used in 1979. The Y85 Pace car edition was available only with the 301-ci Turbo and included special striping around the bumper and wheel well opening, as well as the rear spoiler and hatch roof openings. On the tail it used a special decal that commemorates the Indy 500.   This package was offered again in 1981 but with NASCAR decal instead of Indy decals

An example of a three-tone stripe used on the 1979 Formula

Another view of the 1979 W50 appearance package.

Stripes were used around the mirrors in the W50 option group.

Example of gold striping on a 1979 Trans Am

Cordova Top

A vinyl top was optional on all hardtop Firebirds, except those with the optional T-top or the D98 accent stripe, and the 1970-1972 Trans Am, or with Special Edition packages. The vinyl top is more common on Esprits and the 1970-1973 models than other models; it is externally rare on the 1973-1977 Trans Am models. It came is variety of colors; the color can be determined by the code used on the Fisher body tag for the upper body color.

Cordova Vinyl Top Color Codes

1970

Code	Color
1	White
2	Black
5	Sandalwood
7	Dark Gold

1971-1972

1	White
2	lack
5	Sandalwood
7	Dark Brown
9	Dark Green

Cordova Vinyl Top Color Codes

1973		1979	
A		11T	White
B	Black	15T	Platinum Poly
D	Med. Blue	19T	Black
F	Med Chamois	22T	Light Blue
G	Med. Green	40T	Pastel Green
H	Maroon	61T	Medium Beige
T	Lt. Neutral	79T	Dark Carmine

1974		1980	
A	White	11T	White
B	Black	19T	Black
D	Medium Blue	21T	Light Blue
E	Cream Beige	44T	Dark Green
F	Brown	63T	Camel
G	Med. Green	76T	Dark Claret
H	Maroon	85T	Gray
L	Russet		
R	Med. Saddle		
W	Silver Taupe		

1975		1981	
11T	White	11T	White
13T	Silver	19T	Black
19T	Black	29T	Dark Blue
28T	Dark Blue	36T	Waxberry
44T	Med. Green	45T	Jadestone
55T	Sandstone	63T	Pastel Sandstone
68T	Cordovan	64T	Doeskin
74T	Maroon	77T	Maple
75T	Red	85T	Med. Slate

1976	
11T	White
13T	Silver
19T	Black
35T	Dark Blue
36T	Firethorn
37T	Mahogany
65T	Light Buckskin

1977	
11T	White
13T	Silver
19T	Black
22T	Light Blue
36T	Firethorn
44T	Medium Green
61T	Light Buckskin

1978	
11T	White
15T	Platinum Poly
19T	Black
22T	Light Blue
79T	Dark Carmine
44T	Medium Green
61T	Light Buckskin

Interior

Instrument Panel
1970-1981

The instrument panel consisted of a two-part design, the upper panel and a instrument panel pad that was originally molded in a color that was keyed to the interior trim. These part numbers were only used a couple of years, and then deleted as a black colored panel took their place as the replacement part. This way instead of listing all the original part numbers we have focused on the black colored panel only, as that is what the reproduction parts are. The panel will have to be repainted to match the interior trim this requires a special paint. We have listed the original interior paint part numbers, to help you achieve the proper color and gloss.

The base pad was listed as part number 496352 for 1970-1977, the instrument panel was restyle for 1978 and given part number 10018005, which continued to be used till the end of the 1981 model year. The glove box compartment was listed as part number 479592 all 12 years. The glove box door, like the instrument panel, was originally molded in a color that matches the instrument panel in color. As time went by the black color door became the replacement part. The door should be painted the same color and shade that is used on the instrument panel. The important thing to remember about the door is that a different unit was used on cars with air conditioning than those without air conditioning. The following doors were used.

Glove Box Door Part Numbers

Year	W/O Air Conditioning	With Air Conditioning
1970	478167	478168
1971-81	483468	483462

It is reported that the 1971-81 style will fit the 1970 models.

A glove box door with air conditioning, note the slot that is cut into it, for an air duct.

Giving it a sports car feel was the use of an assist handle that placed on the instrument panel above the glove box door. Originally this handle and the attaching bezels were molded in color that matched the instrument panel in color. Again as it was consolidated into replacement parts only the black colored handle was used. This handle must be painted the same color as the instrument panel but was done in flat finish and not a semi-gloss like the panel. It was listed as part number 479872 with the bezels as part number 479437 for all 12 years. This handle was not used in all Firebirds, but only those with the custom trim option group.

The assist handle was used only in cars with the custom trim group.

1970 Interior Color Part Numbers

Codes	Color	Flat Dupont	Ditzler	Rinshed-Mason	Semi-Gloss Dupont	Ditzler	Rinshed-Mason
207, 217, 227, 208,218, 228, 209, 219	Black	4428-L	9317	168C41	99-L*	9266	170B40
201,211	Med Bright Blue	9696-L	13966	170B25	9540-L	13572	168B24
213	Dark Brown	9702-L	23309	170B87	9713-L	23320	170B89
214	Med. Red Dark Red*	9699-L*H	71826	170B50R	9709-LH	71827	170B51R
205,215	Med. Saddle Dk. Saddle*	9703-L	23310	170B88	9714-L	23321	170B800
206, 216	Midnight Green	9582-LH	43993	169V36	9593-LH	44010	169V35
207,217, 227	Med. Sandalwood Dk. Sandalwood*	9704-L	233311	170B74	9716-L	23323	170B76

*Flat finishes are in a darker shade *- Number is actually full gloss flattener must be added

1971 Interior Color Part Numbers

Codes	Color	Flat			Semi-Gloss		
		Dupont	Ditzler	Rinshed-Mason	Dupont	Ditzler	Rinshed-Mason
207, 217, 227, 208,218, 228, 209, 219 212	Black	4428-L	9317	168C41	99-L**	9266	170B40
201,211	Dark Blue	9818	14103	171B25	9807-L	14104	172B27
201,213	Dark Saddle	9817	23453	171B86	9801-L	23436	172B88
214	Dk. Sienna	9820	23454	170B87	9813	23451	172B79
206,216	Dark Jade		44316	17B36	9808-L	44315	172B38
207,217, 227	Med. Sandalwood Dk. Beige*	9819	23452	171B85	9716-L	23434	172B76

*Flat finishes are in a darker shade (212 is ivory trim door panels and other trim use part number 8850 semi gloss (ivory-color) Ditzler paint. **- Number is actually full gloss flattener must be added

1972 Interior Color Part Numbers

Codes	Color	Flat			Semi-Gloss		
		Dupont	Ditzler	Rinshed-Mason	Dupont	Ditzler	Rinshed-Mason
207, 217, 227, 208,218, 228, 209, 219 121,221, 207, 217, 227	Black	4428-L	9317	168C41	99-L*	9266	170B40
131,231	Dark Saddle	9817	23453	171B86	9801-L	23436	173B88
141,241	Dark Green	9920-L	44504	17B31	9911-L	44508	173B33
251,351	Dark Blue	9818-L	14103	171B25	9807-L	14104	173B27

Flat finishes are in a darker shade (207,217,227 are white trim door panels and other trim use part number 8892 Ditzler 9909-l Dupont semi gloss (white-color) paint. Black is used on instrument panel. *- Number is actually full gloss flattener must be added

1973 Interior Color Part Numbers

Codes	Color	Flat			Semi-Gloss		
		Dupont	Ditzler	Rinshed-Mason	Dupont	Ditzler	Rinshed-Mason
236,246 232,242	Black	4428-L	9317	168C41	99-L*	9387	170B40
233,243	Dark Saddle	10014-LH	23774	173B84	9997-LH	23778	17B852
247	Dk.Oxblood	10016-LH	72007	173B53R	10000-LH	72008	173B50R
255	Lt. Neutral Dk neutral*	10012-LH	23787	173B79	9992-L	23779	173B74

*Flat finishes are in a darker shade (232,242 are white trim door panels and other trim use part number 8892 Ditzler 9909-L Dupont semi gloss (white-color) paint. Black is used on instrument panel.

1974 Interior Color Part Numbers

Codes	Color	Flat			Semi-Gloss		
		Dupont	Ditzler	Rinshed-Mason	Dupont	Ditzler	Rinshed-Mason
576,596,586, 572,592	Black	4428-L	9317	168C41	99-L*	9387	170B40
581	Med. Blue Dk Blue*	10006-LH	14510	173B23	9983-LH	14493	173A20
573,593,583	Dk Saddle	42913-LH	23988	174B86	10004-LH	23942	174B80
594	Med. Green Dk Green*	42914-LH	44898	173B33	49901-LH	44862	173B31
590	Med. Red Dk. Red*	42917-LM	72073	174B63	42907-LH	72054	174850R

*Flat finishes are in a darker shade (572,592 are white trim door panels and other trim use part number 8892 Ditzler 9909-L Dupont semi gloss (white-color) paint. Black is used on instrument panel. * *- Number is actually full gloss flattener must be added

1975 Interior Color Part Numbers

Codes	Color	Flat			Semi-Gloss		
		Dupont	Ditzler	Rinshed-Mason	Dupont	Ditzler	Rinshed-Mason
19W, 19V, 11W,11V	Black	4428-L	9317	168C41	99-L*	9387	170B40
26W	Dark Blue	43625-LH	14796	A4403	43615-LH	14783	A4404
63V, 63W	Dk Saddle	10014-LH	23774	A4407	9997-LH	23778	A4408
73W	Oxblood	10016-LH	72007	A4405	10000-LH	72008	A4405

Flat finishes are in a darker shade (11W ,11V are white trim door panels and other trim use part number 8855 Ditzler 9625-L Dupont semi gloss (white-color) paint. Black is used on instrument panel. *- Number is actually full gloss flattener must be added

1976 Interior Color Part Numbers

Codes	Color	Flat			Semi-Gloss		
		Dupont	Ditzler	Rinshed-Mason	Dupont	Ditzler	Rinshed-Mason
11M, 11N, 19M, 91M, 19N,91N	Black	4428-L	9317	168C41	99-L*	9387	170B40
26N, 92N	Dark Blue	43625-LH	14796	A4403	43615-LH	14783	A4404
64M, 64N	Buckskin	42913-lh	23988	A4558	42900-lh	23942	A4559
71N, 97N	Firethorn	43965-lh	72158	A4733R	43961-lh	72145	A4734R

Flat finishes are in a darker shade (11M, 11N are white trim door panels and other trim use part number 8855 Ditzler 9625-L Dupont semi gloss (white-color) paint. Black is used on instrument panel. *- Number is actually full gloss flattener must be added

1977 Interior Color Part Numbers

Codes	Color	Flat			Semi-Gloss		
		Dupont	Ditzler	Rinshed-Mason	Dupont	Ditzler	Rinshed-Mason
11R, 11N 19R, 19N, 19B	Black	4428-L	9317	168C41	99-L**	9387	170B40
24N, 92N,24B	Light Blue Dark Blue*	43625-l	14796	a-4403	43617-lh		a-4741
64R, 64N	Buckskin	42913-lh	23988	A4558	42900-lh	23942	A4559
71R, 97R ,71N,97N,71B	Firethorn	43965-lh	72158	A4733R	43961-lh	72145	A4734R

*Flat finishes are in a darker shade (11R,11N are white trim door panels and other trim use part number 8855 Ditzler 9625-L Dupont semi gloss (white-color) paint. Black is used on instrument panel. * *- Number is actually full gloss flattener must be added

1978 Interior Color Part Numbers

Codes	Color	Flat			Semi-Gloss		
		Dupont	Ditzler	Rinshed-Mason	Dupont	Ditzler	Rinshed-Mason
11R, 11N 19R, 19N, 19B	Black	4428-L	9317	168C41	99-L**	9387	170B40
24N,24B	Lt. Blue Dark Blue*		15149			14782	
62R, 622 62B,62N	Dark Camel		24530			24542	
74R, 74B,74N	Dark Carmine		72291			72273	

*Flat finishes are in a darker shade (11R,11N are white trim door panels and other trim use part number 8855 Ditzler 9625-L Dupont semi gloss (white-color) paint. Black is used on instrument panel. * *- Number is actually full gloss flattener must be added

1979 Interior Color Part Numbers

Codes	Color	Low Gloss			Semi-Gloss		
		Dupont	Ditzler	Rinshed-Mason	Dupont	Ditzler	Rinshed-Mason
19R, 19N, 19B	Black	4428	9433	A9609	99-L**	9387	170B40
24N,24B	Lt. Blue Dark Blue*		15149			14782	
62R, 62B,62N	Dark Camel	45873	24659	A9985	45222	24542	A9565
74R, 74B,74N	Dark Carmine	45243	72291	A9616	45224	72273	A9567
152	Silver		33034			33163	

*Flat finishes are in a darker shade (12R,12N are Oyster trim door panels and other trim use part number 90101 Ditzler semi gloss (oyster-color) paint.. **- Number is actually full gloss flattener must be added

1980 Interior Color Part Numbers

Codes	Color	Low Gloss			Semi-Gloss		
		Dupont	Ditzler	Rinshed-Mason	Dupont	Ditzler	Rinshed-Mason
19R, 19N, 19B, 12R 12N	Black	4428	9433	A9609	99-L*	9387	170B40
26D, 26R, 26N, 26B	Dark Blue	C8014	15345	116959	C8005	15344	A11641
62B, 62 N, 62R. 62D	Dark Camel	45873	24659	A9985	45222	24542	A9565
74R, 75N.75B	Dark Carmine	45243	72291	A9616	45224	72273	A9567

Flat finishes are in a darker shade (12R,12N are Oyster trim door panels and other trim use part number 90101 Ditzler semi gloss (oyster-color) paint. . *- Number is actually full gloss flattener must be added

1981 Interior Color Part Numbers

Codes	Color	Low Gloss			Semi-Gloss		
		Dupont	Ditzler	Rinshed-Mason	Dupont	Ditzler	Rinshed-Mason
19R, 19N, 19B	Black	4428	9433	A9609	99-L*	9387	170B40
26D, 26R, 26N, 26B	Dark Blue	C8014	15345	116959	C8005	15344	A11641
63B	Lt. Sandstone	C8148	24927	12399	C8105	24899	12260
15V,15W	Silver	C8126	33456	12389	43622	33163	2901
75R,75N,75B	Med. Red				C8114	72416	12270R
64D, 64R, 64B, 64N	Med Doeskin	C8148	24927	12399	C8110	24867	12265

*Flat finishes are in a darker shade (12R,12N are Oyster trim door panels and other trim use part number 90101 Ditzler semi gloss (oyster-color) paint. *- Number is actually full gloss flattener must be added

Instrumentation and Controls
1970-1981

Basically three different types of instrument clusters were used. The standard instrument cluster, and the Rallye cluster with clock, and Rallye cluster with tachometer/clock. The Rally cluster with the clock was standard on Formula models and the unit with tachometer and clock were standard in the Trans Am.

Laid out in front of the driver was the main instrument cluster. On the standard cluster this consisted of the far left-hand side warning lamps for the oil, water and alternator, to the far right was the speedometer, and in the center was the fuel gauge. On models with the RPO W30 clock and Rally Cluster, the warning lamp pod

was displaced with a clock. The fuel gauge was moved to separate pod right of the speedometer, which stayed in same position as the standard set up, and taking it's place was combination oil pressure/ water temperature gauge. The ammeter was placed in a separate pod to the right of the fuel gauge. Trans Am and those with the RPO U30 Rally Cluster used the same set up as the W30, except the clock and tachometer combination was used in the far left-hand pod.

Standard Firebird instrumentation, note the pod with the warning lamps to the far left.

An example of the Rally cluster with the tachometer, shown is a 1979 model, with a 100 mph speedometer

1970-1981 Speedometer Part Numbers

Model Year	Part Number
1970-1971	6492882
1972	6492882-*
	6497947-**
1973-1974	6497947
1975	8986779
1976-1979	25024034++
Except Y89-1979	25024035+
1979 Y89	25024038
1980	$25022022_{(1)}$
	$25022023_{(2)}$
	$25022037_{(3)}$
	$25024928_{(4)}$
1981	$25044621_{(5)}$
	$25044622_{(6)}$
	$25044625_{(7)}$
	$25048107_{(8)}$

*-First part of year with out seat belt warning
**-Second part of year with seat belt waringin
++- Without gauges
+-With Gauge package
(1)- without gauge/ Calf. 305 without gauges
(2)- 4.3 Liter with Gauges except Calif.
(3)- 4.3 Liter with gauges Calif.
(4)-With RPO Y85
(5)- Without gauge except Canada
(6)-With Gauges except U18, Z49 or Export
(7)- With Gauges Export
(8) _ With Y85 package.

1970-1981 Tachometer Part Numbers

Model Year	Part Number
1970-1971	6469962
1972-1973	5657931
1974-1975	6469784
1976	6469784*
	5659020**
1977-1978	5659020
1979	5659391
1980-1981	5659849

*-First part of year **-Second part of year

1970-1981 Fuel Level Gauges Part Numbers

Model Year	Part Number
1970-1972	6431309 +
	6431428 ++
	6431393 +++
1973-1974	6431746+
	6431428++
1975-1979	6432003+
	6432039++
1980-1981	6432891+
	6432975++

+-With Rally clusters ++-With Rally Cluster
+++-With Warning Lamp

1970-1981 Ammeter Gauges Part Numbers*

Model Year	Part Number
1970-1979	6473740
1980-1981	6474616

*- With Rally Cluster only

1970-1981 Oil Pressure/Water Temp Gauges Part Numbers*

Model Year	Part Number
1970-1978	6493193
1979	8993338+
	8993714++
1980-981	8993699

*-With Rally Clusters only
+Except Y89 ++-With Y89 only

1970-1974 Firebirds used a 160 mph speedometer.

Formulas, even with the 455-ci SD and rally cluster used the wood grain bezel. Not the Trans Am's engine turned bezel.

Trans Am models used this engine-tuned bezel

Basically there were two different types of bezels those used in Trans Am, which featured a engine turned pattern, which added to the sporty road racer feel, having driven both there is a certain feel that you get behind the wheel of Trans Am that you can't get behind a Camaro, and part of that feel is the instrument bezel, which gives you the sensation that you're behind the wheel of a true sports car. The other bezel was used in all other models and it is a wood grain pattern.

Besides the texture, other factors affecting the bezel usage is whether or not the car was ordered with air conditioning, or the Rally Cluster option. A Firebird medallion, part number 481542 1970-1975, was used on the instrument cluster bezel of all Firebird models except Trans Am or those with the Rallye gauge package. For 1973-1979 models with the radial turned suspension option, the RTS medallion part number 494299 was used on the instrument panel, including the Trans Am models. Several different instrument bezels were used throughout the scope of this guide. There were rare options indicated here, one is the 1979-1981 Trans Am without the gauge package, it still used the engine turned bezels, but did not have provisions for air conditioning or gauges. It came in both gold and silver tints. The gold tint was also used on the Redbird models.

Firebirds without the Rally Cluster instrumentation used this medallion in this location all 12 years.

The RTS nameplate was located here

1970-1981 Instrument Bezel Part Numbers					
Model Year	Except Trans Am				Trans Am
	Except Rally Cluster		With Rally Cluster		Without A/C	With A/C
	Without A/C	With A/C	Without A/C	With A/C		
1970	478549	481736	481737	481738	481740	481741
1971	483519	481736	481737	481738	481740	481741
1972	478549	481736	489248	481738	481740	481741
1973-1975	478549	481736	489248	481738	481740	481741
1976	10012499	10012500	10012501	10012502	10012504 10012506*	100012503 10012507*
1977	10012499	10012500	10012501	10012502	10012504 10012506*	10012503 10012507*
1978-1979	10012499 10005647**	10012500 10012505**	10012501	10012502	10012504 10012506* 10015647**	10012503 10012507*
1980	10012499	10012500	10012501	10012502 10010603***	10012504 10012506* 10015647**	10012503 10012507*
1981	10010601	10012500 10012505**	10012501	10012502 10010603**	10012504 10012506* 10020676****	10012503 10012507*

*-With Y82/Y84 Special Edition package Gold trim **- Gold trim aluminum has no provisions for gauges used on Esprit with W68 package 1978-81 and Y82/Y84/Y88 package in Trans Am very rare in Trans Am models. ***- Used in 1980 Yellow Bird package. ****-Without gauges.

Removing Instrument Panel
1970-1981

The instrument panels in the second generation Firebirds were basically one big crash pad. This has advantages and disadvantages. The advantages are that it is lightweight and fairly easy to remove and replace, compared to all steel dashes that are used in other GM models. Since little change in design occurred there is a big interchange range, the vinyl makes it easy to change the color. Disadvantages, replacement dashes can be expensive and because they are made of all vinyl they are prone to damage. The sun cracks and easily fades them and just a minor impact can total the pad.

To remove the pad, make sure the battery is disconnected. Next remove all the lower air conditioning ducts, this will allow you access to the mounting screws. Remove the ashtray, console and upper and lower instrument panel trim plates, this includes the instrument bezel. Remove glove box, disconnect and separate fuse box at firewall. Disconnect all instrument cluster and lamp wiring harness from the back of the cluster.

Disconnect the parking brake control. Next remove the screws that secure the steering column tow cover plate to the dash and lower the steering column support column temporarily with knee, or better yet disconnect wires and lower column to floor. Remove hold bolts and then remove instrument cluster, watching for any connected leads that you may have missed. Remove instrument panel attaching bolts and lift unit from car.

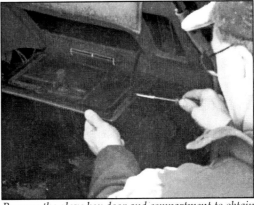

Remove the glove box door and compartment to obtain access to the instrument panel hold screws.

197

Lower the steering column, then remove instrument cluster watching for any connections that may remain.

1970 Standard and Deluxe Steering Wheels

Trim Code	Wheel Color	Steering Wheel Part Numbers		Notes
		Standard	Deluxe	
207, 217, 227, 208,218, 228, 209, 219	Black	9751053*	9751059	*-Black used in all standard trim s
201,211	Lucerne Blue	N/A	9752013	
213	Dark Brown	N/A	9752014	
214	Cardinal Red	N/A	9752009	
205,215	Saddle	N/A	9752010	
206, 216	Midnight Green	N/A	9751060	
207,217, 227	Sandalwood	N/A	9752011	

Steering Wheel
1970

Standard steering wheel was a two-spoke unit that was molded in black color regardless of the interior trim color. It was listed as part number 9751053. The horn shroud matched the steering wheel in color and was listed as part number 9796889 and featured the Pontiac symbol in the middle. This steering wheel was standard on the Base Firebird models only.

The Deluxe steering wheel was available as a separate option RPO N30 or as part of the custom interior group. It was also standard in the Esprit and Formula models. It used a three-spoke design, which was color keyed to the interior trim, except white, which used a black colored wheel. The center cover matched the wheel in color and featured soft touch vinyl horn buttons that too matched the steering wheel in color.

1970 Deluxe Steering Wheel Center Cap

Black	9797158
Lucerne Blue	478992
Dark Brown	478989
Cardinal Red	478988
Saddle	478990
Midnight Green	9797387
Sandalwood	478987

The custom sport wheel was not available on the Firebird models; instead the simulated leather rim Formula steering wheel was used. Listed as part number 546296 it was standard in Trans Am models and optional in all other Firebird models, under option RPO NK3. It used a notched black colored center cap listed as part number 480444, this cap is unique to the Firebird line and if you are swapping from a GTO or Grand Prix the horn cap on this wheel is incorrect for your Firebird. This wheel also required a special extension part number 546280 to mount the steering wheel.

1971-1974

It may appear that the base Firebird received the three spoke deluxe steering wheel, as it is listed that the deluxe steering wheel is standard. What happened was that Pontiac juggled the names of the steering wheels around a little. What was listed standard in 1970 was now listed as deluxe, and the deluxe steering wheel was given the name custom cushion. What this accomplished was that instead of just a black colored steering wheel, the wheels were color keyed to the interior trim.

The cover was like that in 1970 but was color keyed to the interior. The following colors were used; black, dark blue , dark jade and beige was used with the sandalwood interior trim.

Now referred to as custom cushion in the service manuals and sale material but still referred to as a deluxe steering wheel in the parts catalogs, the three spoke steering wheel with colored horn buttons was standard on the Esprit and Formula models, and was used in the Base Firebirds as an option or as part of the custom interior group. The cover and the steering wheel matched the interior trim, except for ivory/white, which used a black colored steering wheel and cover.

Deluxe steering wheel 1973 is shown 1970-1972 is similar. Called a cushion custom from 1971-1974.

Formula steering wheel was standard in Trans Am models. Shown is the black colored wheel part number 549296.

1971-1972 Deluxe Steering Wheel Center Cap

Black	9797158
Dark Blue	482283
Dark Jade	482284
Dark Beige	482285

1971-1972 Custom Cushion Steering Wheel Center Cap

Black	9797158
Dark Blue	482273
Dark Jade	482274
Dark Beige	482275
Dark Saddle	482276
Dark Sienna	482277

1971 Standard and Deluxe Steering Wheels

Trim Code	Wheel Color	Steering Wheel Part Numbers		Notes
		Standard	Deluxe	
207, 217, 227, 208,218, 228, 209, 219 212	Black	9756443	9755889	
201,211	Dark Blue	9753001	9753006	
201,213	Dark Saddle	N/A	9753009	
214	Dk. Sienna	N/A	9753010	
206,216	Dark Jade	9753002	9753007	
207,217, 227	Dk. Beige	9753003	9753008	

1972 Standard and Deluxe Steering Wheels

Trim Code	Wheel Color	Steering Wheel Part Numbers		Notes
		Standard	Deluxe	
207, 217, 227, 208,218, 228, 209, 219 121,221, 207, 217, 227	Black	9756443	9755889	
131,231	Dark Saddle	N/A	9753009	
141,241	Dark Green	9753002	9753007	
251,351	Dark Blue	9753001	9753006	

Beginning in 1973 Pontiac begin to revamp the way they held inventory of older parts. Steering wheels were still color-keyed but the colored steering wheels were only kept in inventory till the supply ran out, after that than a black colored steering was used and painted to match the instrument panel. However the same basic design on the deluxe and cushion custom wheel remained till the end of 1974.

Trans Ams still came standard with the simulated leather covered Formula steering wheel; it used the same part number as in 1970, as did the horn button. This set up was used till the end of the 1975 model year.

1975

The same sets of three different steering wheels were used again. However, the covers on the Deluxe and Custom Cushion were restyled and are visually different; while the steering wheel is the same as those used in 1974, the covers are not. As before the steering wheel and the covers matched the interior trim, except for white, which used a black steering wheel and cover.

As before the base Firebird used the deluxe steering wheel, the Esprit and Formula models were standard with the custom cushion steering wheel and the Trans Am was standard with the simulated leather rim steering wheel. The Custom cushion steering wheel was optional on the base Firebird models, and the formula wheel was optional on all Firebird models.

1976 Special Edition Trans Ams used a Formula steering wheel with gold colored spokes. All other models used black colored spokes.

Beginning in 1978 the Formula steering wheel came in different colors that matched the interior trim, except for white, which used a black colored steering wheel. The spokes are silver in this photo.

1977-1981

The two-spoke steering wheel was gone for 1977. The standard wheel was the 3-spoke unit that was molded in color to match the interior trim, except for white which used a black colored steering wheel. This wheel is different than those in previous years but it still uses a color matching plastic cover. This wheel was used in all Firebirds except the Trans Ams, which continued to use a Formula style steering wheel. However, the wheel received some modifications. One was the simulated leather material which was now offered in colors that matched the interior trim , except for white which used black color simulated leather.

The Black Special Edition models used a blacked rim with gold colored spokes. Listed as part number 100013871, this wheel was used all five years with all Special Edition models except the 1979 Y89 package where a steering wheel with gray colored simulated leather and silver spokes were used. This wheel was listed as part number 1009536, and was the wheel used on the 1980-81 pace car editions.

An important thing to remember while most of the same steering wheels that were used in the Trans Am were also used in other Firebird models, providing the interior trim was the same, there was an exception. The wheel used in 1981 Esprits with the NK3 wheel option used different steering wheels than those in other Firebirds; this is due to the fact that the Esprits used a different center cap than those in other Firebirds.

Also the RPO N31 custom sport steering wheel became optional from the factory on Firebirds in 1981.

1976

The same wheels that were used in 1975 were used again in 1976, with one addition: the custom sport wheel now became available as an option on all Firebirds except the Trans Am models, as a dealer installed option. This steering wheel featured a deep inset with a large center horn bezel button that was color keyed to the interior trim, except with white trim, which used a black colored bezel. The bezel was topped off with a horn ornament cap with the Pontiac arrow logo it was listed as part number 10003056. For this add on to be considered correct there must be written proof it was installed by the dealer before the customer took delivery of the car. Another variation was the Formula steering wheel used in the Trans Am Special Edition package; this steering wheel used gold color spokes, instead of the standard flat black.

Standard steering wheel for 1978.

Formula steering wheel used in 10th Anniversary Special edition model.

Formula steering wheel used on 1979 Trans Am with the gray interior, except 10th anniversary Special Edition

Push the seat all the way back and remove the front mounting screws that hold the seat to the floor, then push all the seat all the way forward and remove the rear mounting screws. You may have to use a shallow socket or an open-end wrench to get to some bolts.

With the front seats free pull up and out of the car.

Seats
1970

Buckets seats were standard in all 1970 Firebirds, but three different levels of trim were used. All models, except the Esprit used the standard all vinyl trim that consisted of Madrid grain inserts and skirts with horizontal stitch bar pleats, with a plain outer border. The custom interior trim was standard on the Esprit and optional on the other Firebird models. It consisted of comfort weave inserts and Madrid vinyl skirts. The horizontal pleats continue over past the inserts and there is no border surrounding this pattern. Deluxe trims with cloth inserts were available in either Sandalwood or black.

To remove the back seat cushion push inward with force to unhook it from the retaining hook in the floor.

1971

Standard trim was in all Madrid grain vinyl. The bucket seats featured wide horizontal stitched pleats, that were not all uniform in size, at the top of the rounded seat back the pleats traced the entire width of the seat back, they then narrowed down to the insert width then transfer back to the seat cushion with the widest pleats being at the front edge of the cushion. The custom trim group used seats with a comfort weave insert and Madrid grain skirts. The horizontal pleats here are more uniform in width. This option was standard on the Esprits and optional on all but the base Firebird models.

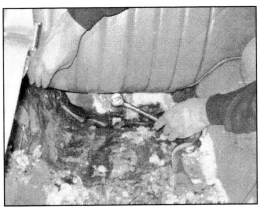

The rear seat backs are held in place with small bolts.

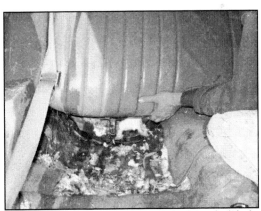

Once the bolts are removed the seat back can be lifted out of place. When removing the rear seat be on the outlook for the build sheet. This is a computer print out that will list all the option on your car.

1972

The standard trim consisted of all Madrid grain vinyl skirts and inserts with wide horizontal stitched pleats. The pattern looked much like the 1971 standard trim. It was standard in all models except the Esprit models. The Esprit was standard with the custom trim group but used black Potomac cloth inserts and vinyl skirts. Optional on the Trans Am and Formula models was the custom trim done in Tetra grain inserts with Madrid grain skirts, and featured wide full width horizontal stitched pleats. This trim group was not available for the base Firebird models.

1973

The standard trim consisted of all Madrid grain vinyl skirts and inserts with wide horizontal stitched pleats, using the same pattern as the standard trim in 1972. . It was standard in all models except the Esprit models. The Esprit was standard with the custom trim group, which used Tetra grain inserts with Madrid grain skirts, and featured deeply inset very wide pleats. This trim group was optional on the Formula and Trans Am models only, it was not available for the base Firebird models.

1972 deluxe interior trim

1974-1975

The standard interior was done in wide Madrid grain vinyl for both the inserts and the skirts. The Custom trim was standard in the Esprit and optional on all other Firebirds. The pattern and grain of both the standard and the custom trim was the same as in 1973.

1976

The standard interior was done in Oxen grain vinyl inserts with Madrid grain vinyl skirts. The insert featured vertical stitched pleats that were crossed by two horizontal pleats in the back and the cushion. This trim was standard in all models except the Esprits, which came standard with the custom trim, which was optional in all other Firebird models.

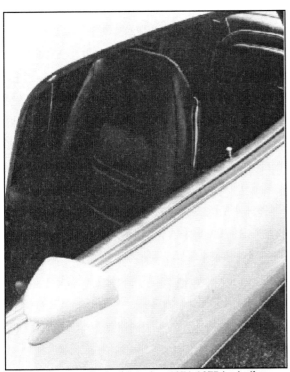

1973 Custom all vinyl interior, 1974-1975 is similar

1978 custom trim in white

1976 custom trim, 1977 is similar, but is done in a different grain

205

1977

The standard interior was done in Oxen grain vinyl inserts with Sierra Grain vinyl skirts. The insert featured vertical stitched pleats that were crossed by two horizontal pleats in the back and the cushion. This trim was standard in all models except the Esprits, which came standard with the custom trim, which was optional in all other Firebird models. The custom interior trim used Doeskin grain vinyl inserts that featured double-needle stitched vertical pleats with decorative welt stitching and no horizontal crossing pleats, and Sierra Grain vinyl grain skirts.

1978-1979

The standard interior was done in Oxen grain vinyl inserts with Sierra Grain vinyl skirts. The insert featured vertical stitched pleats that were crossed by two horizontal pleats in the back and the cushion. This trim was standard in all models except the Esprits, which came standard with the custom trim, which was optional in all other Firebird models. The custom interior trim used Doeskin grain vinyl inserts that featured raised pillow inserts that were separated by horizontal pleats. The skirts were done in Sierra grain vinyl. The 10th Anniversary Special Edition Trans Am in 1979 used special trim that looked similar in style to the custom trim but was done in silver leather inserts and skirts. Cloth covered seats were also available both years in a variety of colors. Cloth seats were not available in the base Firebird, or on the Special Edition models.

1979 10th Anniversary Special Edition Trans Am with silver leather interior trim

1980-1981

The standard interior was restyled and was done in Elk grain vinyl inserts with Sierra Grain vinyl skirts. The insert featured vertical stitched pleats that were crossed by two horizontal pleats in the back and the cushion, but the stitching did not extend up into the headrest area. This trim was standard in all models except the Esprits, which came standard with the custom trim, which was optional in all other Firebird models. The custom interior trim used Doeskin grain vinyl inserts that featured raised pillow inserts that were separated by horizontal pleats. The skirts were done in Sierra grain vinyl. Cloth trim was available both years.

1979 cloth trim with hobnail cloth inserts was optional on all but the base Firebird and those with the Special Edition packages like the Redbird and 10th Anniversary Trans Am.

The hinges were covered with injection-molded plastic covers that had a pebble-grain finish and were molded in a color that matched the seat trim. Reproductions are usually in black, and should be painted to match the interior trim in a 30-degree gloss finish.

The bucket seats used a protective ABS plastic cover. Originally these covers were molded in color that matched the seat trim in color. Most reproduction parts are in black only, or they are available as used parts only so they will most likely not match your trim and will have to be painted to match your trim. But before applying paint the panel should be thoroughly cleaned using Naphtha or equivalent solvent, then lightly scuff the surface with #400 grit sandpaper. Clean again with the solvent cleaner, and dry thoroughly, with a lint free cloth. Coat with acrylic lacquer that matches the trim. Color part numbers can be found under the instrument panel heading; use gloss finish. Allow to dry completely then rubbing out and polishing.

Door Panels
1970-1971
There is a physical difference between the standard trim and custom trim door panels, and they cannot be interchanged. The panels were covered in colored vinyl that matched the seat trim in color. The standard panels featured a pattern of multiple diagonal pleats that were dielectrically pressed into Madrid grain vinyl and divided into two separated sections by three horizontal pleats that cross at the same axis as the window crank handle's location.

You can use a special tool or a flat blade screwdriver to push the retaining clip out that holds the window crank handle in place.

207

Use a long blade Phillips head screwdriver to remove the arm rests.

With the door handle cup and locking knob removed the door panel can be popped loose of its retaining clips and removed from the door.

The custom panels had a feel of the custom panels in 1969, which featured images that were used on Corvettes at the time. It featured a pleated insert with diagonal pleats, but no crossing horizontal pleats. A matching pull handle was placed in the center of the insert with the custom trim Originally this pull strap was molded in color that matched that of the door panel, in later years the black color handle part number 9643788 was used and was painted to match the door panel.

Be aware that there was a change in the door panel design in 1971. Early models use panels that contained a map and pull up cup set up, while the later models did not use these items.

Kick panels were made from color-molded plastic that matched the interior trim, except for ivory/white, which used black. Two different seats of kick panels were used with each color, regardless of whether or not air conditioning was used.

1972

Basically the same design that was used in 1971 was used again for 1972, on both the standard and the custom door panels. The difference was that these were a two-part design. The lower panel featured molded in storage bins and armrests; unlike the upper panels these panels were not molded in color but were painted to match the upper panels in color. Listed as part numbers 9600954 right-hand and 9600955 left-hand, they were used with standard and the custom trim options. Kick panels had the same general design that was used in the 1971 models.

Standard door panel 1970-early 1971

1979 10th Anniversary Special Edition models required special door panels with multiple colored embroidery logo.

1973-1977

The standard trim door panels used the same design and format with upper and lower panels. The lower panels even used the same part numbers as before. The custom trim got a new look for the upper panels with breathable pigskin vinyl inserts that were not pleated. Door panels matched the interior color trim, including white. A medallion part number 1700550 was used on the panels over the window regulator hole if power windows were ordered; this medallion was used with both the standard and the custom trim, it was also used in 1970-1972 models with power windows, but it was listed as part number 984416. Both have a black and red bird, those with special packages such as the Black Special Edition. Redbird, Skybird, have a gold colored medallion when power windows were used, power windows were part of many of the packages, and it was listed as part number 3063896. Skybird used special light blue interior trim. The Redbird package used red colored trim.

1978

For the first time since 1970 the standard door panel got a new look. Done in Sierra grain vinyl it featured vertical stitched pleats, in the center bordered by two horizontal strips. The upper strip was straight across but the lower strip angled upward towards the front edge of the panel matching the length of the vertical pleats. Arm rests were separate items that matched the panel in color.

The custom trim door panels were also restyled. They were cleaner looking than before with carpet along the bottom edge. And like the standard trim panels they no longer used built in arm rests, they were separate items that matched the trim in color. In fact the same armrests were used on both the standard and custom trim. A medallion was used over the window regulator hole when power windows were ordered. Part numbers were the same as in 1977.

1979-1981

The same patterns were used again that were used in 1978 for both the standard and custom trim, with one exception the 1979 10th Anniversary Special Edition Trans Am used special door panels. They were available in silver leather with multiple color embroidery. Since power windows were a standard and not deleteable item for this model no provision for the window crank handle was used and this panel did not use a medallion on the door panel. Special silver colored carpet was used on the bottoms of the door panels.

1976 door panel with custom trim, door speakers are not original units.

209

Console
1970-1979

The console was an option on all Firebirds, and had to be ordered in early 1970-1974 models. In order to get a floor shifted automatic cars, this includes the rare Super Duty cars. There are reports that five cars were built in 1973 with the 455-ci Super Duty. There were basically two different designs of consoles those used on 1970-1979 models, and those used on the 1980-1981 models. This further breaks down to transmission type. Basically two bases were used: part number 480104 with manual transmissions and part number 479536; these numbers would be changed in coming years, but the parts remained the same till the end of the 1979 model year. The base held to the floor with a pair of support brackets. These brackets should be painted the same color as the car, as they were in place when the car was painted.

An escutcheon panel that trims the shift lever opening was used according to transmission type. All manual transmission used part number 478571. Two-speed automatics used a different trim plate than the three-speed automatics. Those 1970-1972 two-speed automatic used part number 480730 while the three speed automatics used part number 478569 till the end of the 1979 model year; except those with the Y85, Y89 and W73 Special Edition packages, which required special trim plates

The box compartment was listed as part number 478562 all ten years and the door was listed as originally molded in color to match the interior trim, except with ivory/white trim which used a black, or one that match the carpet. That became a black colored unit and had to be painted the same color and shade that the console was. The door was listed as part number 10019554.

A rear console was also available as a separate option RPO D58 from 1971-1977. Like the front console it was originally molded in color and later only black was used, which had to be painted to match the front console. It was listed as part number 9790585. It was mounted to the floor with a support bracket. This bracket should be painted the same color as the exterior of the car. The rear console held a support escutcheon that held the seat belts in place and ashtray part number 7770646.

1980-1981

The console was restyled for the 1980 model year. Again two bases were used. Those with a manual transmission used part number 10011164, while those with the automatic transmission used part number 10011163. In 1981 the bases were changed to part numbers 14034977 with an automatic transmission and 10013238 with a manual transmission. All bases should be painted to match the interior except with white, which used black in a 30-degrees gloss.

The base held to the floor with a pair of support brackets. These brackets should be painted the same color as the car, as they were in place when the car was painted.

An escutcheon panel that trims the shift lever opening was used according to transmission type. All manual transmission used part number 478571 and automatics used part number 478569 both years.

The box compartment was listed as part number 478562 both years, and the door was listed as part number 10019554, which is the same door and box that was used on the 1970-1979 models. A special cover was used over the map pocket, and two different parts were used. All but those with a turbocharger used part number 10011175, while those with a turbocharger used part number 10016344, but these covers were used only on 1980 models.

An example of a console with a manual transmission, 1979 model is shown.

An example of a console with an automatic transmission, a 1973 model is shown.

Sun Visors, Headliners, and Seat Belts

The 1970 to early 1973 models used two distinct types of headliners according to the type of interior. Those models with the standard interior trim used a Premier no-perforated vinyl while those with the custom interior used a Premier perforated vinyl headliner. In late 1973 the headliner material was changed due to a change in the supplier. From late 1973 till the end of the 1981 foam backed perforated vinyl was used. This headliner has larger holes and is sturdier than the earlier style. The headliner, and the wind lace used to mount the headliner matched the seat trim in color.

Sun visors also matched the interior trim in color, but not material. Like the headliners two different types of material were used on the early models (1970-early 1973) and were used according to the interior trim type. Those with the standard trim used Premier non-perforated vinyl, while those with the custom trim used Premier perforated vinyl. In late 1973 at the same time the headliners changed, so did the sun visors, they now used Madrid vinyl regardless of the interior trim grade.

Seat belts came in two styles: the standard belt and the custom belt. The seat belt usually matched the seat trim in color. There were exceptions. Those with white or ivory colored seat trim used a black colored belt interior in 1970-71. And 1973-1981 models with the standard belts, which used black colored belts and buckles. Those with the deluxe belts were colored keyed to the interior, except white, which still used black belts, and the buckles were metal. However, color keyed belts were also used from 1977-1981 with the custom trim, but without the custom seat belt option, these belts have a larger buckle, that was the same color as the belt but are not brushed metal.

There is also one other thing to remember about the seat belt and that was change over from a four-point hitch to a three-point hitch, which occurred on late built 1972 models. This change over occurred on both the standard and custom belt options and happened on January 1, 1972. In fact, the change over is when black colored seat belts became used in all standard forms. Only the deluxe or custom belts were color-keyed.

211

The change over also required a seat belt buzzer that warned the occupants to fasten the seat belts.   This change over was a government mandated change. All vehicles were affected.   The changed is believed to have happened January 1, 1972.

Information about the belt, such as manufacture can be found on the back of the buckle, it was not uncommon to have different manufacturers in the same car.

Standard belt for 1970-1972

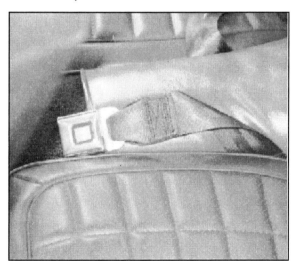

1972 Deluxe seat belt, featured a bright buckle

Custom belt for 1979. The buckle and belt were color-keyed to the trim, except with white, which was black.

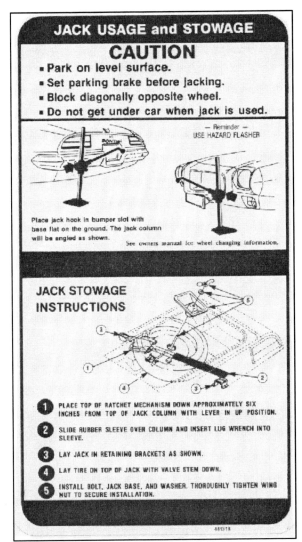

Early 1970 Jacking decal featured a dark blue background. Decal courtesy of Jim Osborne Reproductions

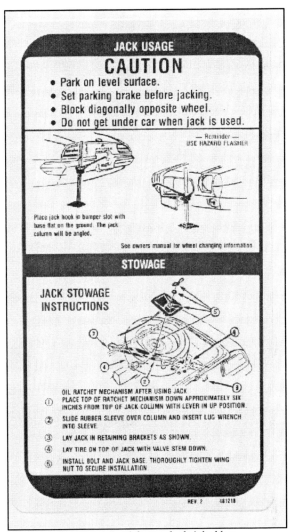

Early 1970 Jacking decal featured a bright blue background. Decal courtesy of Jim Osborne Reproductions.

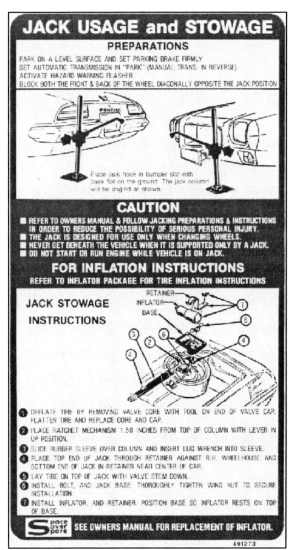

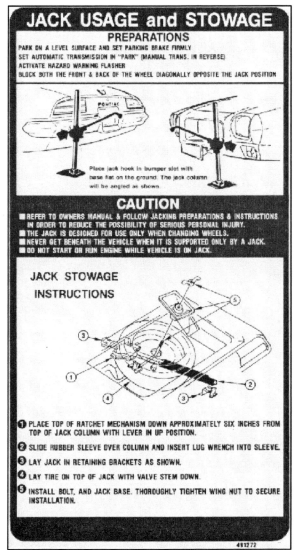

1971-1974 Jacking decal used with space saver spare tire. Decal courtesy of Jim Osborne Reproductions.

1971-1974 Jacking decal used with regular spare tire. Decal courtesy of Jim Osborne Reproductions.

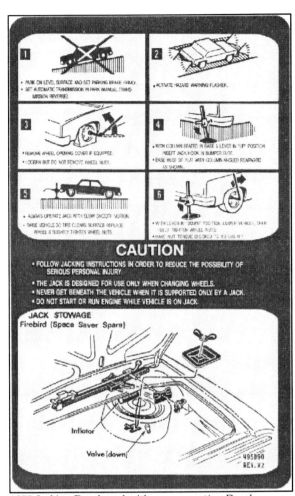

1975 Jacking Decal used with space save tire. Decal courtesy of Jim Osborne Reproductions.

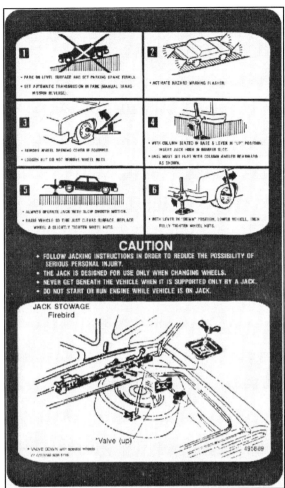

1975-1978 Jacking decal for use with regular spare wheel. Decal courtesy of Jim Osborne Reproductions.

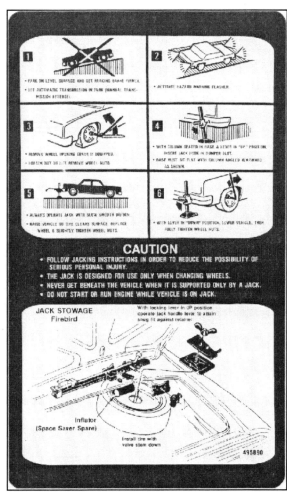

1976-1978 Jacking decal with space saver spare tire. Decal courtesy of Jim Osborne Reproductions.

1979-80 Jacking decal with space save spare tire. Decal courtesy of Jim Osborne Reroductions.

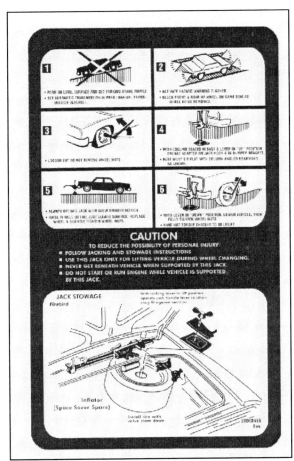

Jacking decal used on late (built after January 1, 1979) 1979 models with Space Save spare tire. Decal courtesy of Jim Osborne Reproductions.

Jacking decal used on 1979-1980 with regular spare wheel. Decal courtesy of Jim Osborne Reproductions.

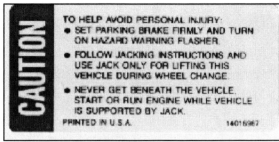

Warning decal placed on jack base of 1980 models.
Decal courtesy of Jim Osborne Reproductions.

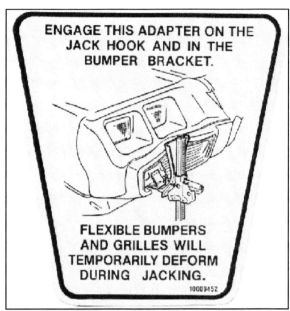

Front bumper jacking decal for 1980 models. Decal
courtesy of Jim Osborne Reproductions.

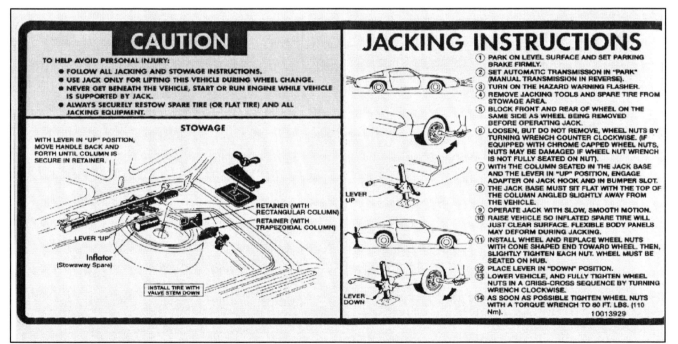

1980 Jacking decal with space saver spare tire. Decal courtesy of Jim Osborne Reproductions

218

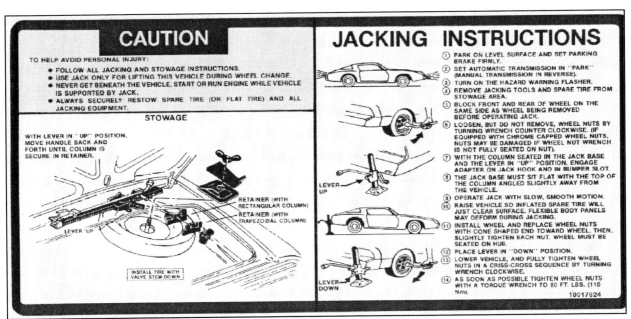

1981 jacking decal. Decal courtesy of Jim Osborne Reproductions

Inside Mirror

Two different types of inside rear view mirrors were used in 1970. Early models used the first type and was listed as part number 911261 and required a support arm listed as part numbers 9816721 and 98167722 and a screw part number 9809937. The late built 1970-71 models used a windshield mounted mirror and was listed as part number 917493 and did not require support arms. In 1972 a 10 in. tilt type mirror part number 911582 that was mounted on the windshield was used and became the replacement part for the Late 1970-1971 models in 1973. The same mirror was used till the end of the 1981 model year.

An example of a support mounted inside rear view mirror

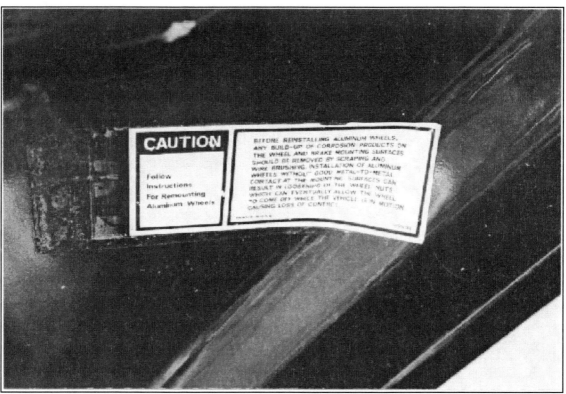

Warning decal used with snowflake wheels that was placed on the under side of the deck lid.

Late 1972-1981 style mirror

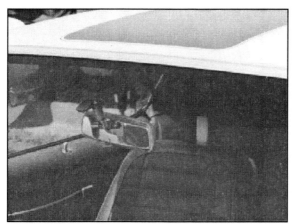

Windshield mount type used in 1970-early 1972 models.

Electrical Systems

Starting and Ignition
1970-1971

A Delco-Ramey top post 12-volt battery was standard in all Firebird models. A Y59 type battery was standard in models with the 350-ci V-8, unless air conditioning was ordered then the R-59 type battery was used, this battery was also the standard unit used on those models with a 4-bbl power-plant except those with Ram Air which used the heavy-duty unit a type R89S. All Firebirds, regardless of the battery type used the same battery tray listed as part number 478611. The battery tray should be painted semi-gloss black. A black colored twin lead positive cable was routed from the battery to the starter motor. Cable part number depends on the engine size.

1970-1971 Positive Battery Cable Part Numbers

Application	Part Number
All 1970 V-8	6296738
1971 V-8 Except 455-ci	8907357
1971 455-ci Ex. H.O.	8907039
1971 455-ci H.O.	8907040

1970-1971 Negative Battery Cable Part Numbers

Application	Part Number	Cable Length
All	6289160	26

Standard battery in 1970 Firebird was the R-59 Delco.

The start motor assembly was based on the original engine that was installed in your Firebird. Those with the 350-ci V-8 used (part number 11084450) a different unit than the 400/455-ci (part number 1108446) powerplants. Those with Ram Air or the High Out package used a different (part number 1108436) starter also. The starter housing should be painted semi-gloss (60-degrees) black.

The distributor was keyed to the engine size and a band or a number that is stamped directly on the housing can identify distributors.

1970 Distributors

CID	Carb	Transmission	Part Number
350-ci	2-bbl	All	1112008
400-ci	2-bbl	Automatic	1111148
400-ci	4-bbl	Manual	1111176
400-ci	4-bbl	Automatic	1111148
400-ci*	4-bbl	Manual	1112010
400-ci*	4-bbl	Automatic	1112009
400-ci#	4-bbl	All	1112011

* Ram Air III #-Ram Air IV

1971 Distributors

CID	Carb	Transmission	Part Number
350-ci		Manual+	1112063
350-ci		All++	1112090
		Automatic	1112069
400-ci	2-bbl		1112068
400-ci	4-bbl		1112070
455-ci *	4-bbl		1112072
455-ci#	4-bbl		1112073

* Except H.O. #- High Output + Early ++-Late

Packard Electric supplies most of the spark plug cables, and they will have the Packard logo on them. Year One has a correct supply of these cables and they are correctly date coded. The date code will consist of a four-character placement, which will look similar to this: 1Q70. The first digit is the quarter of the year that the cable was made. Be aware that most production was in the first and third quarters, which is signified by the letter "Q". The last two digits are the year of manufacture, not the model year. So the model year and the year of manufacture may not always agree. For example the code 3Q69 would be third quarter 1969 and be for a 1970 model while the code 3Q70 would be for the third quarter of 1970 and be for a 1971 model. The date code on the cables must precede the build date of your car. If for example your car were built in September 1970, it would be incorrect for it to use cables dated 1Q70.

1972-1977

The battery was changed in 1972; a top post battery is no longer correct for V-8 equipped Firebirds. Instead all batteries are side post mounted type. A Delco-Ramey built battery was still being used, but several different types were used. Also a new option appeared. The C-89 Maintenance Free Battery was optional only on cars with the 455-ci V-8 rated at 80-amps this battery can be identified by the lack of vent caps. The entire case was sealed. The non-sealed type battery featured a date code on the battery case, it is located between the first and second vent cap from the negative post.

1972 Side Mount Battery Usage

Standard	A/C	Heavy Duty	Maintenance Free
		350-ci	
Y88	R88	R88S	N/A
		400-ci	
R88	R88	R88S	N/A
		455-ci	
R88S	R88S	R88X	C89
AMP RATING			
Y88	**R88**	**R88S**	**R88X**
53	61	62	72

1973 Side Mount Battery Usage

Standard	A/C	Heavy Duty	Maintenance Free
		350-ci	
Y89	Y89	R89S	N/A
		400-ci	
R89	R89	R89S	N/A
		455-ci	
R89S	R89S	R89X	C89
AMP RATING			
Y89	**R89**	**R89S**	**R89X**
53	61	62	73

1974 Side Mount Battery Usage

Standard	A/C	Heavy Duty	Maintenance Free
		350-ci	
R89	R89	R89S	C-89
		400-ci	
R89	R89	R89S	C-89
		455-ci	
R89S	R89S	R89W	C89

1975-1977 Side Mount Battery Usage

Standard	A/C	Heavy Duty	Maintenance Free
		350-ci	
R87P	R87P	R87SP	C-89
		400-ci	
R87P	R87P	R89SP	C-89
		455-ci	
R87SP	R87SP	R87WP	C89

From 1970-1977 a type A (square-head) ignition key was used for the ignition switch. The starter motor was determined by engine size. The 350-ci V-8's used different part number than the 400-ci and 455-ci powerplants. The Super Duty 455-ci used a special starter motor both years. The starter housing should be painted semi-gloss (60-degrees) black.

1972-1977 Starter Motors

Engine Size	Part Number	Notes
1972		
350-ci	1108445	
400/455-ci	1108446	1108436 High Output
1973-1974		
350-ci	1108498	1-Shunt winding
400/455-ci	1108500	1108436-S.D.
1975-1976		
350-ci	1108758	1-Shunt winding
400/455-ci	1108759	
1977-1977		
305-ci	1109064	Man. Trans.
	1109074	Auto. Trans.
350-ci (Chevy)	1109067	Man. Trans.
	1109065	Auto. Trans.
350-ci/403-ci Oldsmobile	1109072	
400-ci	1108759	

1972 Distributors

CID	Carb	Transmission	Part Number
350-ci		Manual	1112140
		Automatic*	1112118
		Automatic**	1112143
400-ci	2-bbl	All*	1112119
		All**	1112189
	4-bbl	All	1112121
455-ci	4-bbl	All+	1112133
		All++	1112126

* Except California **-California only
+- With Transistor ignition ++- Without Transistor ignition

1973 Distributors

CID	Carb	Transmission /Item	Part Number
350-ci		Manual	1112202*
			1112806**
		Automatic	1112510*
			1112804**
		High Altitude	1112216*
			1112808**
		Calif.	1112201
400-ci	2-bbl		1112511*
			1112805**
		High Altitude	1112224*
			1112809**
		Calif.	1112199*
			1112224**
	4-bbl	Manual+	1112233*
		Automatic+	1112812**
		Manual++	1112231*
		Automatic++	1112813**
		High Altitude	1112232*
			1112814**
455-ci	4-bbl		1112191*
		High Altitude	1112507+
			1112220**++
455-ci S.D.	4-bbl		1112206

* Before March 15, 1973 **After March 15, 1973
+With Transistor Ignition ++-Without Transistor ignition

1974 Distributors

CID	Carb	Transmission /Item	Part Number
350-ci		Manual	1112236
		Automatic	1112234
		High Altitude	1111235
400-ci	2-bbl		1112237
		High Altitude	1111238
		Calif.	1112834
	4-bbl	Manual	1112239++
			1112812+
		Automatic	1112512++
			1112812+
		High Altitude	1112240++
455-ci	4-bbl		1112513++
			1112810+
		High Altitude	1112860
		Super Duty	11112243

1975 Distributors

CID	Carb	Transmission /Item	Part Number
350-ci	2-bbl	All	1112950
	4-bbl	Manual;	1112498
		Automatic	1112946
		Calif.	1112947
400-ci	4-bbl	Manual	1112495
		Automatic	1112928
455-ci	4-bbl		1112923

1976 Distributors

CID	Carb	Transmission /Item	Part Number
350-ci	2-bbl	Automatic	1112497
	4-bbl	Manual	
			1103206*
		Automatic	
		Calif.	1103206
400-ci	4-bbl	Manual	
		Automatic	1112928
			1103205*
455-ci	4-bbl		1112923

1977 Distributors

CID	Carb	Transmission /Item	Part Number
301-ci	2-bbl	Manual	1103273
		Automatic	1103272
350-ci	4-bbl		1103346
			1103323*
403-ci	4-bbl		1103347
			1103325*
400-ci	4-bbl	Manual	1103271
		Automatic	1103269+
			1103271++

* California only + With 2.92 axles or under ++- 2.93 axles and over

1978-1981

A sealed no-maintenance battery was standard on all Firebird models beginning in 1978. This battery was a side mount unit made by Delco Ramey and featured a built hydrometer. If the eye featured a green dot it was okay, if the eye was dark it might need to be jumped started, if the eye was yellow or bright battery was to be replaced. All but the 403-ci V-8 came standard with a type R85-5 battery; the 403-ci came standard with a R87-5 type. And a type R89-5 was the heavy-duty unit.

In 1980 the battery was still the same basic design that was used in 1978, but new models were used. All V-8 models, including the Turbo used a type 83, the heavy-duty battery was listed a type 87A.

The battery tray part number 547043 was the same unit that was used in 1976, which had became the replacement part for the 1970-1975 models. This same tray would continue till the end of the 1981 model year.

The start motor assembly was a type 10MT, several different units were used according to engine manufacturer. Those with the Pontiac built 301-ci used part number 1109523, those with the Oldsmobile built 350-ci or 403-ci used part number 1109072, those with the Chevrolet built 350-ci part number 1109065 those with the 305-ci V-8 used part number 1109074 with manual transmission and part number 1109064 with automatic. The 400-ci Pontiac used part number 1108759The starter housing should be painted semi-gloss (60-degrees) black.

1978 Distributors

CID	Carb	Transmission /Item	Part Number
305		Manual	1103281
		Automatic	1103282
			1103353**
350-ci		Manual	1103337
		Automatic	1103353
			1103285*
400-ci	4-bbl	High Perf.	1103315
	4-bbl	Automatic	1103359
403-ci	4-BBL		1103347**
			1103325*

*-Calif. **-High Altitude

1979 Distributors

CID	Carb	Transmission /Item	Part Number
301-ci	2-bbl		1103314
	4-bbl	Manual	1103400
		Automatic	1103399
305-ci		Manual	1103281
		Automatic	1103379
			1103285*
400-ci	4-bbl		1103315
403-CI	4-BBL		1103325

*-Calif.

1980 Distributors

CID	Carb	Transmission /Item	Part Number
301-ci		Except Perf	1103425
		`Turbo	1103444
305-ci			1103386

1980 Distributors

CID	Carb	Transmission /Item	Part Number
301-ci		Except Perf	1103453
		`Turbo	1103444*
			1103453**
305			10497135**
267-ci			1103370

*-Export **- with NB1 closed loop

A unit type distributor. The identification number is imprinted into the body as shown.

Charging Systems
1970-1981

A Delco-Ramey built alternator was used in all applications. For the most part a 37-amp alternator was standard with all powerplants, and a 55-amp alternator was used if air conditioning or the heavy alternator was ordered. As electrical systems were pushed to the limits and more powerful batteries became available, the ratings were revised in 1978. Standard rating was now 42-amps with 61 amps if the air conditioning was ordered with the 63-amp alternator with the heavy-duty unit. In 1981 this was again revised upwards as the standard rating was anywhere from 55-70 amps depending on the engine.

The identification part number along with the rating was stamped into the alternator housing. The alternator case should have a natural appearance.

1970 Alternators

Amp Rating	ID Number	Notes
V-8		
37 amp	1100902	
55-amp	1100903	
61 amp	1100904	A/C and rear window defroster or heavy Duty

1971-1974 Alternators

Amp Rating	ID Number	Notes
V-8		
37 amp	1100927	
55-amp	1100928	
80 amp	1101015	A/C and rear window defroster or heavy Duty

1975-1977 Alternators

Amp Rating	ID Number	Notes
V-8		
37 amp	1102481	
	1102384	
55-amp	1102482	
	1102385	
80 amp	1101027	A/C and rear window defroster or heavy Duty
	1101016	

1978-1979 Alternators

Amp Rating	ID Number	Notes
V-8		
42-amp	1102848	
61-amp	1102849	
63-amp	1105360	A/C and rear window defroster or heavy Duty

1980 Alternators

Amp Rating	ID Number	Notes
42-amp	1103060	
61-amp	1103061	
63-amp	1105360	A/C and rear window defroster or heavy Duty

Exterior Lighting
1970-1972

The headlamp switch was located to the left of the driver, it was listed as part number 1995154 and was the same unit used in 1968-1969 Firebirds and 1969-1971 Tempest and Grand Prix models. The knob was listed as part number 479773, and this is unique to the Firebird line. Two different bezels were used the 1970 models used part number 479766 while the 1971-1972 models used part number 482351. The switch controlled the twin-headlamp arrangement and tail amps, along with the instrument cluster lamp level.

The headlamps were listed as part numbers 5962996 and fit either side of the car. The tail lamps consisted of a design of two modified rectangular shapes that sloped downward at the outer ends. Bright trim finished the design on the outside of the red colored lenses. A gasket was used to seal the tail lamp to the body and between the lenses to the housing.

An example of the clear lens used in 1970-1971 front parking lamp

1970-1972 Tail Lamp Part Numbers

Housing	Lens	Trim
917146-RH	5962963- RH	5963094- RH
917145-LH	5962965- LH	5963095- LH

The signal lever was listed as part number 9786981 unless cruise control was also ordered then part number 6465256 was used. The front turn lamps were positioned under the front bumper and in the front valance pan. The individual lamps were made up of a housing, lens, and cross hair bezels, with a gasket in between the lens and the housings. The entire unit fit into a filler cup (part numbers 480705-RH and 480706 –LH 1970, and 483960-RH 483961-LH- 1971- early 1972) that was placed in the front valance pan. For late 1972 part numbers see the 1973 section.

1970-1972 Front Parking Lamp Part Numbers

Housing	Lens	Trim
916814-LH/RH	5960508 LH/RH	5960557 LH/RH

Notes:
Lens were clear for 1970-1971 models Early 1972 models used clear lens and the later models used amber colored lens.

Side marker lamps were placed at each corner with an amber colored lens at the front and rear at the rear with a bezel that, was painted the same color as the body, was used to frame the lens.

1970-1972 Side Marker Lamp Part Numbers

Lens		
Front	Rear	Notes
917400-RH	917402-RH	
917399-LH	917401-LH	
Bezels		
Front	Rear	
479083-RH	479630-RH	
479084-LH	479631-LH	

Late 1972-1973 models used a amber colored lens in the front parking lamp.

1973

There were very little changes in the 1973 models. The headlamp switch was the same as was the knob, and the bezel used the same part number it used in 1972.

The headlamps were the same as before, but the front parking lamp was given an amber colored lens. This change occurred in late built 1972 models. Early 1972 models used the 1970-71 styles where the bulb was part of the parking lamps, with the later style the bulb was part of the front-end harness assembly. The later 1972 style was continued over into the 1973 models year. The housing was listed as part number 5963966 and was used on either side. The cross hair bezel part number 5960557 was the same unit used on 1971 models.

Tail lamps were also slightly restyled. The overall design was the same but the housings were now listed as part number 5963088 right-hand and 5963089 left-hand. The lenses were listed as part numbers 5964664 right-hand and 5964663 left-hand and the bezel was listed as part numbers 5963094 right-hand and 5963093 left-hand. These parts became the replacement parts for the 1970-1972 models, and are the same except that the lights plug in from the rear of the housing as opposed to the bottom like they were in earlier years.

1974-1975

With the minor face-lift in 1974 some new components were used. The headlamp switch was listed as part number 1995199, which became the replacement part for the 1970-1973 models. The knob was the same part that was used in previous years, as was the bezel. These parts were used both years.

The headlamps were restyled to fit the new front end. The headlamp assembly was listed as part number 5964573 and fit either side. Bright bezel part numbers 492666 right-hand and 492667 left-hand were used and featured a more sloped appearance.

The tail lamps were an evolution of design. They featured the overall shape of the earlier units, but were more graduated and larger appearing. The housings part numbers 5968978 right–hand and 5968977 left-hand supported three turn/stop/tail lamps plus the back up lamps on the far inward side. A gasket was used to seal the housings and lens part numbers 5949828 right-hand and 5949827 left-hand together. An outer bezel part numbers 5949286 right hand and 5949285 left-hand was also used. The right-hand bezel supported the license plate lamp part number 928790.

Front turn lamps were different each year. The 1974 models used a very plain looking Ventura II lamp assembly listed as part numbers 912166 right-hand and 912165 left-hand. While the 1975 models used similar design ,they were made especially for the Firebird models and featured an outer bezel with a cross-hair design. The lamp housings were listed as part numbers 912464 right-hand and 912463 left-hand, and the bezels were listed as part numbers 496660 right-hand and 496661 left-hand. The side marker lamps were the same and used the same part numbers as the years before.

1970-1973 style tail lamp bezel, 1973 model is shown.

1976

The 1976 model was similar in design to the 1975 models. The headlamp switch used the same part number, as did the knob and bezel. Also using the same part numbers were the headlamps and the bezels.

The tail lamps featured the same general design that was used in 1975. However the bezels part numbers 5949286 right-hand and 5949285 left-hand were slightly restyled and the left-hand unit now supported the license plate lamp, which used the same part number as before. Even though the bezels changed the housings remained the same as those in 1975. All Firebirds used the same pair of lenses; they were listed as part numbers 5949828 right-hand and 5949827 left-hand.

Front parking lamps had a design that was similar to the 1975 model year , but used different part numbers. The lamp assemblies were listed as part numbers 912992 right-hand and 912991 left-hand. The cross hair bezels were listed as part numbers 499855 right-hand and 499856 left-hand and attached over the front parking lamp with a #8x3/4 screw with 18-thread count. Side marker lamps were a constant and used the same part numbers, including the bezels, which were painted to match the body, they were used since the 1970 model year.

1977-1978

Quad headlamps returned, although the same switch, knob and bezel were used to turn them on that was used in previous years. The headlamps were rectangular in shape and unique to each side. The outboard headlamps were listed as part numbers 5973930 right-hand and 5973929 left-hand while the standard inward lamps were listed as part number s 5973932 right-hand and 5973931 left-hand. Quartz inward headlamps were optional and they were listed as part number 16501996 right-hand and 16501995 left-hand.

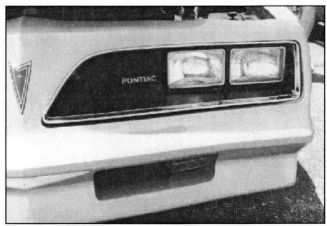

1977-78 Firebirds used quad headlamp

The tail lamps were the same units including part numbers that were used on the 1976 models for 1977. In 1978 two different sets of tail lamps were used. Most of the birds still used the set of tail lamps that were used in 1977 Trans Ams and those Formulas with the W50 appearance package used special blacked out tail lamp lens listed as part numbers 5970348 right-hand and 5970347 left-hand. However, the bezels part numbers 5949286 right-hand and 5949285 left-hand remained the same with both sets of lens.

1979-1981 Firebird used this headlamp arrangement. Note the front parking lamp tucked away in the grille in the front bumper.

The front parking lamps were restyled and resided in the front bumper. They were listed as part number 913648- right hand and 913647 left-hand, and were covered by a cross hair bezel listed as part number 499855 right-hand and 499856 left-hand, which are the same part number used in 1976. The side marker lamps and bezels used the same part numbers that they used in the years before.

1979 -1981

Quad headlamps remained but were sheltered by the huge front nosepiece. However, the headlamps used the same part numbers as the 1978 model year. Due to the inset in the body bezels had to be added. Two different sets were used. Bright chrome bezels were used on the base Firebird models, and black colored bezels were used on all the other models. It is incorrect for a chrome bezel to be used on a Trans Am.

Front parking lamps were restyled and integrated into the grilles that placed in the front bumper. They were listed as part number 914010 right-hand and 914009 left-hand. No bezel was used over the face of these lamps. The front marker lamps were still the same as in previous years.

The entire lamp assembly was restyled. A total of four different housings were used, the standard set up, and those which used the custom extension which added an extra lamp on the inward side of each housing. Those models with the custom extension will have a smokey gray colored outer lens, while those without it will have a red colored inner lens only. Trans Ams and Formulas were standard with the custom extension; other models with this included the 1980 Esprit, and others with appearance packages. The look of full width tail lamps was carried out by the use of a cover that was used over the fuel door. Part number 5973207 was used without the custom extension and part number 5973205 was used with the custom extension. A close out filler part number 5930701 was required on the left-hand side without the custom extension; no filler was needed on the right-hand side.

An example of the full width with custom extension tail lamps used on the 1979-81 Trans Am.

A close up of the custom extension outer lens.

1979-1981 Tail Lamp Part Numbers

Type	Housings		Inner Lens		Outer Lens		Notes
	Right-Hand	Left-Hand	Right-Hand	Left-Hand	Right-Hand	Left-Hand	
Without Extension	5970714	5970713	5970720	5970719	Not Used	Not Used	
With Extension	5970794	5970793	5970806	5970805	5937036	5937035	
With Extension	5970794	5970793	5970806	5970805	5937874*	5937873*	With 1980 Yellowbird only *-Yellow in color.

1979-1981 Tail lamps without rear extensions.

Engine Harness Part Numbers

Engine Type	Part Number	Notes
1970		
V-8 Except Ram Air	8903743	Coded 3743
Ram Air	8903830	Coded 3830
1971		
V-8 Except 455-ci H.O.	8904423	Manual Transmission
V-8 except 455 H.O.	8904564	Automatic Transmission
455-ci H.O.	8904375	Coded 4375
1972		
All Except 455 H.O.	8912112	
445-ci H.O.	8912113	Wm or YB code
455-ci H.O.	8912266	With WD or YE codes
1973		
Early V-8	N/A	
Late V-8	8915286	
1974		
All V-8	8915154	Except unit distributor or HE.I.
1976		
Early V-8	N/A	
Late V08	12003023	Coded 2362
1977-1978		
Pontiac built V-8	12003023	Coded 2362
Oldsmobile built V-8	12002727	Coded 2727
Chevrolet built V-8	12006635	Coded 6635
1979		
Pontiac built V-8	12006628	Coded 6628
Oldsmobile built V-8	12008872	Coded 8872
Chevrolet built V-8	12006635	Coded 6635
1980		
301-ci without gauges	12009338	Coded 9338
301-ci with gauges and T.H. 350	12009349	Coded 9349
301-ci with gauges, ex. T.H. 350	12009575	Coded 9575
305-ci without gauges	12005774	Coded 5774
301-ci Trubo	12009893	Coded 9893
1981		
267-ci Export with gauges 305-ci with gauges	12009991	Coded 9991
267-ci Export without gauges	12016128	Coded 6128
305-ci without gauges	12016128	Coded 6128
265-ci or 301-ci without gauges	12009961	Coded 9961
265-ci or 301-ci with gauges	12009962	Coded 9962
301-ci Turbo Export	12009993	Coded 9993
301-ci Turbo	12009923	Coded 9923

Note harness is label with a tag that reads the part number or the last four digits of the part number.

Wiper Systems
1970-1981

A two-speed electric windshield wiper motor was standard all 12 years. The base Firebird for 10 years came with standard wiper. Which means that the wiper arms can be seen in the park position. All other models came with the concealed wipers (the arms cannot be seen in the park position) as standard equipment. The concealed wipers were available as an option on the base Firebird. Beginning in 1980 the standard wiper on all Firebird models was the concealed unit. The standard (non-concealed) wipers used a square shaped motor, while the concealed wiper motor has a round shape.

A Pulse control wiper was first offered as an option in 1977. Option RPO CD4 remained available until the end of the 1981 model year. Basically a delayed wiper system this unit used a round shaped motor and can be identified by a green wire leading to the timing circuit.

A total of 7 different motors were used in the 12 year run. Note that there was a change in design of the concealed type motor in the 1973 model year. Early models used the same motor that was used in the 1970 1972 models. This unit will have separate magnet switch assembly and terminal board, while the later style will have an integrated magnet switch and terminal board as one part, and has an opening in the washer pump frame and cover for the terminals. The motor assembly should have a two-tone finish. The terminal case should be painted 30-degrees semi-gloss black. The upper motor housing should also be painted gloss black, but the lower motor case should have a natural appearance.

Wiper Motor Part Numbers		
Model Year	Standard	Concealed
1970-1973*	4918442	4939586
1973**-1975	4918442	4960951
1976-1979	22048242	22048252 22048344

The type of wiper system in the car regulated the wiper switch. Those with the non-concealed wipers used a different part number than those with the concealed wipers. Part number 1994090 was used on the base 1970-1971 Firebirds without the concealed wipers and part number 1994089 was used on all the other 1970-1972 models. The switch was restyled in 1973 and those base Firebirds without the concealed wiper arms used part number 1994178, while the other models used part number 1994179. These part numbers continued over till the 1977-model year., where they were joined by part number 497234 which was used on the pulse wiper option, and all three continued till the end of the 1979 model year. The wiper switches were again restyled in 1980 and those without the pulse wiper option used the same part number as in 1979, which was when the pulse wiper option was changed to part number 12505681.

A total of 5 washer jars were used. 1970-1974 used part number 3961557, a replacement part number of 3990892 took its place in 1975. The washer jar was restyled in 1975 and given part number 499857, which remained till the end of the 1976 model year. Then part number 248324 took its place and was used up till the middle of the 1978 model year, except with the pulse wiper option. Later built 1978 models used part number 461252, which was used with all wiper options till the end of the 1981 model year. Even though the washer jar was changed the bracket part number 480893 remained the same from 1970-1981.

Only two different sets of washer nozzles were used: the 1970-1976 models used part number 480753, while the 1977-1981 models used part number 100013928. These nozzles were used on either side of the car in both cases.

The type of wiper system in the car also regulated the wiper arms. Those with the exposed wiper arms used part number 9806040 and fit either side, while those with the concealed wipers used wiper arms that were designed for each side of the car. They were listed as part numbers 9806042 right-hand and 9806043 left-hand all 12 years. Either an Anco or Trico blade insert was used.

Wiper switch with Pulse wiper option

Heater Systems
1970-1981

All Firebirds were equipped with an upper ventilation system, because they did not have vent windows. The heater motor assembly part number 4918686 all three years, is the standard heater motor. Those with air conditioning used a different motor for these part numbers see the Options chapter of this guide. The motor assembly is attached to a blower case part number 3016905, which is located on the right-hand side of the firewall all 12 years.

Standard wiper switch

The heater controls were located in the center of the instrument panel. For 1970-All except Trans Am models used part number 7312272, Trans Am models used part number 7930582. In 1971 the Trans Am models used the same part number but the other models used part number 7935372, For 1972 the face of the panels were restyled and read defrost instead of de ice as the earlier models. The above part numbers that were used in 1971 were used as replacement part numbers till the end of the 1976 model year. While they will fit they are incorrect as they read de ice, instead of defrost. The part numbers for 1972 models were listed as 7938572, except Trans Am models, which used part number 7938582. The control was replaced with part number 16004442, which was used with all 1976 Firebird models, and would remain till the end of the 1981 model year.

Regular Production And Dealer Installed Options

Both Regular Production (those installed at the assembly plant) and Dealer Installed options (installed solely by the dealer) were available all 12 years. The option codes begin with a letter, which indicates the option group, (for example the letter "L" indicates the engine option group) the additional code represents that individual option.

In this section listed first are the options that were available each year. Note that some options like power brakes or power steering are covered elsewhere in this guide under that particular heading. For example: the option power steering is covered under the heading steering systems.

Dealer installed options may some time mirror the factory installed option, such as outside mirrors. The difference between these options was, besides being installed by the dealer, was that dealer installed options are coded by a part number, instead of a sales or RPO code. For a dealer-installed option to be considered correct there must be paperwork that backs up the claim and that the dealer for the original owner installed it, mostly before they (the original owner) took delivery of it.

1970 Firebird Dealer Installed Options	
Sales Number	**Option**
988698	16-in wiper blade
994124	Power brakes
988863	Electric clock
988826	Compass
988761	Tissue Dispenser
988700	Front License plate frame
988865	Fender splash guards
988823	Door edge guards
984642	Engine block heater 750Watt
988958	2.00in Hitch ball
988859	Hood hold downs
988834	Hood Lock package
988605	4-speed knob
993997	Luggage lamp
988824	Under hood lamp
986602	Littercontainer-Blue
986603	Littercontainer-Fawn
986607	Liter container-Black
986608	Littercontainer-Red
984825	Locking gas Cap
984701	Locking Rear Spare
988845	Front floor mat Black
988846	Front floor mat Dark Green
988847	Front floor mat Dark Brown
988848	Front floor mat Dark Red
988849	Front floor mat Dark Saddle
988850	Front floor mat Dark Sandalwood
988851	Front floor mat Bright Blue
988852	Front floor mat Ivory
988842	Rear Floor mat Black
988790	Rear Floor mat Blue
988792	Rear Floor mat Green
988793	Rear Floor mat Sandalwood
988794	Rear Floor mat Saddle
988795	Rear Floor mat Brown
988796	Rear Floor mat Red
988856	Remote control mirror LH
988857	RH Mirror
988860	Power Steering
988832	Pushbutton radio
988830	AM/FM Radio
988831	AM/FM Stereo
988855	Deck Lid release
988854	Rear Speaker
988829	Tape Player without console
988828	Tape player with console
988827	Hood mounted tachometer
988836	Tire pump
988870	Wheel trim with N98 wheels

1970 Firebird Factory Installed Options

Sales Code	Option	Sales Code	Option
A01	Tinted glass ,all	M53	2-speed Automatic
A02	Tinted glass, Windshield only	N30	Deluxe Steering wheel Base Firebird only
A31	Power Windows	N33	Tilt Steering column
A90	Remote Deck lid Release	N41	Power Steering
AK1	Custom Seat Belts	N65	Space Saver Spare Tire
AU3	Power Door Locks	N98	Rally II wheels
B32	Front floor mats	NK3	Formula steering wheel
B33	Rear Floor Mats	P02	Custom wheel Covers
B42	Rear Compartment Floor mat	P05	Honey Comb wheels
B80	Roof Drip rail moldings	P06	Chrome Trim rings
B84	Vinyl Side moldings	Pl3	E78x14 white wall
B85	Belt Reveal Moldings	PL4	F70x14 white letter tires
B93	Door edge guards	PM7	F60x15 tires
B96	Front and rear wheel moldings	PX6	F78x14 Whitewalls
C08	Vinyl Top	PY6	F70x14 Blackwall tires
C24	Concealed wipers Base Firebird only	TP1	Heavy Duty Delco Battery
C49	Electric Rear window defroster	U05	Dual Horns Base Firebird only
C50	Rear Window Defogger	U30	Rallye instruments with tach/clock
C60	Custom Air Conditioning	U35	Electric clock
D34	Right-hand visor Vanity mirror	U55	Cassette Tape Player
D35	Dual sport mirrors	U57	8-track Tape player
D55	Front Console	U58	AM/FM Stereo
D58	Rear Console	U63	AM Radio
D80	Rear Spoiler	U69	AM/FM Radio
D98	Sport Stripes	U80	Rear Seat Speaker
G80	Safe-T-Track rear axle	V01	Heavy Duty Radiator
G90-G92	Performance axles	W54	Custom trim package
J50	Power Brakes	W63	Rally instruments with clock
K45	Dual stage air cleaner	Wt5	High Altitude Package
L30	350 ci V-8 2-bbl	Wu1	Self charging flashlight
L65	400 ci 2-bbl	Y88	Basic Group
L67	400-ci Ram Air IV	Y92	Convenience lamps
L74	400-ci H.O. Ram Air III	Y96	Handling package
L78	400-ci 4-bbl		
M12	3-spd manual on floor		
M13	H.D. 3-spd Manual on floor		
M20	4-spd Manual		
M21	4-spd. Close Ratio		
M22	4-spd Close ratio Heavy Duty		
M38	T.H. 350		
M40	T.H. 400		

1971 Firebird Factory Installed Options

Sales Code	Option	Sales Code	Option
A01	Tinted glass, all	M53	2-speed Automatic
A02	Tinted glass, Windshield only	N30	Custom Cushion Steering wheel Base Firebird only
A31	Power Windows	N33	Tilt Steering column
A90	Remote Deck lid Release	N41	Power Steering
AK1	Custom Seat Belts	N65	Space Saver Spare Tire
AU3	Power Door Locks	N98	Rally II wheels
B32	Front floor mats	NK3	Formula steering wheel
B33	Rear Floor Mats	P02	Custom wheel Covers
B42	Rear Compartment Floor mat	P05	Honey Comb wheels
B80	Roof Drip rail moldings	P06	Chrome Trim rings
B84	Vinyl Side moldings	Pl3	E78x14 white wall
B85	Belt Reveal Moldings	PL4	F70x14 white letter tires
B93	Door edge guards	PM7	F60x15 tires
B96	Front and rear wheel moldings	PX6	F78x14 Whitewalls
C08	Vinyl Top	PY6	F70x14 Blackwall tires
C24	Concealed wipers Base Firebird only	TP1	Heavy Duty Delco Battery
C49	Electric Rear window defroster	U05	Dual Horns Base Firebird only
C50	Rear Window Defogger	U30	Rallye instruments with tach/clock
C60	Custom Air Conditioning	U35	Electric clock
D34	Right-hand visor Vanity mirror	U55	Cassette Tape Player
D35	Dual sport mirrors	U57	8-track Tape player
D55	Front Console	U58	AM/FM Stereo
D58	Rear Console	U63	AM Radio
D80	Rear Spoiler	U69	AM/FM Radio
D98	Sport Stripes	U80	Rear Seat Speaker
G80	Safe-T-Track rear axle	V01	Heavy Duty Radiator
G90-G92	Performance axles	W54	Custom trim package
J50	Power Brakes	W63	Rally instruments with clock
K45	Dual stage air cleaner	W74	Warning /Clock lamps
L30	350 ci V-8 2-bbl	Wt5	High Altitude Package
L65	400 ci 2-bbl	Wu1	Self charging flashlight
L75	455-ci 4-bbl	Wu3	Ram Air for Formula models with LS5
L78	400-ci 4-bbl	Y88	Basic Group
LS5	455-ci H.O.	Y92	Convenience lamps
M12	3-spd manual on floor	Y96	Handling package
M13	H.D. 3-spd Manual on floor		
M20	4-spd Manual		
M21	4-spd. Close Ratio		
M22	4-spd Close ratio Heavy Duty		
M38	T.H. 350		
M40	T.H. 400		

1972 Firebird Factory Installed Options

Sales Code	Option	Sales Code	Option
A01	Tinted glass, all	N41	Power Steering
A02	Tinted glass, Windshield only	N65	Space Saver Spare Tire
A31	Power Windows	N98	Rally II wheels
A90	Remote Deck lid Release	NK3	Formula steering wheel
AK1	Custom Seat Belts	P02	Custom wheel Covers
AU3	Power Door Locks	P05	Honey Comb wheels
B32	Front floor mats	P06	Chrome Trim rings
B33	Rear Floor Mats	PX6	F78x14 whitewall tires
B42	Rear Compartment Floor mat	PL3	E78x14 whitewall tires
B80	Roof Drip rail moldings	PY6	F70x14 balckwall tires
B84	Vinyl Side moldings	Pl4	White letter F70 tires
B85	Belt Reveal Moldings	UA1	Heavy Duty Delco Battery
B93	Door edge guards	U80	Rear Seat Speaker
B96	Front and rear wheel moldings	U30	Rallye instruments with tach/clock
C08	Vinyl Top	U35	Electric clock
C24	Concealed wipers Base Firebird only	U55	Cassette Tape Player
C49	Electric Rear window defroster	U57	8-track Tape player
C60	Custom Air Conditioning	U58	AM/FM Stereo
D34	Right-hand visor Vanity mirror	U63	AM Radio
D35	Dual sport mirrors	U69	AM/FM Radio
D55	Front Console	U80	Rear Seat Speaker
D58	Rear Console	V01	Heavy Duty Radiator
D80	Rear Spoiler		
G80	Safe-T-Track rear axle		
G92	Performance axles		
K45	Dual stage air cleaner		
L30	350 ci V-8 2-bbl		
L65	400 ci 2-bbl		
L75	455-ci 4-bbl		
L78	400-ci 4-bbl		
LS5	455-ci H.O.		
M12	3-spd manual on floor		
M13	H.D. 3-spd Manual on floor		
M20	4-spd Manual		
M21	4-spd. Close Ratio		
M22	4-spd Close ratio Heavy Duty		
M38	T.H. 350		
M40	T.H. 400		
N30	Custom Cushion Steering wheel Base Firebird only		
N33	Tilt Steering column		

1973 Firebird Factory Installed Options

Sales Code	Option	Sales Code	Option
A01	Tinted glass, all	M38	T.H. 350
A02	Tinted glass, Windshield only	M40	T.H. 400
A31	Power Windows	N30	Custom Cushion Steering wheel Base Firebird only
A90	Remote Deck lid Release	N33	Tilt Steering column
AK1	Custom Seat Belts	N41	Power Steering
AU3	Power Door Locks	N65	Space Saver Spare Tire
AV6	Electric Door locks	N98	Rally II wheels
B32	Front floor mats	NK3	Formula steering wheel
B33	Rear Floor Mats	P01	Deluxe Wheel Covers
B42	Rear Compartment Floor mat	P02	Custom wheel Covers
B80	Roof Drip rail moldings	P05	Honey Comb wheels
B84	Vinyl Side moldings	P06	Chrome Trim rings
B85	Belt Reveal Moldings	P85	Gr7x14 whitewall tires
B93	Door edge guards	PL3	E78x14 whitewall tires
B96	Front and rear wheel moldings	Pl4	White letter F70 tires
C08	Vinyl Top	PX5	F78x14 Blackwall tires
C24	Concealed wipers Base Firebird only	PX6	F78x14 Whitewall tires
C49	Electric Rear window defroster	PY6	F70x14 Blackwall tires
C50	Rear Window defogger	TP1	Maintenance Free Battery
C60	Custom Air Conditioning	U30	Rallye instruments with tach/clock
D34	Right-hand visor Vanity mirror	U35	Electric clock
D35	Dual sport mirrors	U55	Cassette Tape Player
D55	Front Console	U57	8-track Tape player
D58	Rear Console	U58	AM/FM Stereo
D80	Rear Spoiler	U63	AM Radio
G80	Safe-T-Track rear axle	U69	AM/FM Radio
G92	Performance axles	U80	Rear Seat Speaker
K45	Dual stage air cleaner	U80	Rear Seat Speaker
K65	Unitized ignition required with LS5	UA1	Heavy Duty Delco Battery
L30	350 ci V-8 2-bbl	V01	Heavy Duty Radiator
L65	400 ci 2-bbl	V32	Front and rear bumper guards
L75	455-ci 4-bbl	VJ9	California Emission package
L78	400-ci 4-bbl	W51	Special Paint
LS2	455-ci Super Duty	W63	Rally Gauges with clock
M12	3-spd manual on floor	Wt5	High Altitude Package
M13	H.D. 3-spd Manual on floor	Wu3	Ram Air for Formula models mandatory with LS5
M20	4-spd Manual	WW7	Screaming Chicken hood decal
M21	4-spd. Close Ratio	WW8	Rally Cluster with tach/clock
		Y90	Custom Trim Group
		Y92	Convenience lamps
		Y96	Handling package
		YH99	Formula Handling package

1974 Firebird Factory Installed Options

Sales Code	Option	Sales Code	Option
A01	Tinted glass, all	M38	T.H. 350
A02	Tinted glass, Windshield only	M40	T.H. 400
A31	Power Windows	N30	Custom Cushion Steering wheel Base Firebird only
A90	Remote Deck lid Release	N33	Tilt Steering column
AK1	Custom Seat Belts	N41	Power Steering
AU3	Power Door Locks	N65	Space Saver Spare Tire
AV6	Electric Door locks	N98	Rally II wheels
B32	Front floor mats	NK3	Formula steering wheel
B33	Rear Floor Mats	P01	Deluxe Wheel Covers
B42	Rear Compartment Floor mat	P02	Custom wheel Covers
B80	Roof Drip rail moldings	P05	Honey Comb wheels
B84	Vinyl Side moldings	P06	Chrome Trim rings
B85	Belt Reveal Moldings	P85	Gr7x14 whitewall tires
B93	Door edge guards	PL3	E78x14 whitewall tires
B96	Front and rear wheel moldings	PI4	White letter F70 tires
C08	Vinyl Top	PX5	F78x14 Blackwall tires
C24	Concealed wipers Base Firebird only	PX6	F78x14 Whitewall tires
C49	Electric Rear window defroster	PY6	F70x14 Blackwall tires
C50	Rear Window defogger	TP1	Maintenance Free Battery
C60	Custom Air Conditioning	U30	Rallye instruments with tach/clock
D34	Right-hand visor Vanity mirror	U35	Electric clock
D35	Dual sport mirrors	U55	Cassette Tape Player
D55	Front Console	U57	8-track Tape player
D58	Rear Console	U58	AM/FM Stereo
D80	Rear Spoiler	U63	AM Radio
G80	Safe-T-Track rear axle	U69	AM/FM Radio
G92	Performance axles	U80	Rear Seat Speaker
K45	Dual stage air cleaner	U80	Rear Seat Speaker
K65	Unitized ignition required with LS5	UA1	Heavy Duty Delco Battery
L30	350 ci V-8 2-bbl	V01	Heavy Duty Radiator
L65	400 ci 2-bbl	V32	Front and rear bumper guards
L75	455-ci 4-bbl	VJ9	California Emission package
L78	400-ci 4-bbl	W51	Special Paint
LS2	455-ci Super Duty	W63	Rally Gauges with clock
M12	3-spd manual on floor	Wt5	High Altitude Package
M13	H.D. 3-spd Manual on floor	Wu3	Ram Air for Formula models mandatory with LS5
M20	4-spd Manual	WW7	Screaming Chicken hood decal
M21	4-spd. Close Ratio	WW8	Rally Cluster with tach/clock
		Y90	Custom Trim Group
		Y92	Convenience lamps
		Y96	Handling package
		YH99	Formula Handling package

1975 Firebird Factory Installed Options

Sales Code	Option	Sales Code	Option
A01	Tinted glass, all	N41	Power Steering
A02	Tinted glass, Windshield only	N65	Space Saver Spare Tire
A31	Power Windows	N98	Rally II wheels
A90	Remote Deck lid Release	NK3	Formula steering wheel
AK1	Custom Seat Belts	P01	Deluxe Wheel Covers
AU3	Power Door Locks	P02	Custom wheel Covers
AV6	Electric Door locks	P05	Honey Comb wheels
B32	Front floor mats	P06	Chrome Trim rings
B33	Rear Floor Mats	P85	Gr7x14 whitewall tires
B42	Rear Compartment Floor mat	QBU	FE78x14 blackwalll tires
B80	Roof Drip rail moldings	QBW	FR78x14 Whitewall tires (credit option)
B84	Vinyl Side moldings	QBX	Gr70x15 tires (radial)
B85	Belt Reveal Moldings	QFL	F78x14 tires Blackwall tires Credit option
B93	Door edge guards	QXY	GR70x15 white letter tires (radial)
B96	Front and rear wheel moldings	T63	Headlamp on buzzer
Bs1	Added insulation Stand in Esprit	TGJ	Radial Tuned Suspension with whitewall tires.
C08	Vinyl Top	TGK	Radial Tuned Suspension with Whiter letter tires
C24	Concealed wipers Base Firebird only	THB	E78x15 white letter tires
C49	Electric Rear window defroster	TML	White letter F70 tires
C50	Rear Window defogger	TP1	Maintenance Free Battery
C60	Custom Air Conditioning	U18	Export Speedometer/Clock
D34	Right-hand visor Vanity mirror	U30	Rallye instruments with tach/clock
D35	Dual sport mirrors	U35	Electric clock
D55	Front Console	U55	Cassette Tape Player
D58	Rear Console	U57	8-track Tape player
D80	Rear Spoiler	U58	AM/FM Stereo
G80	Safe-T-Track rear axle	U63	AM Radio
G92	Performance axles	U69	AM/FM Radio
JL1	Pedal Trim	U80	Rear Seat Speaker
K05	Engine block heater	U80	Rear Seat Speaker
K45	Dual stage air cleaner	UA1	Heavy Duty Delco Battery
K65	Unitized ignition required with LS5	UR1	Fuel economy gauge
L30	350 ci V-8 2-bbl	V01	Heavy Duty Radiator
L65	400 ci 2-bbl	V32	Front and rear bumper guards
L75	455-ci 4-bbl	VJ9	California Emission package
L78	400-ci 4-bbl	W51	Special Paint
M15	. 3-spd Manual on floor	W63	Rally Gauges with clock
M20	4-spd Manual	Wt5	High Altitude Package
M21	4-spd. Close Ratio	Wu3	Ram Air for Formula models mandatory with LS5
M38	T.H. 350	WW7	Screaming Chicken hood decal
M40	T.H. 400	WW8	Rally Cluster with tach/clock
N30	Custom Cushion Steering wheel Base Firebird only	Y90	Custom Trim Group
N33	Tilt Steering column	Y92	Convenience lamps
		Y96	Handling package
		YH99	Formula Handling package

1976 Firebird Factory Installed Options

Sales Code	Option	Sales Code	Option
A01	Tinted glass, all	N41	Power Steering
A02	Tinted glass, Windshield only	N65	Space Saver Spare Tire
A31	Power Windows	N97	Body colored Rally II wheels
A90	Remote Deck lid Release	N98	Rally II wheels
AK1	Custom Seat Belts	NK3	Formula steering wheel
AU3	Power Door Locks	P01	Deluxe Wheel Covers
AV6	Electric Door locks	P02	Custom wheel Covers
B32	Front floor mats	P05	Honey Comb wheels
B33	Rear Floor Mats	P06	Chrome Trim rings
B42	Rear Compartment Floor mat	P85	Gr7x14 whitewall tires
B80	Roof Drip rail moldings	QBP	Fr78x15 white letter tires
B84	Vinyl Side moldings	QBU	FE78x14 blackwall tires
B84	Color-Keyed Vinyl body	QBW	FR78x14 Whitewall tires (credit option)
B85	Belt Reveal Moldings	QBX	Gr70x15 tires (radial)
B93	Door edge guards	QFL	F78x14 tires Blackwall tires Credit option
B96	Front and rear wheel moldings	QXY	GR70x15 white letter tires (radial)
Bs1	Added insulation Stand in Esprit	T63	Headlamp on buzzer
C08	Vinyl Top	TGJ	Radial Tuned Suspension with whitewall tires.
C24	Concealed wipers Base Firebird only	TGK	Radial Tuned Suspension with Whiterletter tires
C49	Electric Rear window defroster	THB	E78x15 white letter tires
C50	Rear Window defogger	TML	White letter F70 tires
C60	Custom Air Conditioning	TP1	Maintenance Free Battery
CB7	Canopy Top	U18	Export Speedometer/Clock
CC1	T-tops	U30	Rallye instruments with tach/clock
D34	Right-hand visor Vanity mirror	U35	Electric clock
D35	Dual sport mirrors	U55	Cassette Tape Player
D55	Front Console	U57	8-track Tape player
D58	Rear Console	U58	AM/FM Stereo
D80	Rear Spoiler	U63	AM Radio
G80	Safe-T-Track rear axle	U69	AM/FM Radio
G92	Performance axles	U80	Rear Seat Speaker
JL1	Pedal Trim	U80	Rear Seat Speaker
K05	Engine block heater	UA1	Heavy Duty Delco Battery
K45	Dual stage air cleaner	UN9	Radio Accommodation package
K65	Unitized ignition required with LS5	UR1	Fuel economy gauge
L30	350 ci V-8 2-bbl	V01	Heavy Duty Radiator
L65	400 ci 2-bbl	V32	Front and rear bumper guards
L75	455-ci 4-bbl	VJ9	California Emission package
L76	350-ci 4-bbl	VQ2	Heavy Duty Cooling
L78	400-ci 4-bbl	W50	Formula Appearance package
M15	. 3-spd Manual on floor	W51	Special Paint
M20	4-spd Manual	W63	Rally Gages with clock
M21	4-spd. Close Ratio	Wt5	High Altitude Package
M38	T.H. 350	WW7	Screaming Chicken hood decal
M40	T.H. 400	WW8	Rally Cluster with tach/clock
N30	Custom Cushion Steering wheel	Y81	Black Special edition trans AM without T-tops
N33	Tilt Steering column	Y82	Black Special edition trans AM with T-tops
		Y90	Custom Trim Group
		Y92	Convenience lamps
		Y96	Handling package
		YH99	Formula Handling package

1977 Firebird Factory Installed Options

Sales Code	Option	Sales Code	Option
A01	Tinted glass, all	N33	Tilt Steering column
A02	Tinted glass, Windshield only	N41	Power Steering
A31	Power Windows	N65	Space Saver Spare Tire
A90	Remote Deck lid Release	N97	Body colored Rally II wheels
AK1	Custom Seat Belts	N98	Rally II wheels
AU3	Power Door Locks	NK3	Formula steering wheel
AV6	Electric Door locks	P01	Deluxe Wheel Covers
B32	Front floor mats	P02	Custom wheel Covers
B33	Rear Floor Mats	P06	Chrome Trim rings
B42	Rear Compartment Floor mat	P85	Gr7x14 whitewall tires
B80	Roof Drip rail moldings	QBX	Radial Tuned Suspension
B84	Vinyl Side moldings	QCY	Radial Tuned Suspension Rally type
B84	Color-Keyed Vinyl body moldings Except Trans Am	T63	Headlamp on buzzer
B85	Belt Reveal Moldings	THB	E78x15 white letter tires
B93	Door edge guards	TML	White letter F70 tires
B96	Front and rear wheel moldings	TP1	Maintenance Free Battery
Bs1	Added insulation Stand in Esprit	U18	Export Speedometer/Clock
C08	Vinyl Top	U30	Rallye instruments with tach/clock
C24	Concealed wipers Base Firebird only	U35	Electric clock
C49	Electric Rear window defroster	U55	Cassette Tape Player
C60	Custom Air Conditioning	U57	8-track Tape player
C95	Dome reading lamp	U58	AM/FM Stereo
CB7	Canopy Top	U63	AM Radio
D34	Right-hand visor Vanity mirror	U69	AM/FM Radio
D35	Dual sport mirrors	U80	Rear Seat Speaker
D55	Front Console	U80	Rear Seat Speaker
D58	Rear Console	UA1	Heavy Duty Delco Battery
D80	Rear Spoiler	UN8	CB Radio requires Console and UN9 package
G80	Safe-T-Track rear axle	UN9	Radio Accommodation package
G92	Performance axles	UR1	Fuel economy gauge
JL1	Pedal Trim	V01	Heavy Duty Radiator
K05	Engine block heater	V32	Front and rear bumper guards
K30	Cruise Control	V81	Trailer tow package
K45	Dual stage air cleaner	VJ9	California Emission package
K65	Unitized ignition required with LS5	VQ2	Heavy Duty Cooling
L27	301-ci 2-bbl	W50	Formula Appearance package
L76	350-ci 4-bbl	W51	Special Paint
L78	400-ci 4-bbl	W60	Skybird Option Package
L80	403-ci 4-bbl	W63	Rally Gauges with clock
M15	. 3-spd Manual on floor	Wt5	High Altitude Package
M20	4-spd Manual	WW7	Screaming Chicken hood decal
M21	4-spd. Close Ratio	WW8	Rally Cluster with tach/clock
M38	T.H. 350	Y81	Black Special edition trans AM without T-tops
M40	T.H. 400	Y82	Black Special edition trans AM with T-tops
N30	Custom Cushion Steering wheel	Y90	Custom Trim Group
		Y92	Convenience lamps
		Y96	Handling package
		YH99	Formula Handling package
		YJ8	Snowflake aluminum wheels

Due to space limitations some options have been omitted.

1978 Firebird Factory Installed Options

Sales Code	Option	Sales Code	Option
A02	Tinted glass, Windshield only	QBX	Radial Tuned Suspension
A31	Power Windows	QCY	Radial Tuned Suspension Rally type
A90	Remote Deck lid Release	TP1	Maintenance Free Battery
AK1	Custom Seat Belts	U18	Export Speedometer/Clock
AU3	Power Door Locks	U30	Rallye instruments with tach/clock
AV6	Electric Door locks	U35	Electric clock
B37	Front/ Rear floor mats	U55	Cassette Tape Player
B42	Rear Compartment Floor mat	U57	8-track Tape player
B80	Roof Drip rail moldings	U58	AM/FM Stereo
B84	Vinyl Side moldings	U63	AM Radio
B84	Color-Keyed Vinyl body moldings Except Trans Am	U69	AM/FM Radio
B85	Belt Reveal Moldings	U80	Rear Seat Speaker
B93	Door edge guards	U80	Rear Seat Speaker
B96	Front and rear wheel moldings	UA1	Heavy Duty Delco Battery
Bs1	Added insulation Stand in Esprit	UN8	CB Radio requires Console and UN9 package
C08	Vinyl Top	UN9	Radio Accommodation package
C24	Concealed wipers Base Firebird only	UR1	Fuel economy gauge
C49	Electric Rear window defroster	V01	Heavy Duty Radiator
C60	Custom Air Conditioning	V32	Front and rear bumper guards
C95	Dome reading lamp	V81	Trailer tow package
CB7	Canopy Top	VJ9	California Emission package
CC1	T-tops- Fisher	VQ2	Heavy Duty Cooling
CD4	Pulse control wipers	W50	Formula Appearance package
D34	Right-hand visor Vanity mirror	W51	Special Paint
D35	Dual sport mirrors	W63	Rally Gauges with clock
D55	Front Console	W68	Redbird Option Pkg.
D58	Rear Console	W72	400-ci High Perf.
D80	Rear Spoiler	WS6	Trans Am High Perf. Pkg.
G80	Safe-T-Track rear axle	Wt5	High Altitude Package
G92	Performance axles	WW7	Screaming Chicken hood decal
JL1	Pedal Trim	WW8	Rally Cluster with tach/clock
K05	Engine block heater	WW8	Hurst Hatch roof
K30	Cruise Control	Y81	Black Special edition trans AM without T-tops
K45	Dual stage air cleaner	Y82	Black Special edition trans AM with T-tops
K76	Heavy duty alternator 61 amp	Y88	Gold Special Edition package.
K81	Heavy Duty Alternator 63 amp	Y90	Custom Trim Group
L78	400-ci 4-bbl	Y92	Convenience lamps
L80	403-ci 4-bbl	Y96	Handling package
Lg3	305-ci V-8	YH99	Formula Handling package
LM1	350-ci 4-bbl	YJ8	Painted Snowflake wheels
MM3	. 3-spd Manual on floor	YJ8	Snowflake aluminum wheels
MM4	4-spd Manual	A46	Power Seats
MX1	Automatic transmission		
N30	Custom Cushion Steering wheel		
N33	Tilt Steering column		
N41	Power Steering		
N65	Space Saver Spare Tire		
N97	Body colored Rally II wheels		
N98	Rally II wheels		
NK3	Formula steering wheel		
P01	Deluxe Wheel Covers		
P02	Custom wheel Covers		

Due to space limitations some options have been omitted.

1979 Firebird Factory Installed Options

Sales Code	Option
A02	Tinted glass, Windshield only
A31	Power Windows
A90	Remote Deck lid Release
AK1	Custom Seat Belts
AU3	Power Door Locks
AV6	Electric Door locks
B37	Front/ Rear floor mats
B42	Rear Compartment Floor mat
B80	Roof Drip rail moldings
B84	Vinyl Side moldings
B84	Color-Keyed Vinyl body moldings Except Trans Am
B85	Belt Reveal Moldings
B93	Door edge guards
B96	Front and rear wheel moldings
Bs1	Added insulation Stand in Esprit
C08	Vinyl Top
C24	Concealed wipers Base Firebird only
C49	Electric Rear window defroster
C60	Custom Air Conditioning
C95	Dome reading lamp
CB7	Canopy Top
CC1	T-tops- Fisher
CD4	Pulse control wipers
D34	Right-hand visor Vanity mirror
D35	Dual sport mirrors
D55	Front Console
D58	Rear Console
D80	Rear Spoiler
G80	Safe-T-Track rear axle
G92	Performance axles
JL1	Pedal Trim
K05	Engine block heater
K30	Cruise Control
K45	Dual stage air cleaner
K76	Heavy duty alternator 61 amp
K81	Heavy Duty Alternator 63 amp
L78	400-ci 4-bbl
L80	403-ci 4-bbl
L27	301-ci 2-bbl
L37	301-ci 4-bbl
MM3	. 3-spd Manual on floor
MM4	4-spd Manual
MX1	Automatic transmission
N30	Custom Cushion Steering wheel
N33	Tilt Steering column
N41	Power Steering
N65	Space Saver Spare Tire
N97	Body colored Rally II wheels
N98	Rally II wheels
NK3	Formula steering wheel
P01	Deluxe Wheel Covers

Sales Code	Option
QBX	Radial Tuned Suspension
QCY	Radial Tuned Suspension Rally type
TP1	Maintenance Free Battery
U18	Export Speedometer/Clock
U30	Rallye instruments with tach/clock
U35	Electric clock
UP5	AM/FM Radio CB
UM1	Am Radio 8-track
U58	AM/FM Stereo
U63	AM Radio
U69	AM/FM Radio
U80	Rear Seat Speaker
U83	Power antenna
UA1	Heavy Duty Delco Battery
UN8	CB Radio requires Console and UN9 package
UN9	Radio Accommodation package
UR1	Fuel economy gauge
V01	Heavy Duty Radiator
V32	Front and rear bumper guards
V81	Trailer tow package
VJ9	California Emission package
VQ2	Heavy Duty Cooling
W50	Formula Appearance package
W51	Special Paint
W63	Rally Gauges with clock
W68	Redbird Option Pkg.
W72	400-ci High Perf.
WS6	Trans Am High Perf. Pkg.
Wt5	High Altitude Package
WW7	Screaming Chicken hood decal
WW8	Rally Cluster with tach/clock
Y81	Black Special edition trans AM without T-tops
Y82	Black Special edition trans AM with T-tops
Y88	Gold Special Edition package.
Y90	Custom Trim Group
Y92	Convenience lamps
Y96	Handling package
YH99	Formula Handling package
YJ8	Painted Snowflake wheels
YJ8	Snowflake aluminum wheels
LG3	305-ci V-8
LM1	350-ci 4-bbl
Y84	Limited Edition Appearance package
J65	4-wheel Disc Brakes
UM2	AM FM 8track
UP8	Dual rear Speakers
N89	Turbo Cast Wheels
UP6	40channel CB with AM/FM radio

Due to space limitations some options have been omitted.

1980-81 Firebird Factory Installed Options

Sales Code	Option	Sales Code	Option
A02	Tinted glass, Windshield only	QBX	Radial Tuned Suspension
A31	Power Windows	QCY	Radial Tuned Suspension Rally type
A90	Remote Deck lid Release	TP1	Maintenance Free Battery
AK1	Custom Seat Belts	U18	Export Speedometer/Clock
AU3	Power Door Locks	U30	Rallye instruments with tach/clock
AV6	Electric Door locks	U35	Electric clock
B37	Front/ Rear floor mats	UP5	AM/FM Radio CB
B42	Rear Compartment Floor mat	UM1	Am Radio 8-track
B80	Roof Drip rail moldings	U58	AM/FM Stereo
B84	Vinyl Side moldings	U63	AM Radio
B84	Color-Keyed Vinyl body moldings Except Trans Am	U69	AM/FM Radio
B85	Belt Reveal Moldings	U80	Rear Seat Speaker
B93	Door edge guards	U83	Power antenna
B96	Front and rear wheel moldings	UA1	Heavy Duty Delco Battery
Bs1	Added insulation Stand in Esprit	UN8	CB Radio requires Console and UN9 package
C08	Vinyl Top	UN9	Radio Accommodation package
C24	Concealed wipers Base Firebird only	UR1	Fuel economy gauge
C49	Electric Rear window defroster	V01	Heavy Duty Radiator
C60	Custom Air Conditioning	V32	Front and rear bumper guards
C95	Dome reading lamp	V81	Trailer tow package
CB7	Canopy Top	VJ9	California Emission package
CC1	T-tops- Fisher	VQ2	Heavy Duty Cooling
CD4	Pulse control wipers	W50	Formula Appearance package
D34	Right-hand visor Vanity mirror	W51	Special Paint
D35	Dual sport mirrors	W63	Rally Gauges with clock
D55	Front Console	W68	Redbird Option Pkg.
D58	Rear Console	W72	400-ci High Perf.
D80	Rear Spoiler	WS6	Trans Am High Perf. Pkg.
G80	Safe-T-Track rear axle	Wt5	High Altitude Package
G92	Performance axles	WW7	Screaming Chicken hood decal
JL1	Pedal Trim	WW8	Rally Cluster with tach/clock
K05	Engine block heater	Y81	Black Special edition trans AM without T-tops
K30	Cruise Control	Y82	Black Special edition trans AM with T-tops
K45	Dual stage air cleaner	Y88	Gold Special Edition package.
K76	Heavy duty alternator 61 amp	Y90	Custom Trim Group
K81	Heavy Duty Alternator 63 amp	Y92	Convenience lamps
W72	301-ci E/C	Y96	Handling package
Lu8	301-ci Turbo	YH99	Formula Handling package
Lg4	305-ci V-8	N90	Snowflake wheels
L37	301-ci 4-bbl	UQ1	Extended range rear speakers
MM3	. 3-spd Manual on floor	UX6	Dual front speakers
MM4	4-spd Manual	UP8	Dual front and rear speakers
MX1	Automatic transmission	Y84	Limited Edition Appearance package
N30	Custom Cushion Steering wheel	J65	4-wheel Disc Brakes
N33	Tilt Steering column	UM2	AM FM 8track
N41	Power Steering	UX6	Dual rear Speakers
N65	Space Saver Spare Tire	N89	Turbo Cast Wheels
N97	Body colored Rally II wheels	UP6	40channel CB with AM/FM radio
N98	Rally II wheels		
NK3	Formula steering wheel		Due to space limitations some options have been omitted.
P01	Deluxe Wheel Covers		

1971-72 Firebird Dealer Installed Options	
Sales Number	Option
988698	16-in wiper blade
993989	Power brakes
988863	Electric clock
988826	Compass
988761	Tissue Dispenser
988700	Front License plate frame
988865	Fender splash guards
989004	Door edge guards
984642	Engine block heater 750Watt
988958	2.00in Hitch ball
988968	Hood hold downs
993997	Luggage lamp
988824	Under hood lamp
986602	Littercontainer-Blue
986603	Littercontainer-Fawn
986607	Littercontainer-Black
986608	Littercontainer-Red
984825	Locking gas Cap
984701	Locking Rear Spare
988845	Front floor mat Black
988937	Front floor mat Dark Blue
988938	Front floor mat Dark Jade
988939	Front floor mat Dark Beige
988940	Front floor mat Dark Saddle
988941	Front floor mat Dark Sienna
988852	Front floor mat Ivory
988842	Rear Floor mat Black
988932	Rear Floor mat Dark Blue
988933	Rear Floor mat Dark Jade
988934	Rear Floor mat Dark Beige
988935	Rear Floor Dark Saddle
988936	Rear Floor mat Dark Sienna
989007	Remote control mirror LH
989010	RH Mirror
988899	Power Steering
988832	Pushbutton radio
988830	AM/FM Radio
988831	AM/FM Stereo
988855	Deck Lid release
988854	Rear Speaker
988829	Tape Player without console
988828	Tape player with console
988827	Hood mounted tachometer
988836	Tire pump
988870	Wheel trim with N98 wheels
993862	Luggage Rack
993537	Emergency Road Package
988947	Light-Duty Trailer Tow

RPO A31 Power Windows

Optional all 12 years as a factory installed option and was available on all Firebird model lines. The two-button single switch unit was placed in the console. Two different switches were used. The 1970-early 1977 models used part number 4432793; the late 1977-1981 models used part number 1725092. The earlier switches needed a retainer, part number 4757731, and a reinforcement part number 899901, the later style switch included a built in retainer. A special motor/regulator assembly was required to operated the door glass.

Power Window Regulator And Motor

Model Year	Driver's	Passenger's
Regulator		
1970-1981	9723313	9723312
Motor		
1970-1975	5045588	5045587
1976-1979	4999678	4999678
1980-1981	1697345	22048341

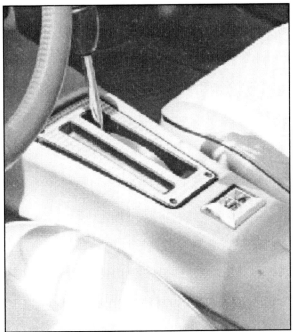

An example of console mounted power window switches.

Power Seats

With this option seat adjustment (up, down, forward and back) was accomplished by the touch of a switch that used a button listed as part number 4309920. That controlled a small motor part number 4939203 and was used to control the driver's side bucket seat. Special adjustment rails were required when the power seats were ordered. Only the driver's side was changed, the passenger's side bucket seat was not available as a power option.

RPO C50 Rear Window Defogger
RPO C49 Electrical Defroster

Two distinct options that did basically the same things but could not be ordered together. Option C50 used a special blower motor that was placed below the rear shelf tray. Cut in the tray was covered by a grille that was painted to match the rear shelf tray The blower case should be painted 30-degrees gloss black. The switch assembly was mounted in the instrument panel and featured a control of high and low fan speeds, plus on and off. While option C50 was good at clearing inner fog off the window, it wasn't beneficial in removing frost from off the glass. Option C49 that placed an electrical grid across the back windows was better at this.

RPO C60/582 Air Conditioning

An extensive option that consisted of many different components that lived coherently with the heater system. The blower motor requires a different unit than that when only heat is used. Part number 4914916 was used till the end of the 1976 model year. In 1977 the beginning year used part number 222020947 while the later 1977 models used a short stack motor part number 22020945, which continued on till the end of the 1981 models years. The evaporator unit was attached to the right-hand side of the firewall. In 1970 part number 3020521 was used this was changed to part number 3023010, which continued till the end of the 1973 model year. At this point part number 3029586 took its place the 1974 design is completely different than the earlier style. The inlet has fittings, instead of a baffle, as in the earlier design.

The condenser was listed as part number 3021753 for 1970-early 1972 models, later 1972 models used part number 3027902 which continued to be used on the 1973 to 1975 models. For 1976 part number 3036949 was used which continued to be used on the 1977-1981 models with a Pontiac or Oldsmobile built power plant. The Chevrolet built units used part number 3036950. A thing to remember is that there was a change in the compressor muffler on the 1972 models. Early models used part number 479077, while the later models used part number 481987.

The air conditioning controls were located in the location of that for the heater and were integrated into each other. The control for 1970 models (except Trans Am models) was listed as part number 7312182; the 1971 models used part number 7935382. Trans Am models used part number 7930592 for both the 1970-1971 model years. These units were marked "De-Ice". Beginning in late 1971 the units were replaced with part number 7938592 for all except Trans Am which used part number 7938602, these units were marked "Defrost".

For 1974 the part numbers were listed as 9349732 for all except Trans Am, which used part number 9346502 which were used up till 1976. In 1977 the part number was changed to 16011632 and was used in all Firebird models. This part continued to be used in all Firebirds till the end of the 1981 model except for the 1979-1981 models with the Y85 package, which used part number 16011682.

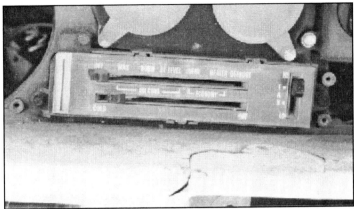

1977-1981 air-conditioning controls were used in all Firebird models.

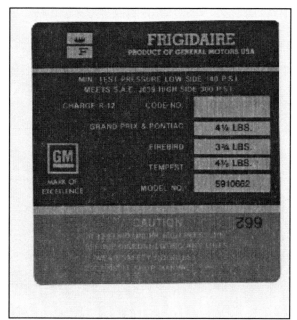

1970 Style air compressor decal. Decal courtesy of Jim Osborne Reproductions.

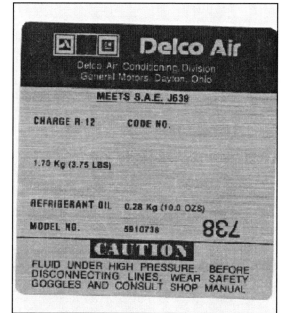

Some 1977 models used this gold, black and silver compressor decal, which was used on the GM, built compressor. Decal courtesy of Jim Osborne Reproductions.

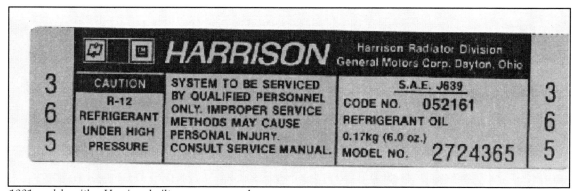

1981 models with a Harrison built compressor used this decal. Decal courtesy of Jim Osborne Reproductions.

Appendix I Firebird Production Totals

1970-1981 Firebird Total Production	
1970	48,739
1971	53,125
1972	29,951
1973	46,313
1974	73,729
1975	84,063
1976	110,775
1977	155,735
1978	187,284
1979	211,453
1980	107,340
1981	70,899
Total 1970-1981 Firebird Production	**1,179,406**

1970-1981 Formula Total Production	
1970	7,708
1971	7,802
1972	5,249
1973	10,166
1974	14,519
1975	13,670
1976	20,613
1977	21,801
1978	24,346
1979	24,850
1980	9,356
1981	5,927
Total 1970-1981 Firebir Formula Production	**165,996**

1970-1981 Trans Am Total Production	
1970	3,196
1971	2,116
1972	1,286
1973	4,802
1974	10,255
1975	27,274
1976	46,704
1977	68,745
1978	93,341
1979	117,108
1980	50,896
1981	33,343
Total 1970-1981 Trans Am Production	**459,055**

1970-1981 Top Ten Rarest Production Firebirds*		
Model	Production	Percentage of Production
1981 Trans Am with 305-ci V-8 and Special Edition package without T-tops	15	.000211
1978 Trans Am with L78 and Y81 package	88	.0004698
1980 Trans Am Special Edition 301-ci	72	.000670
1974 Formula with 455-ci S.D.	58	.000786
1973 Formula with 455-ci S.D.	43	.000928
1976 Trans Am with T-top and Y82 package and 455-ci	110	.000993
1977 Trans Am Black Special Edition with 403-ci V-8	210	.001121
1977 Trans Am with L80 and Y81 package	180	.001155
1970 Trans Am Ram Air IV	88	.0018
1979 Trans Am Special Edition T-top and 301-ci V-8	573	.002798
Based on percentage of total model year production		

Appendix II Firebird Part Suppliers

Name/Address	Phone/ Website	Supplies
Jim Osborne Reproductions 101 Ridgecrest Dr. Lawrenceville, GA 30045	Phone:770-962-7556 www.osborn-reproductions.com	Quality reproduction decals
TexasTransAms.com 4588A Kennedale New Hope Road Fort Worth TX 76140	Phone: 817-563-2121 www. texastransams.com	A selection of Firebird parts and restorable cars for sale. Also a Firebird salvage yard
Warpath Restoration Parts Parma OH 44130	Phone 440-845-4612 www. warpath-parts.com	
The Parts Place 217 Paul St Elburn, IL 60119	630-365-1800 www.thepartsplaceinc.com	A section of Firebird parts
Classic Exhaust 805 Program Parkway Geneva, OH 44041	Phone: 440-466-5460	Exhaust parts
Pontiac Parts	Phone: 800-447-2886 www.pontiacpart.com	
Franks Pontiac Parts Ramona, CA 92065	Phone: 760-789-0669 www.frankspontiacparts.com	Used and new parts
Classic Industries 18460 Gothard Huntington Beach, CA 92648	Phone 800-854-1280 www.classicindustries.com	Selection of reproduction parts.
National Parts Depot	Phone 352-378-9000 www. npdlink.com	Great selection of reproduction parts
Faxon Auto 3901 Carter Ave. Riverside, CA 92501	Phone: 1-800-458-2734	Large section of automotive literature
Paper N Parts 5299 US Hwy. 127 Bryan, OH	Phone: 419-636-8674	
Original Parts 5252 Bolsa Ave. Huntington	1-800-243-8355 www.gmrestoparts.com	Larges selection of reproduction parts
Pontiac Oakland Club Internat. P.O. box 14057 Bradenton, Fl 34280	941-792-4992	Pontiac club
Year One P.O. Box 521 Braselton, GA 30517	1-800-932-7663 www.yearone.com	Selection of reproduction parts.
CST Salvage Aurora MO	417-678-7305 417-678-6994	Salvaged Firebirds in Yard
Henderson Auto Salvage Monett MO	417-235-3719	Salvaged Firebirds in Yard